CHANTAL AKERMAN
AFTERLIVES

LEGENDA

LEGENDA is the Modern Humanities Research Association's book imprint for new research in the Humanities. Founded in 1995 by Malcolm Bowie and others within the University of Oxford, Legenda has always been a collaborative publishing enterprise, directly governed by scholars. The Modern Humanities Research Association (MHRA) joined this collaboration in 1998, became half-owner in 2004, in partnership with Maney Publishing and then Routledge, and has since 2016 been sole owner. Titles range from medieval texts to contemporary cinema and form a widely comparative view of the modern humanities, including works on Arabic, Catalan, English, French, German, Greek, Italian, Portuguese, Russian, Spanish, and Yiddish literature. Editorial boards and committees of more than 60 leading academic specialists work in collaboration with bodies such as the Society for French Studies, the British Comparative Literature Association and the Association of Hispanists of Great Britain & Ireland.

The MHRA encourages and promotes advanced study and research in the field of the modern humanities, especially modern European languages and literature, including English, and also cinema. It aims to break down the barriers between scholars working in different disciplines and to maintain the unity of humanistic scholarship. The Association fulfils this purpose through the publication of journals, bibliographies, monographs, critical editions, and the MHRA Style Guide, and by making grants in support of research. Membership is open to all who work in the Humanities, whether independent or in a University post, and the participation of younger colleagues entering the field is especially welcomed.

ALSO PUBLISHED BY THE ASSOCIATION

Critical Texts
Tudor and Stuart Translations • New Translations • European Translations
MHRA Library of Medieval Welsh Literature

MHRA Bibliographies
Publications of the Modern Humanities Research Association

The Annual Bibliography of English Language & Literature
Austrian Studies
Modern Language Review
Portuguese Studies
The Slavonic and East European Review
Working Papers in the Humanities
The Yearbook of English Studies

www.mhra.org.uk
www.legendabooks.com

MOVING IMAGE

Editorial Committee
Professor Emma Wilson, Corpus Christi College, Cambridge (General Editor)
Professor Erica Carter (King's College London)
Professor Robert Gordon (Gonville and Caius College, Cambridge)
Professor Jo Labanyi (New York University)
Professor Nikolaj Lübecker (St John's College, Oxford)

Legenda/Moving Image publishes cutting-edge work on any aspect of film or screen media from Europe and Latin America. Studies of European-language cinemas from other continents, and diasporic and intercultural cinemas (with some relation to Europe or its languages), are also encompassed. The series seeks to reflect a diversity of theoretical, historical, and interdisciplinary approaches to the moving image, and includes projects comparing screen media with other art forms. Research monographs and collected volumes will be considered, but not studies of a single film. As innovation is a priority for the series, volumes should predominantly consist of previously unpublished material.

Proposals should be sent with one or two sample chapters to the Editor, Professor Emma Wilson, Corpus Christi College, Cambridge CB2 1RH, UK.

APPEARING IN THIS SERIES

1. *Spanish Practices: Literature, Cinema, Television*, by Paul Julian Smith
2. *Cinema and Contact: The Withdrawal of Touch in Nancy, Bresson, Duras and Denis*, by Laura McMahon
3. *Cinema's Inter-Sensory Encounters: Krzysztof Kieślowski and Claire Denis*, by Georgina Evans
4. *Holocaust Intersections: Genocide and Visual Culture at the New Millennium*, edited by Axel Bangert, Robert S. C. Gordon and Libby Saxton
5. *Africa's Lost Classics: New Histories of African Cinema*, edited by Lizelle Bisschoff and David Murphy
6. *Agnès Varda Unlimited: Image, Music, Media*, edited by Marie-Claire Barnet
7. *Thinking Cinema with Proust*, by Patrick ffrench
8. *Blanchot and the Moving Image: Fascination and Spectatorship*, by Calum Watt
9. *Chantal Akerman: Afterlives*, edited by Marion Schmid and Emma Wilson
10. *Screening Work: The Films of Christian Petzold*, by Stephan Hilpert and Andrew J. Webber

Managing Editor
Dr Graham Nelson, 41 Wellington Square, Oxford OX1 2JF, UK

www.legendabooks.com

Chantal Akerman
Afterlives

Edited by
Marion Schmid and Emma Wilson

LEGENDA
Moving Image 9
Modern Humanities Research Association
2019

Published by Legenda
an imprint of the Modern Humanities Research Association
Salisbury House, Station Road, Cambridge CB1 2LA

ISBN 978-1-78188-639-7 (HB)
ISBN 978-1-78188-640-3 (PB)

First published 2019
Paperback edition 2021

All rights reserved. No part of this publication may be reproduced or disseminated or transmitted in any form or by any means, electronic, mechanical, photocopying, recording or otherwise, or stored in any retrieval system, or otherwise used in any manner whatsoever without written permission of the copyright owner, except in accordance with the provisions of the Copyright, Designs and Patents Act 1988, or under the terms of a licence permitting restricted copying issued in the UK by the Copyright Licensing Agency Ltd, Saffron House, 6–10 Kirby Street, London EC1N 8TS, *England, or in the USA by the Copyright Clearance Center, 222 Rosewood Drive, Danvers MA 01923. Application for the written permission of the copyright owner to reproduce any part of this publication must be made by email to legenda@mhra.org.uk.*

Disclaimer: Statements of fact and opinion contained in this book are those of the author and not of the editors or the Modern Humanities Research Association. The publisher makes no representation, express or implied, in respect of the accuracy of the material in this book and cannot accept any legal responsibility or liability for any errors or omissions that may be made.

Trademark notice: Product or corporate names may be trademarks or registered trademarks, and are used only for identification and explanation without intent to infringe.

© *Modern Humanities Research Association 2019*

Copy-Editor: Dr Birgit Mikus

CONTENTS

	Acknowledgements	ix
	List of Illustrations	x
	Notes on the Contributors	xi
	Introduction MARION SCHMID AND EMMA WILSON	1
	In Memory of Chantal Akerman: Passages through Time and Space GIULIANA BRUNO	7
1	A Tree in the Wind: Chantal Akerman's Later Self-Portraits in Installation and Film SANDY FLITTERMAN-LEWIS	13
2	Moeder, Maman, Mom CAROL MAVOR	26
3	Smokescreens: Notes on Cigarettes in Chantal Akerman ALICE BLACKHURST	41
4	Ageless: Akerman's Avatars JENNY CHAMARETTE	54
5	Real Estates: The Comedy of Spaces and Things in Chantal Akerman's *Demain on déménage* HILDE D'HAEYERE AND STEVEN JACOBS	66
6	Diaries, Thresholds and Gazes as Anamnesis in Chantal Akerman's Cinema ANAT ZANGER	77
7	Unknown Deaths in *La Captive* EMMA WILSON	90
8	Texas (is not Paris) is Burning: The Drag of Dis/Orientation in Chantal Akerman's *Sud* SO MAYER	102
9	Vocal Landscapes: Framing Mutable Stories in *De l'autre côté* (2002) and *Une voix dans le désert* (2002) ALBERTINE FOX	115

10 'Like a Musical Piece': Akerman and Musicality 127
ADAM ROBERTS

11 Light out of Joint 139
CYRIL BÉGHIN

12 Chantal Akerman: Filmmaker, Video Artist, Writer 150
MARION SCHMID

Works by Chantal Akerman 164

Select Bibliography of Works on Chantal Akerman 167

Index 168

ACKNOWLEDGEMENTS

We would like to express our warm thanks to Sylviane Akerman, the Fondation Chantal Akerman, Paradise Films and the Cinémathèque royale de Belgique for allowing us to use some of the illustrations in this book. Our special gratitude goes to Lore Gablier (Paradise Films) and Jean-Paul Dorchain (Cinémathèque royale de Belgique) for their kind assistance with sourcing the images.

We would also like to thank Anthony Cummins for his translation of Cyril Béghin's chapter and Adam Roberts and Claire Atherton for their help with compiling the list of Chantal Akerman's installations. Finally, we are indebted to editors and publishers for their permission to reprint material, though in some cases significantly changed. The text of Giuliana Bruno's chapter first appeared in *October*, 155 (2016), 162–67; Marion Schmid's chapter partly draws on material from her 'Between Literature and the Moving Image: The Cinematography of Chantal Akerman', *Revue critique de fixxion française contemporaine*, 7 (2013), 73–84.

E.W., M.S., January 2019

LIST OF ILLUSTRATIONS

Fig. M.1. Portrait of Chantal Akerman © Fondation Chantal Akerman — collection Cinémathèque royale, all rights reserved.

Fig. M.2. Chantal Akerman, *Nightfall on Shanghai* (2009), Courtesy Marian Goodman Gallery, Paris/ New York/ London. Photo: Marc Domage © Fondation Chantal Akerman.

Fig. 1.1. Chantal Akerman, *NOW* (2015), Courtesy Marian Goodman Gallery, Paris/ New York/ London © Fondation Chantal Akerman.

Fig. 1.2. Chantal Akerman, *Marcher à côté de ses lacets dans un frigidaire vide* (2004), Courtesy Fondation Chantal Akerman & Marian Goodman Gallery, Paris/ New York/ London © Fondation Chantal Akerman.

Fig. 2.1. Chantal Akerman, *Marcher à côté de ses lacets dans un frigidaire vide* (2004).

Fig. 2.2. *Femme Maison*, 1947, Louise Bourgeois (1911–2010), detail of announcement for Bourgeois's 1947 solo exhibition at the Norly St. Gallery, New York, DACS.

Fig. 2.3. *Hope*, 1886, George Frederic Watts (1817–1904) © Tate, London, 2018.

Fig. 3.1. Chantal Akerman, *Femmes d'Anvers en novembre* (2008), Courtesy Marian Goodman Gallery, Paris/ New York/ London © Fondation Chantal Akerman.

Fig. 4.1. Chantal Akerman, *Les Rendez-vous d'Anna* (1978).
Fig. 4.2. Chantal Akerman, *Les Rendez-vous d'Anna* (1978).
Fig. 4.3. Chantal Akerman, *Les Rendez-vous d'Anna* (1978).
Fig. 5.1. Chantal Akerman, *Demain on déménage* (2004).
Fig. 5.2. Chantal Akerman, *Demain on déménage* (2004).
Fig. 5.3. Chantal Akerman, *Demain on déménage* (2004).
Fig. 6.1. Chantal Akerman, *Demain on déménage* (2004).
Fig. 6.2. Chantal Akerman, *Demain on déménage* (2004).
Fig. 6.3. Chantal Akerman, *Demain on déménage* (2004).

Fig. 7.1. Chantal Akerman, *La Captive* (1999) © Fondation Chantal Akerman — collection Cinémathèque royale.

Fig. 9.1. Chantal Akerman, *De l'autre côté* (2002) © Roches Noires Productions.
Fig. 9.2. Chantal Akerman, *De l'autre côté* (2002) © Roches Noires Productions.

Fig. 10.1. Chantal Akerman *Les années 80* (1983), Courtesy of Fondation Chantal Akerman © Fondation Chantal Akerman.

Fig. 11.1. Chantal Akerman, *Maniac Summer* (2009), Courtesy Marian Goodman Gallery, Paris/ New York/ London © Fondation Chantal Akerman.

Fig. 11.2. Chantal Akerman, *D'Est* (1993).

Fig. 11.3. Chantal Akerman, *Maniac Shadows* (2013), Courtesy Marian Goodman Gallery, Paris/ New York/ London © Fondation Chantal Akerman.

Fig. 12.1. Chantal Akerman, *Un divan à New York* (1996).

Fig. 12.2. Chantal Akerman, *Marcher à côté de ses lacets dans un frigidaire vide* (2004), Courtesy Fondation Chantal Akerman & Marian Goodman Gallery, Paris/ New York/ London © Fondation Chantal Akerman.

Fig. 12.3. Chantal Akerman, *No Home Movie* (2015).

NOTES ON THE CONTRIBUTORS

Cyril Béghin is a member of the editorial board of *Cahiers du cinéma*, for which he has written since 2004. He regularly contributes to journals, catalogues and collective volumes on cinema. He has prefaced and edited *Duras/Godard Dialogues* (Post-Editions, 2014). Since 2005 he has also been the assistant of the choreographer and performer Valeria Apicella. He contributed to the book *Chantal Akerman: Autoportrait en cinéaste* (Cahiers du cinéma, 2004), co-edited the catalogue *Chantal Akerman. Monographie* (Magic Cinema, 2014) and contributed to a special dossier on Chantal Akerman in *Film Quarterly* (70.1 (2016)).

Alice Blackhurst is a Junior Research Fellow in French and Visual Culture at King's College, Cambridge. She works at the intersection between contemporary critical theory and visual studies; her current research looks at an aesthetics of luxury in relation to modern French thinkers and Francophone visual arts practitioners. Other interests include feminist and gender studies, the use of clothing in contemporary installation projects, and film.

Giuliana Bruno is Emmet Blakeney Gleason Professor of Visual and Environmental Studies at Harvard University. She is internationally known for her interdisciplinary research on visual arts, architecture and media. Her book *Atlas of Emotion: Journeys in Art, Architecture and Film* (Verso, 2002) has gained several prestigious recognitions, including the Kraszna-Krausz prize for best Moving Image Book in the world. Bruno is also the author of *Streetwalking on a Ruined Map* (Princeton University Press, 1993), winner of the Society for Cinema and Media Studies book award, and *Public Intimacy: Architecture and the Visual Arts* (MIT, 2007), and has contributed to numerous monographs on contemporary art, published by the Guggenheim Museum, the Whitney Museum, and the Museum of Modern Art (MoMA). In her latest book, *Surface: Matters of Aesthetics, Materiality, and Media* (University of Chicago Press, 2014), Bruno revisits the impact of surface and materiality in contemporary visual culture.

Jenny Chamarette is Senior Lecturer in Film Studies at Queen Mary, University of London. Her first monograph, *Phenomenology and the Future of Film* (2012), discussed embodiment, affect, and temporality in relation to the films and installations of Agnès Varda, Chantal Akerman, Chris Marker and Philippe Grandrieux. She has published widely on intermediality, embodied and existential phenomenologies, cultural politics and intersectionality in contemporary visual and moving image cultures, particularly in Europe, North America and the Middle East. She is currently at work on her second book, *Cinemuseology: Museum Vitrines, Digital Screens and Cultural Politics*.

Hilde D'haeyere is a photographer and silent film historian who heads the Masters program in film at KASK, school of arts of the University College in Ghent, Belgium. Among her recent publications is 'Slapstick on Slapstick' in *Film History* (2014), 'Frankfurter Slapstick: Benjamin, Kracauer and Adorno on American Screen Comedy', *October*, 160 (2017) co-authored with Steven Jacobs, and 'Ziegfeldized Slapstick, Useful Comedy' in *The Colour Fantastic* (Amsterdam University Press, 2018).

Sandy Flitterman-Lewis is the author of *To Desire Differently: Feminism and the French Cinema*, and co-author of *New Vocabularies in Film Semiotics*. She co-founded two journals, *Camera Obscura: Feminism* and *Film Theory and Discourse: Studies in Media and Culture*. She has authored countless articles on feminist film theory, popular culture, and Shoah memory for numerous collections. She is currently assembling a collection of her essays entitled *Hidden Voices: Childhood, the Family, and Antisemitism in Occupation France*, a study of material culture and memory in WWII France. She teaches courses in film through the English and Comparative Literature departments at Rutgers University in New Brunswick, New Jersey.

Albertine Fox is Lecturer in French Film at the University of Bristol. She is the author of *Godard and Sound: Acoustic Innovation in the Late Films of Jean-Luc Godard* (2017) and her articles have appeared in *Studies in French Cinema*, *SEQUENCE* and *Sight & Sound*. She is currently working on a project that explores the role of interviews in documentaries by French, Francophone and European filmmakers and part of this project is particularly concerned with the work of Chantal Akerman.

Steven Jacobs is an art historian specialized in the interactions between film, the visual arts and architecture. He has published in *Art Journal*, *History of Photography*, *Millennium Film Journal*, *October*, and in numerous edited volumes. He also (co-) authored *The Wrong House: The Architecture of Alfred Hitchcock* (2007), *Framing Pictures: Film and the Visual Arts* (2011), *The Dark Galleries: A Museum Guide to Painted Pictures in Film Noir* (2013), *Screening Statues: Cinema and Sculpture* (2017), and *The City Symphony Phenomenon: Cinema, Art, and Urban Modernity Between the Wars* (2018). He teaches at Ghent University and the University of Antwerp.

Carol Mavor is a writer who takes creative risks in form (literary and experimental) and political risks in content (sexuality, race in America, child-loving and the maternal). Her *Reading Boyishly: Roland Barthes, J. M. Barrie, Jacques Henri Lartigue, Marcel Proust, and D. W. Winnicott* was named by Grayson Perry in *The Guardian* as his 2008 'Book of the Year.' Her sixth monograph is *Aurelia: Art and Literature Through the Eyes and Mouth of the Fairy Tale*, which Maggie Nelson describes as 'enigmatic, and full of magic as its subjects.' Currently Mavor is working on a new book, *Serendipity: The Afterlife of the Object*.

So Mayer is the author of *Political Animals: The New Feminist Cinema* (IB Tauris, 2015) and *The Cinema of Sally Potter: A Politics of Love* (Wallflower, 2009), as well as several collections of poetry, and the co-editor of *Lo personal es politico: feminism y documental* (with Elena Oroz, INAAC, 2011) and *There She Goes: Feminist Filmmaking and Beyond* (with Corinn Columpar, Wayne State UP, 2010). So curates with queer feminist film curation collective Club des Femmes, is a co-founder of industry campaigners Raising Films, and is a regular contributor to *Sight & Sound* and *Literal Magazine*.

Adam Roberts is a film-maker, writer, curator and co-founder with Joanna Hogg of *A Nos Amours*. Adam has made films with dancers (Sylvie Guillem and Jonathan Burrows), which have been shown in festivals and won prizes. *A Nos Amours* curated a Chantal Akerman retrospective at ICA 2013–2015, to date the most exhaustive of the artist's films yet presented. Akerman attended a number of the retrospective screenings. In 2015 *A Nos Amours* curated an exhibition of Akerman's installation work in collaboration with Ambika P3 Gallery in London. Akerman was personally involved in the installation design.

Marion Schmid is Professor of French Literature and Film at the University of Edinburgh. She is the author of *Chantal Akerman* (2010), *Proust dans la décadence* (2008), *Proust at the Movies* (2005, co-authored with Martine Beugnet) and *Processes of Literary Creation: Flaubert and Proust* (1998). Her new book *Intermedial Dialogues: The French New Wave and the Other Arts* is forthcoming with Edinburgh University Press. Together with Kim Knowles (Aberystwyth University) she coordinates the research network 'Film and the Other Arts: Intermediality, Medium Specificity, Creativity'. In 2012, she curated a retrospective of Chantal Akerman's films for the French Film Festival UK.

Emma Wilson is Professor of French Literature and the Visual Arts at the University of Cambridge and a fellow of Corpus Christi College. She is the author of *Sexuality and the Reading Encounter* (1996), *French Cinema since 1950* (1999), *The French Cinema of Krzysztof Kieślowski* (2000), *Cinema's Missing Children* (2003), *Alain Resnais* (2006), *Atom Egoyan* (2009) and *Love, Mortality and the Moving Image* (2012). Her new book *The Reclining Nude* is forthcoming with Liverpool University Press. She is currently writing a study of Céline Sciamma for the Edinburgh University Press series on women directors 'Visionaries'.

Anat Zanger is an associate professor at the Department of Film and Television Film Studies at Tel Aviv University and served as Head of MA studies (2006–2017). Her books include *Film Remakes as Ritual and Disguises: from Carmen to Ripley* (Amsterdam University Press, 2006) and *Place, Memory and Myth in Contemporary Israeli Cinema* (Vallentine Mitchell, 2012). Her projects on Israeli space and film and on Jerusalem in films have received grants from the Israeli Science Foundation (2008–2012; 2013–2017). She is co-editor of *Just Images: Ethics and the Cinematic* (Cambridge Scholar Publishing, 2012) and has contributed to *Chantal Akerman: A Spiral Autobiography* (Tel Aviv Museum of Art, 2006).

INTRODUCTION

If one had only one word to describe the extraordinary trajectory of Chantal Akerman, one of the great visionaries of modern cinema, it should probably be courage. The courage to take to the camera aged 18, without any formal training, doubling up as director and sole actress in her tragi-comic portrait of adolescent crisis, *Saute ma ville*; to show herself naked on screen and engage with her own body in the lesbian lovemaking scene in *Je tu il elle*; to propose a new syntax for filming women in the monumental *Jeanne Dielman*, shot when she was just 25; to commit to an uncompromising *auteur* style at the margins of big production systems, and to make a name for herself in a largely male-dominated industry. Over almost half a century, until her tragic death in 2015, Akerman revolutionized the cinematic landscape with an oeuvre of singular freedom and artistic integrity. Like Jean-Luc Godard or Rainer Werner Fassbinder, to whom she is often compared, hers is a cinema that radically alters our vision, engaging spectators in a demanding — though no less enthralling — interrogation of the forms and conditions of human existence. In their resistance to the lure of easily consumable images, her films trace an alternative, 'critical' cinema, charting different ways of beholding and apprehending reality. Reclaimed by this modernist director, the *audendi potestas* ('the right to dare') of the artist translates into a cinematic language that shakes up our habitual forms of being and seeing.

One of the most significant figures in women's and feminist filmmaking and a radical innovator of forms, Akerman made over forty films, spanning a dazzling array of genres and formats, from minimalist 'single-location' features to exuberant musical comedy, art films on German choreographer Pina Bausch, Austrian pianist Alfred Brendel and French cellist Sonia Wieder-Atherton, not to forget her cinematic self-portraits, creative adaptations of Proust and Conrad and her experimental documentaries 'bordering on fiction'. In the early 1990s, she was one of the first filmmakers to cross over from the projection room to the museum and gallery space, extending her creative work to video art and installation. She was also a gifted writer, gaining critical acclaim with her auto-portrait *Ma mère rit*, shortlisted for the 2013 Prix Médicis. Known for its detached, anti-illusionist style, her work gradually shifted from a 'cinema of the bodies'[1] concerned with female gestures and bodily attitudes to a wider exploration of questions of identity and memory. Attentive to the textures of everyday life, she will be remembered as a 'hero of the intimate', who believed in art's capacity to share and make palpable even the most infinitely private experience.[2] As Nicholas Elliott writes in a homage in *Cahiers du cinéma*, '[s]i nous sommes tant à la pleurer aujourd'hui, ce n'est pas seulement parce qu'elle a fait de beaux films. En partageant son intimité, Chantal Akerman a fait de nous ses intimes. Elle a élargi le champ de l'intime.'³

In terms of periodisation, Akerman belongs to the generation known as the 'post-New Wave'. Her first film, *Saute ma ville*, was made in 1968, the legendary year of civil unrest in France, but also the moment which, in film history, is considered as the ultimate vanishing point of the *Nouvelle Vague*.⁴ Her coming of age, both literally and artistically, coincided with a crucial generational shift, as filmmakers such as Philippe Garrel, Jean Eustache, André Techiné, Jacques Doillon and Benoît Jacquot gave a new direction to the legacy of the New Wave. A truly transnational director, her aesthetic was inflected by, on the one hand, European modernist cinema in the tradition of Robert Bresson, Alain Resnais and Godard and, on the other, her discovery of North-American avant-garde music, performance and film during two extended stays in New York in the 1970s. With their emphasis on time, duration and the viewing experience, the structural films of Michael Snow, Jonas Mekas or Andy Warhol became instrumental for her interest in a cinema that excavates truth by way of a sustained looking process. In her self-portrait *Autoportrait en cinéaste*, she asserts: 'la vérité ne se livre pas si simplement, souvent même elle se refuse. Je mettrai la caméra là, en face, aussi longtemps qu'il sera nécessaire et la vérité adviendra.'⁵ Placed in the corridors of a welfare hotel in *Hôtel Monterey* or in the streets of New York in *News from Home*, interrogating landscapes in *Sud* or lingering on anonymous passengers in a Moscow train station in *D'Est*, the camera scrutinizes faces and places until, in Akerman's words, 'un trouble s'installe': the vertigo of seeing afresh, but also of sensing beneath these images of the here-and-now the passage of time with its traces and inscriptions.⁶ A means to understand — or at least to feel — existence, her signature long takes actively involve spectators in her search for the invisible beneath the deceptively smooth surface of the image.

Their openness to past and becoming ('*advenir*') makes each Akerman film an adventure and a risk, both for the director and her audience. The formal rigour, plastic beauty and meticulous framing of her works — placing her in the tradition of Dutch Golden Age painting and, in cinema, in the wake of Antonioni and Fassbinder — may give the impression of a carefully controlled oeuvre. Yet nothing would be further from her artistic practice. Masterfully assured though it is, hers is an instinctive, spontaneous cinema open to chance encounters and unforeseen events; a cinema that, rather than seeking to shape the materials of reality, lets reality — and what lies beneath it — imprint and reveal itself in filmic form. Akerman often insisted on the role of intuition and what she calls her 'attention flottante' in the filmic process. As she states in conversation with Leonardo Luiz Ferreira in the Brazilian documentary *Chantal Akerman, From Here* (2010): 'If it's totally conscious, it's dead. The unconscious brings out something that you were not expecting, which is usually the richness of the work'. Her long-standing editor and collaborator Claire Atherton testifies to this receptiveness of her work, grounded in a perpetual questioning as well as a personal disquiet: 'Si les images de Chantal sont si profondes et fortes, si elles dépassent ce qu'elles montrent, c'est parce qu'elles ne sont pas enfermées dans des intentions, mais qu'elles sont chargées de tous les questionnements, les obsessions qui l'habitaient.'⁷

Committed to a 'minor cinema' that rebels against the ideologies of the mainstream, denounces social and linguistic conditioning and rejects fixed conceptions of gender, sexuality and belonging, Akerman's work from its inception centered on questions of alterity and exclusion. Her oeuvre is animated by a deep empathy for society's traditional 'others', be they juvenile delinquents and drug addicts (*Hanging out Yonkers*), the residents of a New York welfare hotel (*Hotel Monterey*), members of the Jewish diaspora who have settled in the US (*Histoires d'Amérique: food, family and philosophy*), destitute Eastern Europeans after the collapse of the Soviet Union (*D'Est*), Mexican migrants attempting to cross the Arizona border (*De l'autre côté*) or the descendants of black slaves in the American Deep South (*Sud*). Her films speak of inequality and displacement, of the difficulty of belonging and the longing for (a) home. As the daughter of an Auschwitz survivor, Akerman was all too aware of the continued atrocities in our own present, against which she heeds in the last part of her video installation *D'Est, au bord de la fiction*:

> Yesterday, today, and tomorrow, there were, there will be, there are right now, even, people that history (without a capital H) comes to strike. People who are there, rounded up in herds, waiting to be killed, hit, or starved; people who walk without knowing where they're going, in a group or alone.

In our worrying times of rising populism and chauvinistic nationalism, in the throes of the biggest refugee crisis since World War II and faced with wide-spread fear of otherness, we look to Akerman as a director who put exile and marginality at the core of her filmic preoccupations. Perhaps more than ever, we are in need of her art that summons the past to make us reflect on our present.

Chantal Akerman: Afterlives aims to take stock of this great artist's legacy now that her oeuvre is sadly complete. Special emphasis is on her work since the 1990s as a particularly fertile period during which Akerman diversified her creative practice, but which has received comparatively little critical attention. Focusing on her filmic output, installations and writing, we wish to offer a more comprehensive and inclusive account of an oeuvre that tends to be overshadowed by her pioneering works of the 1970s and 80s, and that is often partitioned within rigid media boundaries.

We open with an essay by Giuliana Bruno, written in the aftermath of Akerman's death and published in the journal *October* in the Winter 2016 edition. The essay was written in that time of heightened emotion, with pain of realization following the filmmaker's untimely death. In some senses this period of mourning, affection, and acute perception offers an affective ground to much of the work collected here where contributors reckon with the work of Akerman in a time when she is no longer living. But Bruno's piece also emerges out of a long period of friendship with Akerman and extensive previous writing on her films, where Akerman's aesthetic practice has seemed directly bound up with Bruno's thoughts about motion and emotion.[8] Bruno's essay is a testimony to the ways, as she says, 'Akerman enriched our world'. She introduces many of the themes dwelt on elsewhere also in our volume, for example, the issues of movement, transmigration and diaspora, and 'reflections on the space of interiority'. Bruno identifies the importance of the period from the mid-1990s forwards for the development of Akerman's works in installation art, as do many contributors here responding to our invitation to think about the last two decades of Akerman's practice, and she thinks in particular about the materiality of these works. Above all Bruno intimates what was very rare, and very precious, about Akerman's work: 'It is as if this woman, this artist, had the ability to relay experiences that come from a place of reflection inside many of us'.

Through this volume, Akerman's latest works, her text *Ma mère rit* (2013) and her last film *No Home Movie* (2015) receive sustained critical attention, and these works, so bound up with thoughts of the illness and death of Akerman's mother, and with the last acts of the filmmaker herself, find their place in her broader corpus. They return, as our contributors consider them variously across their essays, as do the earlier works outside our time span, notably *Jeanne Dielman* that seems to haunt these later works. Sandy Flitterman-Lewis's essay, 'A Tree in the Wind: Chantal Akerman's Later Self-Portraits in Installation and Film', following decades of thinking and writing about Akerman, responds to the filmmaker's later self-portraits, linking her restlessness and her nomadism to her life as a Jewish woman, and arguing for 'the emergent and increasingly central exploration of Jewish identity and history in Akerman's works'. Flitterman-Lewis identifies the nexus of 'Mother, Memory, Shoah and Home' that exists in Akerman. She looks with particular poignancy at *No Home Movie* as a film about no longer having a home after the death of the mother, and ends with words from Delphine Horvilleur, the rabbi who spoke at Akerman's funeral.

These concerns reverberate too in Carol Mavor's intricate three-stranded piece, 'Moeder, Maman, Mom', an intimate reflection on Anne Frank's diary, on Akerman's installation and video featuring the journal of her grandmother who died in Auschwitz, *Marcher à côté de ses lacets dans un frigidaire vide*, and on an autobiographical recording by Mavor's own mother. The reflections here on maternal depression, on the sexuality of adolescent girls, on domesticity, the containment and captivity of the *femme-maison*, on writing, play, and hope, place Akerman's pictorial narratives within a broader corpus of words and images of the lives of women and girls. Alice Blackhurst's 'Smokescreens: Notes on Cigarettes in Chantal Akerman', looks at a particular act, or gesture, of smoking a cigarette in Akerman's works, including *Portrait d'une paresseuse* and *Femmes d'Anvers en novembre*, an act she sees associated with 'maternal modes of agency'. She identifies the rapture in the ordinary of this act, the appetite and curiosity in Akerman's works, as well as their fascination with making the spectator delay and 'feel time'. A third take on mothers and daughters, on generations, comes in Jenny Chamarette's 'Ageless: Akerman's Avatars', where Chamarette sees Akerman creating slippage between women of different generations and so 'queering the temporalities of ageing, particularly and specifically female ageing'.

Hilde D'haeyere and Steven Jacobs, and Anat Zanger, focus in part or in whole on *Demain on déménage*, Akerman's comedy, also of mothers and daughters, moving and smoking. D'haeyere and Jacobs, in 'Real Estates: The Comedy of Spaces and Things in Chantal Akerman's *Demain on déménage*' close in on the sets and spaces of the film, seeing Akerman composing 'cinematic spaces like dollhouse universes'. Working with the permeability between interior and exterior Bruno too identifies, and closing in on claustrophobia and captivity, they consider the film in relation to the history of domestic interiors, their objects and souvenirs, and also to the history of slapstick comedy, in early cinema, and the humour of furniture, pianos, moved and removed. In her contrasting essay 'Diaries, Thresholds and Gazes as Anamnesis in Chantal Akerman's Cinema', Anat Zanger looks at movement between past and present in a discussion more particularly of postmemory, of the traces of the past in the objects of the present. Her essay resonates with Flitterman-Lewis's in seeing Akerman's works consistently tracing 'the presence of memory and postmemory between event and picture and between the first and second generation of Holocaust survivors'. While moving off to look at Akerman's Proust adaptation, *La Captive*, and to consider its scenes of sex and drowning, sleeping and dying, through engagement with Ingeborg Bachmann's readings of Proust, Emma Wilson finds too the return of the unknown suffering of the mother, a first generation Holocaust survivor, in this late film.

So Mayer and Albertine Fox follow Akerman beyond Europe to look, respectively, at her more far flung documentaries *Sud* and *De l'autre côté* and its accompanying installation *Une voix dans le désert*. (The films *D'Est* and *Là-bas* with which these documentaries form a tetralogy are variously treated by other contributors). In 'Texas (is not Paris) is Burning: The Drag of Dis/Orientation in Chantal Akerman's *Sud*', So Mayer responds critically to *Sud*, comparing the documentary to other engagements with the murder of James Byrd Jr. and seeing the film made in the immediate aftermath of the events missing the histories of racism and white supremacy the murder identified. She brings in questions of possible blindspots in Akerman's works. In 'Vocal Landscapes: Framing Mutable Stories in *De l'autre côté* and *Une voix dans le désert*', Albertine Fox responds differently to Akerman in the Americas and her film and installation about the Mexico/US border. For Fox these works 'foster within the spectator an attitude of deep receptivity, placing her/him in an encounter with a compassionate mode of filmmaking that arises from an aural-ethical approach'. She is concerned in particular with acts of listening, 'listening beside'. She sees the director as a sort of 'sensitive sponge', receptive to the tensions of the areas where she films.

Fox's piece looks closely at sound in these works, offering a valuable companion to Adam Roberts's virtuoso essay, '"Like a Musical Piece": Akerman and Musicality'. It is with particular pleasure that we include this piece by Adam Roberts who, together with Joanna Hogg in their collective 'A nos amours', mounted the extraordinary London-based retrospective of Chantal Akerman's films and videos, culminating in the exhibition NOW at Ambika P3 Gallery (jointly curated by Roberts, Hogg and Michael Mazière). It is in the thrall of this long-form retrospective, running over two years, from 2013 to 2015, that a number of our contributors had the opportunity to engage with Akerman's works. Adam's personal passion for the films and delicacy towards Chantal enlivened and rarefied these events. His multi-faceted essay looks at Akerman with John Cage, discusses the span of her musical films, and her collaboration with Sonia Wieder-Atherton, and ends with a coruscating reading of sound and silence in *La Captive*.

We are equally thrilled to include an essay by French film critic and writer for *Cahiers du cinéma* Cyril Béghin. His summative piece, 'Light out of Joint', looks across Akerman's works, including the installations *Maniac Summer* and *Maniac Shadows*, to make an argument for the force of light in her work, mediating between representation and abstraction. He sees Akerman engaging in light-craft from the 1990s forwards, and looks at natural and artificial light in her works, at her focus on the dying of the light, and by contrast the night disappearing in real-time dawn. His essay acts as an invitation to think the form and matter of Akerman's works, as her installation pieces pull away from narrative towards sensation and abstraction.

The volume closes with Marion Schmid's essay, 'Chantal Akerman: Filmmaker, Video Artist, Writer', which appraises Akerman finally as an artist and writer, looking at writing in her works, and her extraordinary acts of autobiographical fiction, placing her alongside Marguerite Duras and Thomas Bernhard, amongst others. Schmid finds a shifting 'je' in Akerman's texts and ghosts of other languages in her writing. She closes with a return to *No Home Movie*, with which our collection of essays begins. For Schmid this is a film of 'silent exits, a sober and deeply moving mise-en-scène of disappearances'. We look in this volume at what remains beyond these disappearances, the dazzling films, installations and texts, their formal brilliance, their intimacy, the traces they offer of Chantal Akerman, her shadow, her afterlives.

Notes to the Introduction

1. Gilles Deleuze, *Cinema 2: The Time Image*, trans. by Hugh Tomlinson and Robert Galeta (Minneapolis: University of Minnesota Press, 1989), p. 196.
2. The term is by Stéphane Delorme in his editorial 'Journal intime', *Cahiers du cinéma*, 716 (2015), p. 5.
3. 'If so many of us mourn her today, it is not only because she has made beautiful films. By sharing her intimacy, Chantal Akerman has made us her intimates. She has broadened the field of intimacy.' Nicholas Elliott, 'Proche', *Cahiers du cinéma*, 716 (2015), p. 83.
4. Having gone their separate ways for some time, members of the New Wave rallied together one last time in 1968 in protest against the government's dismissal of the director of the Cinémathèque, Henri Langlois, and in support of the interruption of the Cannes Festival. See Noël Simsolo, *Dictionnaire de la Nouvelle Vague* (Paris: Flammarion, 2013), p. 12.
5. 'Truth does not give itself away easily, it even often refuses itself. I will place my camera for as long as is necessary and truth will emerge' (Chantal Akerman, *Autoportrait en cinéaste* (Paris: Editions du Centre Georges Pompidou/ Editions Cahiers du cinéma, 2004), p. 30).
6. 'a trouble sets in', Akerman, *Autoportrait en cinéaste*, p. 31.
7. 'If Chantal's images are so deep and powerful, if they go beyond what they show, it's because they are not locked up in intentions, but charged with all the questions, the obsessions that inhabited her'; 'Hommage à Chantal Akerman par Claire Atherton', www.cinematheque.fr./article/726.html (last accessed 19 June 2018).
8. See for example Bruno's extraordinary reckonings with Akerman's films in *Atlas of Emotion: Journeys in Art, Architecture and Film* (London: Verso, 2002).

IN MEMORY OF CHANTAL AKERMAN

Passages through Time and Space

Giuliana Bruno

What viewer of *Jeanne Dielman, 23, Quai du Commerce, 1080 Bruxelles* has not been affected or even changed by the experience of watching this film? With the minimal simplicity of precisely framed 'long takes', Chantal Akerman's breakthrough film, made in 1975, when she was only twenty-five, exposed the strictures of women's time and space while creating a new cinematic language of observation and a filmic *longue durée*. At age eighteen, Akerman had already made an explosive start with *Saute ma ville* (1968), directing herself, shut away and alone in her apartment, blowing up rituals of domesticity and, in the end, blowing herself up, together with her home. Personally full of life and energy but haunted by the dark specter of severe psychic pain, Akerman began her fictional journey with a defiant act of self-destruction that would come to be realized years later, when her life ended suddenly at age sixty-five.

Akerman enriched our world through an extraordinarily ordinary journey composed of images, of places, perceptively explored and executed within a formally rigorous aesthetic. Cities, lands, and homes are intimately portrayed in her frontal long takes, which capture the passing of everyday life — especially that of women — as they intensify our sense of time, memory, and space. Passing through doors, staring through windows, lingering in corridors, we are led to explore sites of transit and separation, instances of cultural movement. The result is our own reflection on processes of displacement, transmigration, and diaspora, as both exterior and interior passages. Akerman's reflections on the space of interiority are particularly affecting — so much so, in fact, that they can become interiorized by the viewer. Her work is not just part of our cultural fabric; it is part of our intimate fabric.

Akerman continued to experiment with moving images much beyond *Jeanne Dielman*. The new filmic form she pioneered in the 1970s was inflected by European modernist cinema and by her encounter with the 'structuralist' paradigms of North American avant-garde artists such as Michael Snow and Hollis Frampton. An encounter with live performance is documented in her 1983 portrait of Pina Bausch's work in *One Day Pina Asked*. Most important, she moved easily between fiction and documentary, and exhibiting in galleries. In the mid-1990s Akerman began to engage in an expanded field of film-based installation art, in an early stage of the cultural movement that drives today's filmmakers and artists to exchange roles and work increasingly between media.

Fig. M.1. Portrait of Chantal Akerman

The position Akerman holds in this expanded field of imaging is unique, for she was able not only to move back and forth between different kinds of cinema and moving-image installation but to interchange these modes of presentation. While she made work specifically for gallery exhibition, she also showed or 'installed' her theatrical films in gallery spaces, generating a dialogue between artistic languages and modes of presentation. Her style of long-durational filming punctuated with minimal or casual action transferred well from the film theater to the art gallery. It resonates with the performative, subjective, roaming style of imaging that has come to inhabit our digital screens today. Her itinerant way of filming was especially suited to the peripatetic mode of reception experienced in the art gallery, where visitors interact with screens that can enhance displacement as well as forms of encounter and liminality.

Akerman thus worked with multiple screens in *Now*, a resounding five-screen projection of traveling shots through desert landscapes that was shown at the 2015 Venice Biennale. She also experimented with the scale of the screen when conjuring the large, futuristic, Turner-like canvas in *Nightfall over Shanghai* (2007). Scrims were interestingly featured in *To Walk Next to One's Shoelaces in an Empty Fridge* (2004), a two-part installation in which the pages of a diary with inscriptions by the artist's grandmother and mother were transformed into a diaphanous screen fabric. Through such experiments in the art gallery, Akerman thus created close encounters with the fabric of time and space. Presenting her feature-length film *D'Est* (1993) on twenty-four separate video monitors, she arranged sequences of interiors and exteriors in triptychs, as if installing paintings of still lifes and landscape in the space of the gallery. Here, as elsewhere in Akerman's work, screens ultimately become the storage space for a mnemonic itinerary, transformed into a moving cultural archive.

Akerman's screen is a porous material that mediates an intensive sense of projection, a relationship between inside and outside, physical and mental space. Her traveling-dwelling in material space forms a psychogeography, and it involves a particular form of spectatorship. With her characteristic frames fixed as if to seize any motion that enters within them, Akerman, in films such as *Toute une nuit* (1982) or *Les Rendez-vous d'Anna* (1978), constructs a geometry of passage and a relational form of screening that empathetically includes us viewers. Typically in her cinema, the camera position is not centered on character identification but tends rather to move independently, remaining steady in time to observe space. It does not ask us to pry but simply to witness. We are made to exist in the space and invited to stay overtime. This 'being there' in time enables us to make a psychic leap, going beyond mere attendance toward a more intimate involvement. Refusing voyeurism and reaching for a closer spectatorial position, the work finally allows us to become participants. In this way, a visitor to Akerman's world can even become sensitized to her own position in it. The placement of her camera sometimes indicates where the author stands in all senses, since it even includes the measure of her slight height. It is a position that marks her presence there, never so close as to interfere or so far that her presence as a fellow traveler is not felt.

Fig. M.2. Chantal Akerman, *Nightfall on Shanghai* (2009)

From Akerman's screens of projection, then, an experience of *Einfühlung* emerges: a 'feeling into' the space of both landscape and streetscape. A sense of material space is enhanced by her careful architectonics of shot composition. Here, a purely formal arrangement, like an empty frame, can convey an affect. As an atmosphere unfolds in slow time-space, we can absorb what is in the air and share in a mood. Akerman's work is, indeed, about this particular affect: a psychic atmosphere that transpires on the surface of things. Shot in what I would ultimately call a distant intimacy, her images are formally arranged to allow for the kind of reserve that is needed to engage us closely. They enable, that is, the kind of analytic detachment — the form of screening — that is necessary to create real empathy.

This particular sense of 'screening' is materialized in a film such as *Là-bas* (2006), which reflects on the very notion of what a screen is, treating it as a space of filtering and an architecture of sifting. Akerman increasingly explored her Jewish identity and family history in recent years, and *Là-bas* chronicles her sojourn in Tel Aviv with an act of screening space that makes ambiguous, even conflicting feelings of belonging clearly felt. Refusing to represent any site of traumatic history directly, she shoots the film mostly from the interior of an apartment. She allows us to see the outside world only through blinds that are made of loosely woven reeds. A screen-partition is constructed to form a delicate physical boundary between inside and outside. This screen functions to filter the outside world but also 'curtains' the space inside, enabling layers of history and memory to sift through. The screen fabric offers Akerman the shelter she needs 'over there' to look out and see inside herself. Such a screen makes a process of introjection possible within its boundaries, which can be crossed. Over time, then, the screen becomes a textured space that retains complex forms of projection within its fabric. The material of this interwoven screen projects the filmmaker's viewpoint and fabrication of intimacy. It is tailored to hold Akerman's particular version of empathy: a position of distant proximity.

We emerge with Akerman into the world only to look inward; we remain inside to look out. In this way, we plunge into the depth of a psychic, subjective space and even into personal history. Regardless of the distance we have traveled, the journey of discovery inevitably turns out to be an inner journey, one of self-analysis. We recognize this particular chamber. We know this curtained world, filtered through the screen of the installation of *Là-bas*, for we have been asked before to dwell in this room. Moving through the architecture of the interior in films such as *Saute ma ville*, *La chambre I* (1972), *Je tu il elle* (1975), or even *Hotel Monterey* (1972) or *Demain on déménage* (2004), we have traversed a textured geography of interiority, through a scene both familiar and familial.

This sense of familiarity invokes the familial because Akerman's inner explorations, in film as in writing, are haunted by the maternal. Akerman's mother, the subject of her 2013 memoir *Ma mère rit*, is present even when she is not there, as in *News from Home* (1976), where the visual chronicle of the filmmaker's life in New York is tied to the sound of her letters. Concern and care, in Akerman's world, also reveal that a mother's traumatic history can live on inside her daughter, who must often struggle to exit her world. This experience is a familiar scene in psychoanalytic terms. Such representations of the ties that bind mother-daughter, and of a chamber turning into confinement — the complex nuances of *oikos* — touch a generational chord. And so even if one was not fortunate enough to know Akerman personally, this inner vision can feel familiarly close.* It is as if this woman, this artist, had the ability to relay experiences that come from a place of reflection inside many of us.

Despite the various media or locations they employ, whether in the cinema or the art gallery, as we step into any of Akerman's many chambers we access rooms of projection that envelop us empathetically, for in these chambers we sense the depth of an intimate experience that we can share. Resting on the border of the screen of projection, this particular 'feeling into' the space can become a mutual boundary to cross. And thus, safely positioned at a distance, we too can engage our own perilous history of projection: a voyage to — and a view from — home.

Until, abruptly, Akerman's journey reaches an end, with the terminal *No Home Movie* (2015). In her final chronicle of women's lives, interior scenes in her mother's Brussels apartment are intercut with moving desert scenes shared with her gallery film *Now*. Akerman documents her mother ailing and dying in her presence, even in virtual presence, as Skype is used as a way not simply of communicating but of making a film where there is no more distance. In this way, she renders the time of aging as it is, not as it is shown in movies. Caring for one's mother is here an everyday occurrence, a quotidian worry, even a tedious experience made of daily chores, constant care, and watching. One waits for that meaningful conversation that might shed some light on traumatic family history and afford release, but in vain. In this personal documentary, time flows as it does in real experience, not as a series of events but as inexorable flux. In the end, after her mother has died off screen, Akerman herself exits the scene, leaving her empty room behind. In film, as in life, that chamber can no longer be inhabited. Akerman's last film was not a home movie, and there will be no more home to look into. The door of that familiar, exploratory chamber has been shut forever, for her and for us.

---

* I am grateful to Annette Michelson for introducing me to Chantal in the early 1980s, initiating a friendship that has much enriched my life and work.

CHAPTER 1

❖

A Tree in the Wind: Chantal Akerman's Later Self-Portraits in Installation and Film

Sandy Flitterman-Lewis

> I am myself the matter of my book.
> MICHEL DE MONTAIGNE

> To tell the truth about oneself, to discover oneself near at hand, is not easy. [Montaigne tells us that] 'tis a rugged road, more so than it seems, to follow a pace so rambling and uncertain, as that of the soul; to penetrate the dark profundities of its intricate internal windings; to choose and lay hold of so many little nimble motions.' There is, in the first place, the difficulty of expression.
> VIRGINIA WOOLF[1]

In her later work, and in the (*auto*)biographical film that punctuates the end of her life and her career, Chantal Akerman has increasingly explored identity as a function of home. But this elusive concept raises more questions about the self than it answers. *No Home Movie* (2015), her last film, a poignant chronicle of her mother dying in her Brussels apartment while Chantal visits or Skypes, with some Israeli desert punctuation, and *Là-bas* (2006), an anti-travelogue in Israel, where stasis replaces movement, space replaces character, and interior replaces the sweep of landscape (as it is mostly shot from within the apartment where Chantal is staying, with occasional forays to the beach) are intensely personal films. The claustrophobic structuring of her final film locates us in the subjective maternal realm, one repeated throughout her oeuvre, while the deceptive travelogue of *Là-bas* depicts intense and memorable moments of landscape and physical space among the main sequences of enclosure and meditation, suggesting both the existence and the impossibility of Eretz Yisroael, the land of Israel. In all of her work the impact of personal stories and subjective experience mingles with glimpses of the natural world and domestic space in order to expand on the wider philosophical terrains of community and memory. Across multiple forms, from films to installations, to novels and multimedia presentations, there are discursive refrains that traverse her work in both manifest and subtle ways: restlessness, nomadism, borders, exile, rootlessness, maternal connection and distance, personal history and collective memory, marginality and displacement, subjective reflection and historical trauma. And all of these radiate from Akerman's central project of continually defining and communicating her complex and contradictory self, a self profoundly embedded in history and intensely cognizant of contemporary realities, especially those impacting on her life as a Jewish woman.

No Home Movie and *Là-bas* are also the films that most reflect an inner subjective core at one with a landscape that Akerman doesn't wholly own, and thus the paradox of identity and place, especially for a peripatetic filmmaker like Chantal Akerman, comes to the fore. *I Don't Belong Anywhere*, the suggestively titled experimental biopic by Marianne Lambert, is equally taken with the Israeli landscape, especially in its closing shot of Chantal walking away from us, Chaplin-like, on a desert road in the Negev, among the tanks and leftover artillery of the Six-Day War. She interrupts her path, in an eerily prescient move, by turning to us and smiling, then receding into the distance, proceeding on her way. Marianne Lambert's film gives the impression that it was Akerman who actually made the film herself (a kind of sequel to the autobiographical *Chantal Akerman by Chantal Akerman* made for *Cinéma de notre temps* in 1996) but has chosen to present it as the work of another. It is filled with her personality, her process, and her prerogatives. And while director Lambert might disagree, this pairing of the documentary with Akerman's own films duplicates the problematic and complicated sense of self in motion while asserting in its recurring images of nature, a fundamental and enduring presence.

A further amplification comes from the relatively simultaneous installations that Akerman has created in gallery and museum spaces that reproduce the thematics of identity and landscape, exile and domesticity, memory and history, while expanding the definitions of visual representation and spectatorship. In fact, Akerman has stated her preference for installation art because it is more direct, more expressive of her sense of self-in-relation, and more evocative of the intersections of the personal and the social. She has referred to installation work as 'pure joy', enabling her to do what she wanted without the burden of film preparation. She further asserts that there is a freedom and a subtlety permitted in these video installations, especially in terms of both landscape and ephemeral personal intuitions. For her, this work is closer to writing, but with a strong visual component; its three-dimensionality brings the viewers closer to experiencing her concerns as their own (what she calls 'the passage from one unconscious toward the other').[2] These installations absorb their viewers in a palpable experience of emotional time, they envelop them in a sensual, contemplative realm where translation is impossible and experience is at the forefront. In addition, and this is a crucial point, these installations trace the emergent and increasingly central exploration of Jewish identity and history in Akerman's work. It is as if the installations liberated her from the cinematic constraints that only allowed for hints and allusions, and this laid the groundwork for the emergence of the complex Jewish self that engages Akerman in so much of her later work. These films and installations trace the philosophy of absence, the geography of the heart that lend the Akerman oeuvre its profound coherence. From Brussels to Tel Aviv, Paris to New York, from Texas to Moscow and California to Shanghai, the nomadic Akerman has sought, through her tender yet observational looks at the 'other', a way of defining herself as an artist, a daughter, a woman, and an inheritor of the Shoah.

Chantal Akerman belongs to the Second Generation of the Holocaust, those children of survivors of Auschwitz and elsewhere who bear the burden of an unspoken trauma that haunts them although they have no direct experience of it. Her mother Natalia (Nelly) had fled pogroms in Poland with her family and settled in Belgium in 1938. Nelly was a teenager when they were denounced by an acquaintance and sent to the concentration camp; although her parents were murdered there, she and her sisters survived the death march and made new lives in Belgium, Canada, and Israel. Although Akerman was born in 1950, she often refers to the fact that her whole life has been in the shadow of the Shoah (she would say in *Là-Bas*, 'The Yellow Star, it is inside of me'). This becomes more and more evident as her work progresses and she finds new ways to articulate the unspeakable, to philosophize absence, and to explore the depths of the ever-present unseen. Something else she mentions frequently: her mother's silence. '[My mother] never wanted to speak about Auschwitz. I asked her once to tell me more, and she said, "No I will get crazy." So we could speak around or after, or before, but the real moment, never. Not directly.'[3] Elsewhere Akerman has said, 'There's nothing to say, my mother said, and it's on this nothing that I continue to work.' Writer Cécile Chich explains: 'This is it, precisely! Chantal's films always are about the unfathomable void which is the mark of her mother's direct experience of the Holocaust.'[4]

While many of Akerman's early films (from the experimental urban texts in Brussels and New York to her landmark first feature of domesticity and suppressed rage, *Jeanne Dielman, 23, Quai du Commerce, 1080 Bruxelles*) contain oblique references to the psychic wound of the Shoah, she does not specifically treat it literally until the question emerges in the space *between* film and installation begun with the duo *D'Est* (1993) and *D'Est: au bord de la fiction* (1995), and carried through the rest of her career with subtle and complex bonds between certain films and video installations, whether in chronology or not. One can say that there is already, in a sense, a specific concern with exile and Jewish identity in 1988 with *Histoires d'Amérique: Food, Family, Philosophy*, but this is Akerman's film closest to a performance piece installation in its frontality, its staged monologues, its ephemeral space, and its ellipses. Even at this point Bérénice Reynaud makes the connection: '[this] is a film of phantoms, filmed in a phantom city, that confronts [...] the symbolic work of death [...] trying to answer the essential question of our time: "how can one make cinema after Auschwitz?"'[5] But with the film *D'Est*, whose images are unaccompanied by Akerman's signature meditative voice (or any voice, for that matter), the explicit posing of this sort of question is hidden under the surface; we must wait two years for the installation to find the articulation of Chantal's deepest concerns with diasporic Jewish identity in complex relation to historical trauma. Taken in tandem, the film and its partner installation provide something of the haunting ephemerality that contrasts the documentary view associated with the quasi-objectivity of the film alone. *D'Est* is a sort of avant-garde look, in static or lateral tracking shots, at the newly constituted Eastern Bloc countries and their people; it invites us to question the harsh reality — and even the strangeness — of Eastern European life. But when it is seen in the context of the installation *Au bord de la fiction*, where unmoored homelessness, endless waiting, and continual wandering (of the camera, of the people) is paired with a meditation on the (largely unanswered) questions of both Jewish identity and the Shoah, these images retroactively take on a significance beyond their literal denoted meaning. This is what Kathryn Potts calls 'the inextricable connections among Eastern Europe, the history of the Jewish people and the memory of the Holocaust.'[6]

It is no accident that both film and installation involve something of a voyage backward in time and space while maintaining a captivating material presence. The film itself literally retraces in reverse direction (that is from East Germany to Poland to Russia) the migration of the Jews as they fled westward from the violence of pogroms and anti-Semitic riots. (This inverts the immigrant's trajectory of *Histoires d'Amérique*, where Eastern Europeans tell their stories and jokes on a vague Brooklyn terrain.) The film's movement is also from Summer to Winter, that is from the carefree oscillation of sunlight and shade to the frozen darkness of ice and snow, with punctuating moments of interior warmth, suggestive of the possibilities of home, but never materialized in an enduring fiction.

The film was made, and shown, in 1993; Akerman was subsequently asked to create an art installation, and she chose, for her first entry into gallery space, to construct a three-dimensional experience around that film, thus simultaneously crystallizing and reinventing cinema spectatorship. In a darkened room twenty-four television screens (eight 'triptychs' as Akerman called them) portrayed portions of the film *D'Est*, allowing viewers to construct their own combinatory representations of that 'East' from which the images flow. The film itself was screened continuously in its entirety in the first room. The final room had one small television screen on the floor, on which, after a fade of a single nighttime image from the film, Akerman read first in Hebrew and then in English, the Second Commandment of the Bible prohibiting representation and idol worship: 'Thou shalt not make unto thee a graven image, or any manner of likeness, of any thing that is in heaven above [...] thou shalt not bow down unto them, nor serve them [...].' In a second text Akerman read from her film notes, culminating in the following meditation:

> whether from long ago or still to come, old images that are barely concealed by other more luminous, even radiant ones: old images of evacuation, of people with packages marching in the snow toward an unknown place, of faces and bodies placed side by side, faces that vacillate between a strong life and the possibility of a death that would come to strike them without their having asked for anything.
>
> And it's always like that.
>
> Yesterday, today, and tomorrow, there were, there will be, there are right now, even, people that history (without a capital H) comes to strike. People who are there, rounded up in herds, waiting to be killed, hit, or starved; people who walk without knowing where they're going, in a group or alone.

There's nothing to be done; it's obsessive and it obsesses me.

Despite the cello, despite the cinema.
The film finished, I say to myself, *that's* what it was; once again *that.*[7]

This is a cryptic statement, one that articulates the unease hovering about the languid flow of images of post-Wall Eastern Europeans that comprise both film and installation. These thoughts in the closing 'monologue' are aporetic, bespeaking the anxiety that arises from knowledge of the insufficiency of representation. The vagueness of this *'that'* simultaneously poses questions and hauntingly suggests possible answers, framing this pronoun without an antecedent in lamentation and meditative anguish. On the soundtrack, in the background, Sonia Wieder-Atherton's cello plays a variant on the sacred chant of Yom Kippur, the Kol Nidre. This music has bound the Jews together through centuries of history and geographic dispersion in a ceremonial request to God that all prior oaths and vows be annulled. The Kol Nidre, like the Second Commandment (and even the Shofar) creates a liturgical space without an edifice, an unspoken bond that allows for an inherited tradition to be transmitted not concretely but obliquely. Thus without ever stating it explicitly, in this installation Akerman's virtual confession evokes the Shoah, whose implicit presence in the film must await the *performance* of this intimate and specific anxiety to gain its meaning.

Watching the film *D'Est* in its sequential unfolding provides the viewer with a two-hour voyage across forbidding terrain and implacable faces, images both mysterious and unyielding yet intriguing and strangely alluring. Waiting, standing, frozen, or sheltered in train or bus stations — locations of transit typical of Akerman's work. Intense visuality suggests the material weight of circumstances. Warm interiors contrast with unyielding cold as fur-hatted and bundled denizens stare bleakly at the surveying eye. Marion Schmid's illuminating analysis gives us an even more precise description of both the film and the implicit philosophical and cultural meanings provided by the installation:

> *D'Est* is arguably Chantal Akerman's most complex and representative work on time, space and memory. Expanding traditional boundaries of the documentary with her stylized images bordering on fiction and letting echoes of the past haunt her portrait of the present, the director creates a multi-layered work which collapses past, present and future into a hallucinatory vision; a work replete with memory, but which eschews explicit commemoration and one which, through its haunted images of destitution, warns of humanity's fragility before the vagaries of History.[8]

The move from the frozen lands of Eastern Europe and Russia to the more temperate climate of one specific place characterizes my next analysis. Israel, and its complicated place in the Akerman quest for self, is at the core of the second pairing of film and installation discussed here, although a period of about nine years separates the film (made in 2006) from Chantal's last installation (2015). Yet the voiceover questions and meditations posed in *Là-bas* — Chantal's only film made in Israel and redolent with reflections on personal and global history, family stories and the Shoah, discourses on food and philosophy (echoes of *Histoires d'Amérique*),

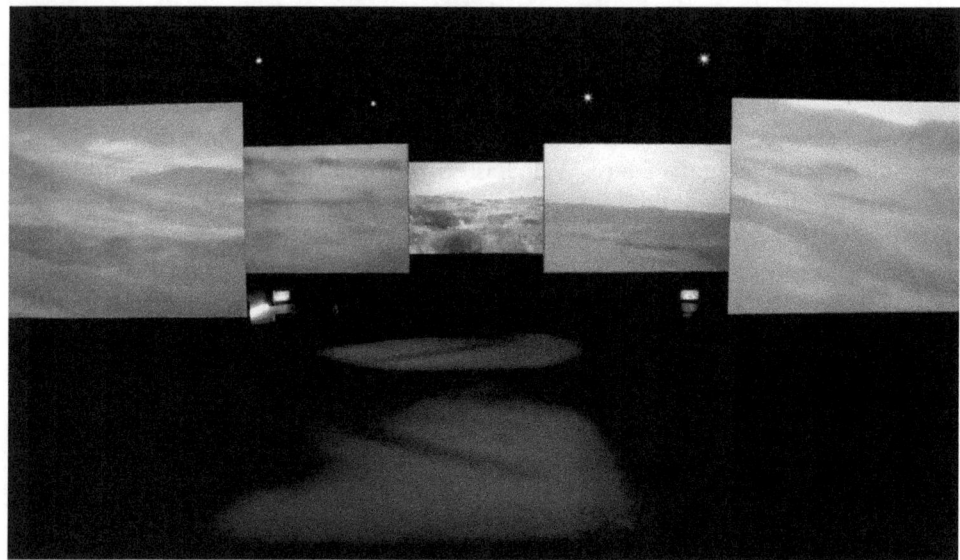

FIG. 1.1. Chantal Akerman, *NOW* (2015)

and reflections on present day geopolitics — are profoundly rooted in a sense of place whose very existence is ceaselessly contested and uncertain. These questions can be seen to find their disturbing culmination in Akerman's final installation, *NOW*, an installation that is at once abstract and very concrete, as open-ended as the most salient text of modernism and as specific as a documentary on the crisis-ridden Middle East and its effects on the contemplative soul. Made for the Venice Biennale and purchased by the Jewish Museum in New York for its permanent collection, *NOW* was created so that its audience would experience 'fear, war, flight, imminent disaster through the entanglement of the soundtracks in space.'[9] Five suspended screens and two floor projections depict violently moving desert landscapes that periodically settle into recognizable views before chaotically resuming the visual turbulence of the terrain. The curious placement of two tiny neon aquariums with electronic fish at the back of the installation provoke further speculation by viewers who seek connections between the realism of the moving landscapes and the fanciful brightness of these unexpected objects. The result is 'a montage architecture that engages the visitor in nomadism typical of Akerman who sees in landscapes "...the idea that the earth we possess is always a sign of barbarism and bloodshed."'[10] As Claire Atherton (who collaborated with Akerman on her installations) explains, Chantal wanted us to live and experience the chaos felt in our world deranged by violence.

Adrian Searle describes it in the following way:

> There is no sign of human presence in Akerman's final gallery work [...]. Horizons rush across the screens, grey deserts sweep away and nearer bluffs of red rock and crumbling stone walls rush from left to right, sometimes faster, sometimes slowing to a halt. Visually relentless, Akerman's *NOW* is also a furious aural cacophony, filled with the sound of skylarks, gunfire, ululations,

calls and cries, the whinny of frightened horses, the sound of helicopter blades, thuds, [whispered prayers], engine noise and armoury. We hear all this but the deserts are empty.[11]

This is truly the culmination of the injunction against image-idolatry that shaped the final sequence of *Bordering on Fiction* (her first installation), and it finally makes sense as a guiding principle of Akerman's art. Marion Schmid, in another context, gives this indecipherability significance: 'Place itself becomes the main protagonist [...] and landscape [...] takes on an important role as a locus of the manifold inscriptions and a repository of memory.'[12] But the visual space of this 'immersive' three-dimensional installation is free of any comforting denotation and the viewer is left to wander through this complex of disturbing sounds and images while the meditative self of *Là-bas* has dissolved into the impossible landscape of contested space. Here the brutalities of the memory of the Shoah (loss, death, destruction, absence, emptiness) are suggested in a refusal of representation as the viewer is made to question the significance of these long travelling shots of the arid Negev, sometimes projected on ancient stones, while Akerman diffuses herself among the perplexing images, present only in suggestions of authorship and a few whispered lines. Here the 'burden of a traumatic history'[13] — the '*that* again' which is at the core of her work — is rendered as a silent, haunting core dispersed among images evoking centuries-old tragic lamentation and contemporary anguish.

When asked by Nicole Brenez for a short description of *Là-bas*, Akerman replied 'Chantal in Israel. Complicated.'[14] Later in the same interview she says, 'I love Israel, even if it's its own form of exile.'[15] The paradox of this homeland that is not a home, this country that is never travelled in a film that purports to be 'about' the land, the subjective musings both philosophical and mundane of a person who is never visible except for the occasional glimpse or shadow, is exactly what one expects from Chantal in a film about Israel. Filled with contradictions, dense with an unexpressed history, signifying both hope and apprehension, Israel as a topic for a film conjures up the ineffable. Always searching for new ways to explore time, space, and memory, to imbue the banal and domestic with the significance of history, Akerman chooses to be present in this film by her voice alone, her characteristic monotone accompanying images exquisite in their visual ordinariness. Yet it is a 'subjective documentary', as much about Akerman's own complex histories as it is about the place that evokes them. Ensconced within the confines of an apartment whose windows are shadowed by matchstick shades, the camera-eye surveys the daily goings-on of Chantal's elderly neighbors in images that conjure up the flat expanses of unexpected beauty in Richard Diebenkorn's abstract paintings. Static shots of inside the apartment combined with views of the outside (hints of a perverse *Rear Window*, sans drama) are accompanied by Akerman's voice reading jottings from a personal journal about Judaism, cinema, her family, and two suicides by women 'who felt exile wherever they were', women that seem to haunt her (her aunt — a survivor of Auschwitz — and novelist Amos Oz's mother, at the beginning of the founding of Israel). Three telephone conversations, with some Hebrew, and a few trips to the beach, suggest a connection with the world outside, but they are tenuous at best. Citing the film's pervasive feeling of loneliness, claustrophobia, and oppressiveness, in spite of its breathtaking visual beauty, writer Dana Gilerman notes:

> Akerman defines her film as a philosophical treatise, an intimate reflection of inner thoughts about [dis]placement and identity and about her constant sense of self as an exile. [...] The dark space, the light that enters from outside, compacted with the inability to go out, create a sense of strangled space. The moments of optimism lie 'down there', in the figures she films on the beach.[16]

The part of the monologue that is the most explicit predicts not only the title, but the overwhelming sense of longing and instability of Marianne Lambert's biographical film nine years later, *I Don't Belong Anywhere*: 'I don't feel like I belong. And that's without real pain, without pride. No, I'm just disconnected. From practically everything. I have a few anchors. And sometimes I let them go or they let me go and I drift. That's most of the time. Sometimes I hang on. For a few days, minutes, seconds. Then I let go again.' In *Là-bas* as elsewhere in her oeuvre, Chantal Akerman asks unresolvable questions (about Israel, about Jewish identity, about the Shoah and its aftereffects) and her films provide only partial resolutions in themselves. Questioning, reflecting, refusing pat answers, so that the open-ended works can engage and speak to us directly, providing us with a series of possibilities and their opposite — that in itself is a kind of resolution.

One of those 'anchors' (especially in this film where the voice at the end of the telephone is like a lifeline) has always been Chantal's mother, Natalia (Nelly) Leibel Akerman. As noted, she is literally at the heart of Akerman's cinematic and video production: Chantal stated in 2011, 'The only subject of my films is my mother.'[17] This must be taken symbolically, because while Natalia is literally absent from many of the films, the complex relationship with her daughter hovers over the work in the feelings of longing and desire, memory and connectedness that are alluded to throughout her oeuvre. Because of the inherited memory of the Shoah, Chantal places herself in a line of matrilineal suffering that embraces her mother, her (unknown) grandmother, and that community of women (including Marceline Loridan-Ivens and Simone Veil) who share, whether articulated or not, stories and memories of an unspeakable past. There is a special poignancy to Akerman's last film, *No Home Movie*, whose ambiguous title complicates the documentation of Nelly's decline into death while Chantal addresses her either from within her Brussels apartment or from work-related distances. Chantal's chronicle in film is at once a final attempt to articulate a connection to her own and her mother's histories and a desperate, passionate attempt to halt the inevitable. In many ways the film is a sort of culmination of Akerman's visual strategies and conceptual concerns, and its emphasis on her relationship to her mother makes it a thematic center as well. It is here that the nexus of Mother, Memory, Shoah and Home coalesce in what will be a final and finite representation.

The film also acts as a kind of bookend to one of Chantal's earliest films, *News From Home*, made some forty years earlier in New York. In that film Nelly's longing for her far away daughter is rendered on the soundtrack; Chantal reads her mother's letters from Nelly's unseen Brussels apartment as her camera discloses varied images of everyday New York. In her final film, it is Chantal who does most of the talking, either from within Nelly's apartment, or in Skyped conversations and deliberations with her editor over the video image. The camera traces every room, every domestic space from kitchen to dining room to living room with the attentiveness we have come to recognize as an Akerman signature. These are relatively empty spaces that we know are imbued with meaning. Now it is the mother who is visually embodied, present even as she is disappearing from life. And Chantal documents the personal tragedy with the same kind of subjective-objective view that characterizes her best work, documenting the ineffable in empty spaces that speak volumes.

Chantal's sense of alterity, of non-belonging, is posed in this film by its very title. As she documents the fading of the home associated with her mother, Chantal's verbal play with the film's subject introduces us to the complexity of the unmooring. *No Home Movie* suggests first that this is not a home movie in the tradition of amateur family recordings. But *No Home Movie* also suggests that this is a movie about 'No Home', about not having a home, a film about rootlessness. This is also a movie about a place that is not a home. And it is also a movie about 'not-home', that is, about the unrepresentable desire for the absent home. But most important, while Nelly's impact is felt in most of Akerman's work, this is the film in which her presence is extensive and explicit. The film is suffused with love, for Chantal's mother is indeed her home, her anchor, her place of return. It is also filled with the devastating realization that this place, both ephemeral and concrete, will cease to exist. Chantal refers to this displacement in an interview about the film: 'Even if I have a home in Paris and sometimes in New York, whenever I was saying I have to go home, it was going to my mother. And there is "no home" anymore because she isn't there, and when I came the last time, the home was empty.'[18]

One of the last shots of the film has Chantal packing her suitcase and tying her shoelaces. This ordinary gesture is full of meaning: it references the installation that I pair with this film (most notably because of the centrality of the maternal relationship and its sorrowful legacies of loss and silence), and, although it precedes *No Home Movie* by about ten years, I consider it to be at the very heart of Akerman's work. 'To Walk Beside One's Shoelaces in an Empty Fridge' (2004), whose cryptic title begins with an expression that means 'to be totally out of it', was inspired by the discovery of a diary that Nelly's mother had kept as a young woman, begun when she was just 15. She died in Auschwitz at the age of 30, leaving Nelly without a mother and Chantal without a grandmother, and thus making the notebook a haunting memento of the ghosts of the Shoah while suggesting the inevitable gaps in personal history that Akerman has been obsessed with. Written in Polish and marginally inscribed with comments by Natalia, the young Chantal, and her sister Sylviane, it becomes a testament to a shared heritage of maternal suffering, but also of creativity and even joy. With a beautiful watercolor sketch of an elegant woman placed at the front and beginning with the audacious statement, 'I am a woman', this diary is central to Akerman's absorbing installation that begins a quest that

No Home Movie can be said to resolve, the installation's probing of Natalia's silence and the first tentative moments of exchange terminating in the conversations that Chantal ultimately has with her mother in her final film.

Dana Gilerman's description of this exquisite installation allows us to be participants:

> [The installation] is made up of spiral-shaped fabric inscribed with text dealing with thoughts on cinema and her own work. The spiral leads into a room where [an image of the journal is projected on a tulle screen and] a film of the director and her mother, who was the inspiration for many of the characters in her films, is projected. The intimate and moving conversation between the two begins with a simple request from the daughter that her mother translate for her (from Polish into French) a single page of the diary written by her grandmother who was murdered in Auschwitz. This is the first time that the mother, 79, talks to Akerman, 56, about the war.[19]

We learn that Chantal's grandmother was an artist and a painter, that she was an independent spirit in a deeply religious community in a Polish village, and that she would paint or go to the cinema instead of observing the Sabbath. From the diaphanous fabric, the inscription of writing on the translucent mobile surface and from the intimate moment of discovery and sharing between mother and daughter, the installation places us within a world of memory, identity, exile and connection, reinforcing in a very direct and absorbing way Chantal's conviction about the piece: 'It touched [my mother]. Not only because of what she said but also because of the beautiful relationship between me and her, mother and daughter. ... [In] all of my films I always speak her name. This time it was she who sat in front of the camera and told her story.'[20]

A Tree in the Wind

Chantal Akerman famously said that her concerns were 'language, documentary, fiction, Jews, and the Second Commandment.' Marianne Lambert's film, *I Don't Belong Anywhere*, seeks to expand on this with Chantal's help: we see clips of her films, we see her working and laughing with her editor Claire Atherton, joking about the lesson in editing that some of Chantal's images provide, we see a biographical sketch amplified by cinematic examples from her oeuvre, we see people that she worked with, such as actress Aurore Clément, and those that were inspired by her. But most important, we see her in the Israeli desert as she contemplates the kind of representation that has been her life's work. As she perches on an abandoned tank near the end of the film, and before her solitary departure down the desert road, she delivers what can be understood as a kind of *ars poetica*: 'From the moment there were concentration camps there were things that could not be shown. Unbearable. A real shaking up of our European civilization, and things would never be the same after that. And that's the reason I film this way. There are things that can't be shown.'

Important for a deeper understanding of how this is represented in the work are two elements contained in Lambert's film, elements that are repeated from

Fig. 1.2. Chantal Akerman, *Marcher à côté de ses lacets dans un frigidaire vide* (2004)

elsewhere in key Akerman texts: the Chasidic tale and the tree. Chantal recites the tale in heavily accented English very close to the opening of *I Belong Nowhere*; its antecedent appearances are in *Histoires d'Amérique*, her first 'Jewish' film, and in *Chantal Akerman par Chantal Akerman*, her first attempt at an autobiographical portrait in film. The repetition of this story gives it a central place in the Akerman oeuvre, linking Jewish tradition, storytelling, and generational transmission. In spite of the injunction and the impossibility suggested by Akerman's discourse on the tank, something human endures in the capacity to share language, to share a connection through narrative:

> A rabbi always passed through a village to get to the forest and there, at the foot of a tree, and it was always the same one, he began to pray and God heard him. His son, too, always passed through the village to get to the forest, but he could not remember where the tree was, so he prayed at the foot of any old tree and God heard him. His grandson did not know where the tree was, nor the forest, so he went to pray in the village and God heard him. His great-grandson did not know where the tree was, nor the forest and not even the village, but he still knew the words of the prayer, so he prayed in his house and God heard him. His great-great grandson did not know where the tree, nor the forest, nor the village were, not even the words of the prayer, but he still knew the story, so he told it to his children and God heard him.

The tree is also graced with a privileged position in this film. This scraggly yet sturdy tree, green and resilient in the driving wind of the Israeli desert, opens *No Home Movie* in a static four-minute shot that leaves us contemplative and engaged before the main matter of Nelly's waning life is on the screen. It is repeated in *I Don't Belong Anywhere* as Chantal and Claire view it on an editing screen, and in this gesture it becomes iconic. The reproduced image of this unexpected strength, this endurance in the face of historical trauma and sorrow, its placement both on the screen and in contested lands, impels us to return to Chantal Akerman's work with the same resisting energy that she herself devoted to it. 'I want people to feel the passing of time', she says after viewing the tree on the screen, 'I want them to feel something.'

It is interesting to note that Chantal's filmmaking career can be said to be framed by two Delphines: Delphine Seyrig, whose unforgettable embodiment of Jeanne Dielman in what the *New York Times* called 'the first film in the feminine', became a touchstone for all discussions of feminist filmmaking, and Delphine Horvilleur, the woman rabbi (one of three in France) whose desire to bring a more secular and inclusive engagement to the Jewish community produced the stunning eulogy for Chantal at Père Lachaise. Image and word, the two poles of Akerman's artistic production, framing a career that produced over forty films, more than a dozen installations, and a number of written texts that redefined autobiography. Seyrig was already a star when the 24 year-old Akerman instructed her to 'walk into the kitchen, go to the sink, turn on the water, wash your hands for five seconds, turn off the water... etc.' And 'think anything you want', thereby defying all traditional forms of actor preparation. Delphine was later to say, when watching the dailies, 'You're right. It works.'[21] And Horvilleur captured the tragic sense of restlessness, exile, and traumatic history, as well as enduring love, in her eloquent eulogy:

> The child of a survivor. The child born after the catastrophe that we call the Shoah. A dark moment for humanity that she carried within her, everywhere she went. This is how, perhaps, the young girl, and then the young woman, learnt to live with her family's ghosts, and the ghosts of a lost world [...]. How to speak of the void? How to speak of loss? Or rather, who will speak of it better than Chantal? How to make presence be, in fact, the constant reminder of absence? Chantal chose to respond to this metaphysical question through her filmmaking, through her oeuvre.[22]

Notes to Chapter 1

1. Virginia Woolf, *The Common Reader* (Harcourt: Brace & World, Inc., 1925), p. 60. Woolf is quoting from *Essays of Montaigne*, translated by Charles Cotton.
2. Nicole Brenez, 'Chantal Akerman: The Pajama Interview', *LOLA*, 2 (2012).
3. Cited by Nicolas Rapold, 'Chantal Akerman Takes an Emotional Path in Film About "Maman"', review of *No Home Movie*, *New York Times*, 5 August 2015.
4. Private conversation with London-based writer.
5. Bérénice Reynaud, 'Histoires d'Amérique', *Chantal Akerman: Autoportrait en cinéaste* (Paris: Cahiers du Cinéma/Centre Pompidou, 2004), p. 202.
6. Kathryn Potts, Assistant Curator and Coordinator of the Jewish Museum's presentation of *D'Est: Au bord de la fiction*, New York, 1996.
7. Chantal Akerman, from the audio-text of *Bordering on Fiction*, 1995.
8. Marion Schmid, *Chantal Akerman* (Manchester: Manchester UP, 2010), p. 107.
9. Text provided by the Jewish Museum press release, January 2018, taken from comments by

Akerman's editor and close collaborator on the installations, Claire Atherton.
10. Ibid.
11. Adrian Searle, 'The Last Picture Show: How Chantal Akerman's Suicide Alters Her Final Artwork', *The Guardian*, 4 November 2015/ 6 March 2017. This description makes one think of Virginia Woolf's final novel, *Between the Acts*, in its harrowing aural evocation of the crisis of modernity.
12. Schmid, *Chantal Akerman*, p. 99.
13. Schmid, *Chantal Akerman*, p. 88.
14. Brenez, 'The Pajama Interview'.
15. Ibid.
16. Dana Gilerman, 'In Exile: Here, There, and Everywhere', *Ha'Aretz*, 11 July 2006.
17. Brenez, 'The Pajama Interview'.
18. Quoted in Rapold, 'Chantal Akerman Takes an Emotional Path'.
19. Gilerman, 'In Exile'.
20. Gilerman, 'In Exile'.
21. Quoted by Henry Bean in his tribute in *The Forward*.
22. This essay is dedicated to my late mother-in-law Miriam Lewis, who, while not a survivor herself, made a loving Jewish home for us all. And gratitude to my twin sister, Sharon Flitterman-King, whose insight and compassion fuelled my writing. Thanks to my mentor Bertrand Augst, who first introduced me to Chantal's work in 1975. And of course joyful thanks to my husband Joel, who keeps me laughing.

CHAPTER 2

Moeder, Maman, Mom[1]

Carol Mavor

'We lay on our bed . . . and I fed you plums the colour of bruises.'
JEANETTE WINTERSON[2]

A bruise marks the distance and closeness of the encounter between an adolescent daughter and mother. A bleeding under the skin. Tender to the touch. Dark as the night, womb, underground. Blue as the sky, the veins that feed us, my mother's eyes. Wounds that keep us thinking about what happened. As the Canadian poet Margaret Atwood writes in her poem entitled 'What Happened':

> Meanwhile on several
> areas of my skin, strange bruises glow
> and fade, and I can't remember
> what accidents I had, whether I was
> badly hurt, how long ago.[3]

The past is irretrievable, but writing can provoke the bruising — give life's blood to the afterlives of those we mourn, including History herself.

A bruise is a wound that lies hiding under the skin.

'Moeder, Maman, Mom' (dark, sweet, tender, fleshy, tough-skinned, stony-hearted) is fed by three secret journals *bruisy* with the maternal.

★ ★ ★ ★ ★

The first journal is Anne Frank's famed diary, known in various edited and more complete forms as *The Secret Annexe [Het Achterhuis]* and *The Diary of a Young Girl*.[4] Her journal was written by Anne in Dutch — for two years between the ages of thirteen and fifteen, whilst hiding in Amsterdam from the Nazis. Anne tells 'Kitty' (the name she gave to her journal) all her secrets. Anne is a moody adolescent (in many ways typical of all girls of her age). She had to struggle to keep writing under the shadow of terror. She does her best to refuse what she calls 'turning the Secret Annexe into the Melancholy Annexe'.[5] Mother is a constant irritant to her. Father is 'the most adorable father' she 'has ever seen' [7].

> ANNE. 'I can imagine Mother dying someday, but Daddy's death seems inconceivable. It's very mean of me, but that's how I feel. I hope Mother will *never* read this or anything else I've written' [51].
> ANNE. '"Paper is more patient than people" [53].

I imagine the kind of mum [*mams*] I'd like to be to my children later on. The kind of mum [*mams*] who doesn't take everything people say too seriously, but who does take *me* seriously. I find it difficult to describe what I mean, but the word 'mum' [*mams*] says it all. Do you know what I've come up with? In order to give me the feeling of calling my mother something that sounds like "Mum" [*mams*], I often call her "Mumsie" [*Mansa*]. Sometimes I shorten it to "Mums" [*Mans*]: an imperfect "Mum" [*Mams*]. I wish I could honour her by removing the "s" [*n*]. It's a good thing she doesn't realize this, since it would only make her unhappy [153–54].'

The Diary of a Young Girl, 'the symbol of a wounded generation',[6] is a book that everyone seems to read as an adolescent in high school — and then it is, most often put away, almost hidden away. In a drawer. Or under a bed. Or tucked into a bookshelf and never turned to again. Or even a cardboard box of childhood things, stored in the attic.

In its English translation, I see Anne's name hiding in the title itself: *Anne*-xe.

★ ★ ★ ★ ★

The second is the teenage journal written by Chantal Akerman's grandmother, Sidonie Ehrenberg, an artist with 'golden hands'.[7] Sidonie's short-lived journal, written between 1920 and 1922, began when she was only thirteen years old, is featured in Akerman's installation and video, *Marcher à côté de ses lacets dans un frigidaire vide* (2004).[8] Like Akerman's *Jeanne Dielman, 23 Quai du Commerce, 1080 Bruxelles* (1975), it is a filmic love letter to Chantal's own mother Nelly, with Sidonie's journal serving as a mouthpiece to speak the unspeakable: Nelly's experiences at Auschwitz. Chantal's mother moved to Brussels 'in 1938 from a small town near Krakow. But strangely enough, in 1942 or 1943, she was taken back to Auschwitz, which was just 30 miles from where she grew up . . . Her parents died there and a lot of her family.'[9]

In Akerman's *Marcher à côté de ses lacets dans un frigidaire vide*, Sidonie's journal is barely seen and is, instead, heard through the voice of Nelly struggling to remember her Polish and to translate it into French, on the spot for Chantal. We watch the split video screen in black and white, going in and out of focus, like taking your reading glasses on and off. The mother and daughter look often into each other's eyes. Chantal asks her mother to read the first page.

> NELLY. 'All right, let's see if I can see with your glasses. Otherwise, mine are on the table there . . . Look her handwriting is already lovely . . . Look how small the writing is. Do you see? And look at this . . . The writing that I admire, so tiny . . .'

Sidonie's journal, written with hopeful adolescent suffering between the years of 1920–22, begins: 'I am woman!' Chantal and Nelly note the exclamation point with pleasure.

★ ★ ★ ★ ★

And lastly, the surprising secret taped journal entry made by my mother, Dorothy

FIG. 2.1. a and b. 'My little darling [*poupée*], I am so happy I have lived for this day.' (Chantal Akerman, *Marcher à côté de ses lacets dans un frigidaire vide*, 2004)

Aileen Mavor — when she was suffering from middle-life — spoken (not written) — when I was grown up: an old child. Like Akerman, 'I always, up to now, feel like an old child.'[10]

My mother's audio-journal is very short: only nine minutes and two seconds long.

My father and I found her secret hidden in a plastic cassette.

My mother made the tape on her mother's birthday. My mother's mother was born in Tennessee.

My mother's mother was thirteen and pregnant on her wedding day.

My mother's childhood memories are American Southern Gothic disturbing: twisted as the uncontrollable kudzu vines that grew all around her, overtaking everything in its path. (The Jack-in-the-Beanstalk vine. The vine that ate the South. The vine that strangled the South.)

My mother's memories are the stuff of Flannery O'Connor.

Desperate Dorothy-Allison poverty: 'shoes that went to paper in the rain'.[11]

> DOROTHY: 'Today is February 4th, 1992. It is my mother's birthday, and if she were alive today, she would be eighty-two years old. But she's not alive. And I'm alive. So what should I talk about?'[12]

Unlike Anne and unlike Sidonie, and, in turn, Nelly, my mother was barely touched by the war. Her wounding (incomparable) was cotton-picking familial. Her abuse was smothered in grey gravy. Her peril included eating greens boiled and drained four times, in hopes of getting the poison out.

Rickets.

Lice.

But like Nelly, whose experiences at Auschwitz greatly affected Akerman's childhood, so my mother's affected mine.

In an interview, Akerman explains: 'my mother was totally different from the mothers of my friends. She would never separate from me. In a way, my life belongs to her [...] My mother was so resentful that she did not have a career because after the war she was broken. She remembered her late mother [Sidonie], who had painted and drawn and made couture clothes, and she saw in me a continuation of her.'[13]

My mother's fears of separation were based on being left behind, ignored, unseen. She was paranoid it would happen again.

While Nelly encouraged her daughter to make something of her life, my mother was more like Akerman's father who wanted her to stay slim and get married. My mother wanted me to be just like her: a problem magnified by the fact that she was not sure who she was.

And unlike Akerman and more like Anne — as an adolescent, my mother was a constant irritant to me.

★ ★ ★ ★ ★

Around my swollen eye, a bruise the size of a new-born's is blossoming. At first, it was a pale-blue hydrangea. Then purple lilacs. Now a black-pansy, as if printed.

If I am not careful the bruise will heal, turning to weeping willow branches, whose pale green will be tinged with a hint of the blue that comes with the onset of summer. Then yellow-green moss. Then yellow freesia. Then nothing.[14]

Nothing cannot happen.

The pain and colour of the bruise must remain.

'There is hope and pain is implanted with hope',[15] writes Marguerite Duras.

DAGBOEK, LE JOURNAL INTIME, DIARY

dagboek

ANNE. 'I hope I will be able to confide everything to you' [1].

So begins Anne's journal.

Anne's red plaid diary, like a school-girl's skirt, which hits just above bruised knees, unfolds the stories of her life in the Secret Annexe. The diary was a gift for her thirteenth birthday: 'I'll begin from the moment I got you, the moment I saw you lying on the table among my other birthday presents' [1].

I have seen her precious diary, with its pages delicately, unashamedly open, in its clear glass box in The Anne Frank Huis.

A sleeping beauty who keeps the world awake.

'Kitty', as Elie Wiesel lacerates is not a book: it is 'a wound.'[16]

When reading *The Diary of a Young Girl*, we become Anne. We too, 'long to ride a bike, dance, whistle, look at the world, feel young', believe we are 'free' [153]. We want what Julia Kristeva calls 'adolescent reverie.'[17] We want to be adolescents.

'Kitty is ourselves, the reader.'[18]

I discover pages written with Anne's beloved fountain pen, with its 'thick nib', which had a 'long and interesting fountain-pen life' [145]. The pen was a gift from her grandmother when she was nine. It travelled with her to the annexe when she was thirteen, but met its demise when Anne was fourteen. Falling accidentally into the stove, like some horrific fairy tale: it burned. 'Not a trace of the gold nib was left. "It must have melted into stone", Father conjectured. I'm left with one consolation, small though it may be: my fountain pen was cremated, just as I would like to be some day' [146].

As a child, Sarah Kofman pinched her father's fountain pen from her mother's purse. Rabbi Bereck Kofman (Sarah's father) was picked up by the Vichy police from their home on Rue Ordener on 16 July 1942. The pulsing heart of the fountain pen writes even in brokenness (like Anne herself):

> I took it one day from my mother's purse, where she kept it along with some souvenirs of my father. It is a kind of pen no longer made, the kind you have to fill with ink. I used it all through school. It 'failed' me before I could bring myself to give it up, patched up with Scotch tape; it is right in front of me on my desk and makes me write, write.
>
> Maybe all of my books have been the detours required to bring me to write about 'that'.[19]

Anne's diary ends abruptly on 1 August 1944, her fountain pen vanished: 'if only there were no other people in the world' [334].

But there were and there still are.

le journal intime

> NELLY [reading Sidonie's journal in Polish and translating into French]. 'I can't tell all my secrets, all my hopes and all my thoughts, in a loud voice. Aloud. I can only suffer in secret my little journal.'
> CHANTAL [turning to her mother, looking into her mother's eyes, the eyes that had seen Auschwitz, the eyes that had seen Sidonie]. 'And this is the only thing you have left?'
> NELLY. 'Yes.'

And then Chantal shows Nelly that she has written in Sidonie's journal.

> CHANTAL. 'There it's you who signed it, that's your writing Maman.'
> NELLY. 'Why did I sign?'

Nelly does not remember writing in her mother's journal.

Then, we watch Nelly's head move gently back and forth as she silently discovers and examines where Chantal has also written in the diary. They laugh quietly together. (We never learn what Chantal wrote.)

Nelly gently takes Chantal's chin in her hand and kisses her daughter. '*Smack.*' A big laugh out of Nelly — and tears. She wipes her runny nose.

> CHANTAL. 'It's incredible . . .'
> NELLY. 'But how did you find it?'
> CHANTAL. 'I found it in a drawer. Obviously, I had no idea of what was written in it. I only saw that you had written in it, so I wrote in it too. I must have been about ten years old . . . and a few years later, Sylviane found it and also wrote in it . . . She must have been seven or eight years old.'
> NELLY. 'Yes she wrote something too.'
> NELLY. 'So . . . It's wonderful. Treasure it, it's all we have left [. . .] My little darling [*poupée*], I am so happy I have lived for this day.'

Sidonie, Nelly, Chantal, and Sylviane (Chantal's younger sister) all secretly wrote in this journal and this emerges in *Marcher à côté de ses lacets dans un frigidaire vide* — like writing in milk held up to the light of a warm candle to make a joy that cannot be extinguished.

What they wrote remains a hush-hush to us.[20]

diary

> DOROTHY. 'I *want* to record a message.' 'I *want* to record a message.'

These are the first two lines of my mother's audio journal. A one-day diary. Her singular repertoire. As an adolescent, I remember her writing a few notes in lined notebooks, like you would use for university. But they are gone. All we have left is her voice: which is a lot.

It is as if I am hearing her voice for the first time. Not only because she speaks with such uncharacteristic lucidity, but also because I listen to her without seeing her face, without seeing the almost disturbing liquid clarity of her pale aquamarine blue eyes, coupled with her high forehead and pronounced cheekbones, which figure so prominently in the old-fashioned roundness of her face.

The voice is hers, but unfamiliar. It is a kind of 'writing aloud'.[21] I admire it.

In her, I hear 'Marcel' hearing his grandmother's voice on the telephone for the first time: 'It is she, it is her voice that is speaking, that is there. But how far away it is!'[22]

That day when my mother spoke into the microphone, I was already thirty-five, living on the other side of the United States, a mother of two children.

I first heard my mother's recorded voice while driving in the car with my father. My mother was dead. The only tape player my father had after her death (now an outdated technology) was in the old Volvo.

We listened as we drove through the blandness of North Carolina suburbia — where housing developments have levelled the ever-abundant pine trees, exposing the red clay soil, like lacerations. We both felt the grain of her voice against the murmuring of what was left of the woodland.

Beginning with the first lines of her nine minutes and two seconds, my mother speaks of wanting — a wanting that cannot be fully expressed. I repeat her desperate repeating lines again.

> DOROTHY. 'I *want* to record a message. I *want* to record a message.'

My mother was a bored middle-class housewife. She went to university for the first time when I was in high school — she graduated, tried her hand at working, including being a teacher, but nothing was fulfilling — nothing stuck.

> DOROTHY. 'Someone should help me . . . somehow I should be able to help myself. But I . . . just go around constantly doing the same thing every day, never changing, never changing anything. Never changing anything.'

She is suffering from desire for desire.[23] She is dangerously waiting for nothing.

The last line comes abruptly.

> DOROTHY. 'That's the way I feel — perhaps I am wrong — I've been wrong before.'

FEMME-MAISON, WOMAN-HOUSE, HUISVROUW

huisvrouw

The house where Anne was hidden was a place of nesting secrets, like Russian dolls. Anne's journal was an infant house enclosing her most intimate thoughts — her teenage body was a child house that enclosed the diary — the Secret Annexe was a mother house (where she lived with her sister and parents, along with Mr and Mrs van Pels and their son Peter, as well as the dentist Fritz Pfeffer) — Prinsengracht 263 was a father house that contained them all, all the way back down to Anne's tiny heart. One beating inside the other, inside the other, inside the other, inside the other . . .

> ANNE. 'I hid inside myself, thought of no one but myself and calmly wrote down all my joy, sarcasm and sorrow in my diary' [157].

The Secret Annexe is where Anne began her period, became a woman.

> ANNE. 'Whenever I have my period (and that's only been three times), I have the feeling that in spite of all of the pain, discomfort and mess, I'm carrying

around a sweet secret. So even though it's a nuisance, in a certain way I'm always looking forward to the time when I'll feel that secret inside me once again' [159].

And she wears heels:

> ANNE. 'Everywhere I go, upstairs of down, they all cast admiring glances at my feet, which are adorned by a pair of exceptionally beautiful (for times like these!) shoes. Miep managed to snap them up for 27.50 guilders. Burgundy-coloured [*wijnrood*] suede and leather with medium-sized heels. I feel as if I'm on stilts, and look even taller than I already am' [129].

Her French vocabulary list recorded when she is age fourteen ends with the word *le sang*.[24]

Women are 'the walking wounded'[25] wrote Jules Michelet.

The Secret Annexe is now a public place: a museum. Anne Frank Huis.

The exterior black paint and the blocked-out glass windows are so shiny black that Prinsengracht 263 appears as a big black mirror: as if the smooth dark canal before it has stood up straight to reach for the sky.

The opening doors of Prinsengracht 263 are now permanently closed. Today people enter in great throngs after waiting in long queues through an entrance around the corner.

On each side of the original doors are two white placards: one with the house number '263', and the other spelling out 'ANNE FRANK HUIS'. People pose in front of the house to be photographed. Especially young girls who pull up their short skirts to make them a bit shorter, bend a knee flirtatiously towards the camera, pull their peasant tops further off their shoulders, take off their dark glasses, smile with their freshly lip-sticked mouths. '*Click*'.

When I first witnessed this, I was appalled. But then I remembered how Anne Frank was full of adolescent reverie: had wanted to be a movie star; liked clothes; liked Peter van Pels; liked girls:

> ANNE. 'Once when I was spending the night at Jacque's, I could no longer restrain my curiosity about her body, which she had always hidden from me and which I'd never seen. I asked her whether, as proof of our friendship, we could touch each other's breasts. Jacque refused. I also had a terrible desire to kiss her, which I did. Every time I see a female nude, such as the Venus in my art history book, I go into ecstasy. Sometimes I find them so exquisite I have to struggle to hold back my tears. If only I had a girlfriend!'

Inside Anne Frank Huis, my eye takes in the adolescent objects of Anne. Like the photograph taken of her sitting at a desk on a plump pillow: writing. The picture was taken not long before she went into hiding. Her eyes meet us, the world. She is adorable. The girl who never grew up. The girl who should have grown up.

(No more photos of Anne, after she went into hiding at age 13.)

There is a film of Anne looking out the window, 22 July 1941. Seeing her moving is overwhelmingly moving to me. I experience the 'unbearable' realism of 'film'.[26]

housewife

When I was twelve, my parents drove me, their only child — in our white Delta 88 Oldsmobile, with a light blue interior — from our home in Los Gatos, California, down to Las Vegas, through Arizona, New Mexico, Texas and up to Arkansas. I sat bored in the backseat, car sick, sleepy, and afraid to be living outside of our usual habits and habitat. We were heading towards the 'Lewis Place' (where my mother grew up) — situated in a non-town, called 'Cross-Roads'. (There are some dozen places in Arkansas with the barren name of Cross-Roads.) One old timber-clad store, leaning and ready to fall. Two roads that, indeed, crossed. When our shiny, clean Olds reached the Lewis Place at the end of an overgrown unpaved skinny road, we found nothing: save for the brick fireplace and part of the chimney. Next to the ruins was a box turtle. When it peaked out of its stone habitat — I saw its eye, (which would have been bright red if it was a male, pale red or dull brown if it was a female). But I clearly remember it as brilliant yellow.

A turtle's shell grows with its body: a perfect fit. But the turtle's shell never falls off and is attached to its internal bones.

Louise Bourgeois's *Femme-Maison* (1947) is a woman's body attached to a shell (a little house) but rather than poking out her face (like a turtle or a snail), she pushes out her legs, arms and genitals, while standing very straight. With a touch of malice, Alice reappears in a Bourgeois's Wonderland: witty and monstrous.

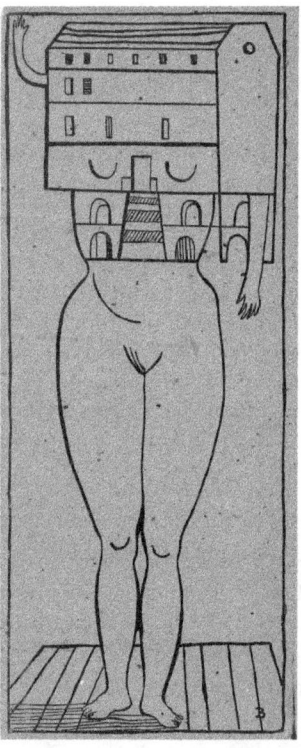

FIG. 2.2. *Femme Maison*, 1947, Louise Bourgeois (1911–2010)

femme-maison

    'It all came very easily, because of course, I had seen it all around me'.
                                Chantal Akerman, speaking about *Jeanne Dielman* [27]

Akerman built her mother's *femme-maison* for us a long time ago: her mother's handsome dollhouse writ large, 'autofictionally',[28] as *Jeanne Dielman*. In the background of *Marcher à côté de ses lacets dans un frigidaire vide* we are reassured to see, once again, Nelly's Belgian apartment furnished with cleanliness, orderliness, and 'women's time'.[29] And we are comforted to see it, yet, again (just as it always was) in *No Home Movie* (2015).

Femme-maison translates as 'housewife': the woman who supposedly does nothing.

    NELLY. 'There's only me . . . the generation that . . . has done nothing.'
    CHANTAL. 'I call it the sacrificed generation.'

Nelly was sacrificed as a Jew during the war and as a woman-wife-mother in the post-war culture of 1950s middle-class life.

Nelly's domestic life and habits, through the filmic hands and eyes of her daughter, are revealed as a replacement of the strict Jewish life that the family once lived, where 'practically every activity of the day is ritualized'.[30] Both ritual practices (strict housekeeping and strict Judaism) 'bring a sort of peace [. . .] knowing every moment of every day brings a sort of peace and keeps anxiety at bay'.[31]

Femme-maison also translates as 'woman-house'. In it, I find a 'room of one's own'. I see Chantal looking out its window.

SPELEN, JOUER, PLAY

    play

Somehow, someone managed to give my mother a Shirley Temple doll.

And she decided to bury it. Bury it in the hard Arkansas dirt, full of clay: the colour of dried blood. Death surrounded my mother, including 'Frankie': her brother who died of typhoid fever. My mother was 'playing' funeral. Burying Shirley in the ground must have taken a great effort.

It rained cats and dogs the night of the burial. It rained so hard that the pitter-patter on the tin roof was not a comfort to the ears. It sounded like bobcats and wolves.

When Shirley was dug up from the earth, that 'devouring mother',[32] she was wrecked.

My mother never learned to play. I have memories of my mother loving me — a caress of my hair — letting me lick the icing bowl from the cake that she made for my birthday — sewing me a dress with a green velvet ribbon along its Jane-Austen bodice that tied in a bow in the back below my shoulder blades — taking me shopping for a new doll. But I have no memories of my mother playing dolls with me, imagining with me, even reading to me. My father was my imaginative playmate, who played board games with me nearly every night, read *Alice in Wonderland* with me . . . My mother, I now understand, was depressed.

She never learned how to make a Winnicottian transitional object to cope with being alone. No blanket with satin trim to rub when no one was there. No song of one's own. No soft object to become other things. No making of something out of nothing. No magic. No play. As D. W. Winnicott teaches us, play enables the child to thrive and is the first entry into spiritual life, creative life. When we feel that we have lost our selves, transitional objects — which are not necessarily material — bring joy. We need to make transitional objects as babies *and* throughout our lives.

My mother never learned to be a child. She never really became adolescent or woman. Robbed of being a little girl, there was nowhere to *become*. No where to play.

jouer

CHANTAL. 'Maman . . .'

'Maman' is the first word of Marcher *à côté de ses lacets dans un frigidaire vide*. And then the pretend play begins. Chantal wants to make something together with her mother (the video that we are watching). Bringing out Sidonie's journal, she places it on the table in front of Nelly.

> CHANTAL. 'Say that they find this under an armchair . . . let's say one of the people who come to visit the apartment find this and come to read it in Polish. Can you read it?'

Chantal (always the 'old child') is helping her mother, by playing with her. They are making a film (art) by playing a game. Their 'toy', their transitional object, is Sidonie's journal.

Nelly, broken by Auschwitz, was broken, could not figure out what to do, how to play when she returned from the camps.

> NELLY. 'I was going to make models and designs and all that [. . .] I drew very well and now not at all. It's gone. [. . .] I would have liked to do something of my own, that's the only thing I regret [. . .] You know, I did nothing [. . .] I was shattered, I was broken, I couldn't do it anymore.'

Like my mother, broken by her childhood, who could not figure out what to do, how to play.

> DOROTHY. 'I keep saying I'm going to do this. I'm going to do that. I don't do anything! [. . .] I don't know how to get an interest for myself [. . .] I just feel like I want to do something creative, something that would, would make me really feel good.'

spelen

Before going into hiding on 6 July 1942 — Anne gave away her tin of marbles — her childishness roundness. The round marbles are warm with the start of summer. Anne's marbles hold all the hope of her return to a life outside of the Secret Annexe.

Life is round. It just is.[33] The pregnant belly. The bird's nest. The earth. And in all this roundness is hope.

In Alain Resnais and Marguerite Duras's *Hiroshima mon amour*, a child's marble rolls into the underground cavern where 'Elle' (the French woman who is being held prisoner by her family for sleeping with a German soldier) is held captive. The marble, 'warm' with 'summer',[34] predicts both the end of the war and the horrific temperatures at the epicentre of the nuclear bomb soon to be dropped on Hiroshima. Elle puts the marble in her mouth.

HUNGER IS THE BASIC ENERGY OF HOPE (Ernst Bloch)[35]

To Walk Next to One's Shoelaces in an Empty Fridge, refers to the fact that Akerman never tied her shoelaces and that the fridge in her home growing up was always empty, because she was being encouraged to eat all the time. As Akerman explains:

When I was a child, she [my mother] complained that I was anorexic so they sent me to places to get me to eat. When I look at pictures of myself, I was just a normal-looking child. It was her fantasy. Because she was starving for such a long time, she wanted to push me to eat. I wanted to eat for her, to give her pleasure, but I became anxious about it.[36]

> NELLY. [After being freed from the camps, the Americans took us] 'to a hospital at Borna and we were cared for there. It was lucky I tell you, lucky because some people started to eat anything, everything they found, and they died . . . they died after . . . after all this suffering . . . they died after . . . at the Liberation.'
> CHANTAL. 'From eating too much?'
> NELLY. 'They couldn't eat . . . you couldn't eat with nothing in your stomach. So, where we were — they fed us by the teaspoon, very gently.'

When Robert Antelme returned to Marguerite Duras's house for the first time after his horrific Nazi internment, the starving man stared at the cherry 'clafoutis sitting on a console table'.[37] And he asked for some. Antelme weighed about eighty-three pounds — 'skin, bones, heart, liver, intestines, brains, lungs, everything'[38] — to eat would be to die. He could not eat, but he had to eat. The doctor said that the fact that Robert wanted to eat cherry clafoutis was a sign of 'a little hope',[39] but that he could only eat gruel, 'by teaspoons. But one teaspoon of gruel choked him — he would cling to our hands, sucking air, and fall back onto his bed. Yet he'd swallow it.'[40]

After seventeen days, his fever dropped — he had bowel movements that smelled human — 'and one morning — "I'm hungry", he said.'[41] And he began to eat everything. 'As soon as he'd eaten and his hunger could feed on itself, it became gigantic and frightening'.[42]

* * * * *

'As a teenager, I ate voraciously',[43] claims Akerman.

* * * * *

Underneath the bed in her childhood home, my mother had collected and hidden three precious chocolate bars: contained in a box, like her Shirley Temple doll. They were too dear to eat. Then one day, my adolescent mother pulled them out

Fig. 2.3. *Hope*, 1886, George Frederic Watts (1817–1904) (c) Tate, London, 2018

of their hiding place and gorged herself on all three, all at once, as fast she could, ridding herself of all that desire under her bed.

★ ★ ★ ★ ★

Anne. 'I'm doing fine, except I've got no appetite' [141].

★ ★ ★ ★ ★

I cannot revive Anne, Sidonie, Nelly, Chantal, my mother.

But to write history is to breathe into the dead — to push onto their stony heart — is Hope.

George Frederic Watts has drawn Hope with 'golden hands', sitting on the round earth: a huge beautiful golden marble. She is blindfolded. Contained. Dreaming. The strings on her lyre are all broken. Save for one.

That's for you . . . to play.

Notes to Chapter 2

1. This essay is dedicated to Hayden White, my paternal-maternal guide, who first directed me to Michael Ann Holly's work on melancholia and art history and encouraged me not to be one of those historians who Nietzsche dubbed as 'epigoni', 'latecomers' one of those 'born with gray hair.' Friedrich Nietzsche *The Use and Abuse of History*, 2nd rev. ed., introduction and translation by Albert Hofstadter (New York: Perennial Classics, 1971), p. 39. As cited by Michael Ann Holly, *The Melancholy Art* (Princeton and Oxford: Princeton University Press, 2013), p. xvi.
2. Jeanette Winterson, *Written on the Body* (London: Vintage, 2014), p. 17. I thank the artist Samantha Sweeting for leading me to this quote.
3. Margaret Atwood, 'What Happened', *The Animals in that Country* (Boston: Little Brown, 1968), p. 27.
4. There are many versions of Anne Frank's journal, beyond its countless translations into other languages.

    A version: The handwritten journals began in the plaid diary and continued in three other notebooks.

    B version: After hearing a request on *Radio Oranje* for stories of the occupation to be kept and published after the war, Anne begins to rewrite the original entries from her diary as a novel. She wants them to be published after the war. These pages are the *B* Version.

    C version: After the war, Anne's father Otto Frank combines the *A* and *B* versions and publishes the combined texts as *The Secret Annexe* (25 June 1947).

    Critical Edition: Contains versions *A, B* and *C*, as well as related articles.

    Definitive Edition: This is the expanded edition compiled by Mirjam Pressler, which works with and expands Otto Frank's original selection. It contains approximately 30 percent more material and has been approved by The Anne Frank-Fonds (Anne Frank Foundation). I have used the Definitive Edition for all my references to Anne Frank's diary.
5. Anne Frank, *The Diary of a Young Girl*, ed. Otto H. Frank and Mirjam Pressler, trans. by Susan Massotty, intro. by Elie Wiesel, trans. by Euan Cameron (London: Penguin Books), p. 73. All further citations will be noted by page number only, in brackets, in the body of my text.
6. Elie Wiesel, introduction to *Anne Frank: The Diary of a Young Girl*, p. vii.
7. Chantal Akerman, *Marcher à côté de ses lacets dans un frigidaire vide [To Walk Beside One's Shoelaces in an Empty Fridge]*, 2004. Courtesy of the Camden Arts Centre, London.
8. I saw the installation in 2008 at the Camden Arts Centre. The first room featured a text in French, by Akerman, projected on two large banderoles of white gauze. A doleful violin could be heard. The text was a spin on the autobiographical footage projected in the second room: the conversation between Chantal and her mother.
9. Interview by Julia Weiner with Chantal Akerman, 'My Family and Other Dark Materials', *The Jewish Chronicle*, 11 July 2008. https://www.thejc.com/culture/film/chantal-akerman-my-family-and-other-dark-materials. Accessed 29 July 2018.
10. Chantal Akerman, interview with Mathias Greuling and Alexandra Zawia, at the Venice Film Festival, Sept 2011. https://www.youtube.com/watch?v=GUStWsegZok. Accessed 13 Aug 2018.

11. Dorothy Allison, *Bastard out of Carolina* (New York: Plume, 1993), p. 224.
12. From my mother's recorded journal, 4 February 1992, as transcribed by Stefania Olafsdottir. All quotes from this recording appear in this same format (with the speaker's name in bold) as if the lines were the script of a play.
13. Akerman, 'My Family and Other Dark Materials'.
14. This description of a bruise is fed by Han Kang's *The Vegetarian*, trans. Deborah Smith (London: Portobello, 2015).
15. Marguerite Duras, *The War: A Memoir*, trans. Barbara Bray (New York: Pantheon, 1986), p. 62.
16. Wiesel, 'Introduction', *The Diary of a Young Girl*, p. xi.
17. Julia Kristeva, 'The Adolescent Novel', in *New Maladies of the Soul*, trans. Ross Guberman (New York: Columbia University Press, 1995).
18. Wiesel, 'Introduction', p. xi.
19. Sarah Kofman, *Rue Ordener, Rue Labat*, trans. by Ann Smock (Lincoln: University of Nebraska Press, 1996), p. 3.
20. Chantal and Sylviane's additions to the diary are cited in Akerman's *Autoportrait en cinéaste* (Paris: Editions du Centre Georges Pompidou/ Editions Cahiers du cinéma, 2004), p. 72.
21. Roland Barthes, *Pleasure of the Text*, trans. Richard Howard (New York: Farrar, 1975), p. 66.
22. Marcel Proust, *In Search of Lost Time*, 'The Guermantes Way', trans. by C. K. Scott Moncrieff and Terence Kilmartin, revised by D. J. Enright (New York: Random House, 1993), p. 174.
23. Adam Phillips, *On Kissing, Tickling and Being Bored: Psychoanalytic Essays on the Unexamined Life* (Cambridge, Mass: Harvard University Press, 1993), pp. 68–78.
24. The French vocabulary list was on display when I visited the Anne Frank Haus in 2016.
25. As quoted by Peter Gay, *The Bourgeois Experience: Victoria to Freud, vol. II, The Tender Passion* (London: Oxford University Press, 1986), p. 82.
26. Marie Darrieussecq, *Tom is Dead*, trans.by Lia Hills (Melbourne: Text Publishing, 2009), p. 73.
27. Chantal Akerman, 'Chantal Akerman on *Jeanne Dielman*', interview for Criterion Collection, 2009. https://www.youtube.com/watch?v=8pSNOEYSIlg. Accessed 13 August 2018.
28. Autobiography (or even the more literary 'memoir') cannot touch real emotions like fiction: *autofiction* (a portmanteau of *autobiographie* and *fiction*) is a French response to this paradox. Serge Doubrovssky is credited with developing this term. The genre is associated with such French authors as Marguerite Duras and Hervé Guibert.
29. Julia Kristeva, defines 'women's time' as outside of the linear time of history and politics — interiorized, multiple, cyclical, monumental (eternal). See 'Women's Time', *The Kristeva Reader*, ed. by Toril Moi (New York: Columbia University Press, 1986), pp. 187–213.
30. Akerman, 'Chantal Akerman on *Jeanne Dielman*'.
31. Ibid.
32. Sally Mann, *What Remains* (Boston: Bullfinch Press, 2003), p. 6.
33. Gaston Bachelard, *The Poetics of Space*, trans. by Maria Jolas (Boston, Mass: Beacon Press, 1994), p. 234.
34. Marguerite Duras, *Hiroshima mon amour; Text by Marguerite Duras, for the Film by Alain Resnais*, trans. by Richard Seaver (New York: Grove Press, 1961), p. 91.
35. Ernst Bloch, *The Principle of Hope*, vol. I, trans. by Neville Plaice, Stephen Plaice and Paul Knight (Cambridge, Mass: MIT Press, 1986), pp. 65–67.
36. Akerman, 'My Family and Other Dark Materials'.
37. Marguerite Duras, *Wartime Notebooks*, ed. by Sophie Bogaert and Olivier Corpet, trans. by Linda Coverdale, as included in *The Lover, Wartime Notebooks, Practicalities*, with an introduction by Rachel Kushner (New York: Knopf, 2018), p. 293.
38. Ibid., p. 294.
39. Ibid.
40. Ibid.
41. Ibid., p. 297.
42. Ibid., p. 290.
43. Akerman, 'My Family and Other Dark Materials'.

CHAPTER 3

Smokescreens: Notes on Cigarettes in Chantal Akerman

Alice Blackhurst

It is only through a serial meandering of substitutions and transformations that we survive desire, that desire survives.
LESLEY STERN[1]

Avec mon grand-père avait disparu le rituel. Avec le rituel, on savait ce qu'on devait faire.
CHANTAL AKERMAN[2]

Introduction

In the final minutes of *Portrait d'une paresseuse,* a little-known Chantal Akerman short film screened as part of the anthology *Seven Women, Seven Sins* from 1986, a young woman played by Chantal Akerman postpones the task of having to make her bed in order to smoke a cigarette. 'Je fume cette cigarette, puis je fais le lit',[3] Akerman announces in declarative, frontal fashion to the camera, before sprawling on the ground and beginning to light up. The shot, overwriting the director's habitual praxis of rigid formal distance, encloses around her face as she takes a drag, her features given over to absorption, reverie, and sensuous contemplation. In the background, the precise strains of Sonia Wieder-Atherton playing her cello can be heard as soundtrack: the sharp chords of the instrument a counterpoint to the aesthetic slackness and chronological anaemia otherwise on screen. The film was made, Akerman suggests in interview with Nicole Brenez, to chronicle the stark polarity between her eponymous laziness and Wieder-Atherton's — Akerman's companion for many years — enduring, indefatigable work ethic.[4] Yet it also, via the cathected object of a cigarette and the arrested motion that the act of smoking permits, atomizes the complex relationship to pleasure, escapism, ritual and sensuality that diffuses through Akerman's filmography at large.

In this essay, I would like to further unravel the motif of smoking in the filmic, and later installation-based, work of Chantal Akerman, arguing that its frequent iteration across the director's both fictional and non-fictional screens mobilizes perennial Akerman questions of embodied experience — or of how to confront the temporality and spatiality of existing as a body in the world — alongside other, less theorized concerns. A recurrent thematisation of smoking — and specifically, of women smoking — I argue, hazes Akerman's persistent labeling as a minimalist formalist, and, via questions of gratuitousness, time-wasting, and feckless indulgence that smoking unfolds, opens space to conceive her as a sensualist, or as someone who invests cinematic time in the afterlives of gestural desire. A cigarette's existence as a token of ambivalence also, I suggest, helps to think through an aesthetics, in Akerman, of liminality and cloudy translucency; of intermediality between absolute, given states. To smoke a cigarette, indeed, both functions as an indexing of time, or a way of measuring time passing — dovetailing with cinema's fabled status as 'art of the index' — but also as a means of circumventing it; or of installing, as John Berger notes, a 'breathing space' or 'parenthesis' in the grind of daily productivity.[5] Testifying to the filmmaker's complex, dialectical and intermedial aesthetics, both these instincts overlap and suffuse one another in Akerman's work. Her corpus — despite its recent enthused embrace by the apparatus of 'slow cinema'[6] — bespeaks both a yearning to slow down, and to ruminate on the vicissitudes of lived experience, and the desire to enact a tear in being's continuity; to — via quick, often devastating acts — take flight from prescribed bourgeois tedium.

In her seminal account of cinematic time, Mary Ann Doane draws a connection between moments of contingency in film and cinephilia. She writes that 'cinephilia hinges not on indexicality, but on the knowledge of indexicality's potential, a knowledge that paradoxically erases itself. The cinephile sustains a certain belief, an investment in the graspability of the asystematic, the contingent, for which the cinema is the privileged vehicle.'[7] A cigarette — a break in the circuit of the everyday, or in *Portrait d'une paresseuse,* a willful deferral of domestic labour — telegraphs the contingency of a desire, or the fugitive life-span of pleasure, which Doane registers as cinephilic, and which recurs as a concern in Akerman's oeuvre. In *Femmes d'Anvers en novembre,* Akerman's 2007 multi-screen installation piece which my essay takes as focal point, the ephemerality of smoking displayed in molecular vignettes thematically rehearses the fragmented, spectral ambience of the exhibition space, its transient existence, which remains illuminated for a time before flaring and contracting once again into darkness.

A structural interest in smoking — or interest in how its unique gestural economy sections or apportions time — becomes, in narrative-based works *Jeanne Dielman, 23 quai du Commerce, 1080 Bruxelles, Toute une nuit* and the text *Ma mère rit,* discussed in the first half of the essay, more affective. In these works, smoking is an act not only fetishized by Akerman herself, but indelibly associated with maternal modes of agency, raising the Kleinian-Winnicottian spectre of the 'good enough mother' haunting the frames of Akerman's oeuvre.[8] In these features, the disjunctive image of the mother who smokes, resonating with the oscillation between drives that marks Klein's thesis, persists as motif, putting pressure on prescribed feminine domestic roles, and exposing the ambivalence that often undergirds maternity. In all three works, smoking has potential as an act of sovereignty and auto-eroticism in the midst of caring for others, re-imagining the domesticated female body not only as a giver, but as a receiver, of pleasure.

In her essay on smoking as cinematic metaphor, Lesley Stern suggests that 'where the gestural often goes unnoticed in the everyday, in the cinema...it moves into visibility.'[9] To give shape to minor gestural economies and to render visible the 'images between the images'[10] often elided by the history of film-making was a well-known aim of Chantal Akerman's broad corpus. That it finds expression through the act of smoking in the pieces under imminent discussion testifies to her ability to locate lyricism in the ordinary, and vitality in finite, perishable objects which circumscribe desires to withdraw from the world through temporal suspension, and reaffirm connection with it via an embodied, sensory and tactile act.

Maternal Ambivalence: The Suspension of Obligation in *Jeanne Dielman*, *Toute une nuit* and *Ma mère rit*

Chantal Akerman's films expose a dialectical relationship to motherhood: indexing the fraught mechanisms which subtend the ambivalent experience of maternity. Kate Rennebohm has noted how 'many of Akerman's films revolve around the filmmaker's efforts, and perceived failure, to connect with her mother';[11] a mother, specifically, who lived her life as an Auschwitz survivor and for whom passing on the traumas of history to her daughters, Chantal and Sylviane Akerman, would have been an unthinkable act. In her autobiographical account *Autoportrait en cinéaste,* Akerman emphasizes the frustration that arose from having to perpetually come up against the blind spot of Natalia ('Nelly') Akerman's experiences, occasioning a childhood cratered by aporetic unknowability, or, in the director's own stark vernacular, a sense of selfhood 'full of holes.'[12] In *News from Home,* Akerman's celebrated epistolary feature from 1977, in which the director narrates letters from her mother as harsh portraits of an alienating New York City loom in tandem on the screen, these lacunae manifest in an asymmetric rendering of the mother-daughter bond as Akerman obscures her own replies. The desire for both intense *rapprochement* to the mother and space to evolve as a woman and an artist on her own terms is framed as Akerman, having relocated to Manhattan from her native Brussels to immerse herself in avant-garde 1970s film-making cultures, both enshrines motherly preoccupations via tender voice-overs and puts literal oceans between her and her matrilineage, both offered and elusive to the viewer's grasp.

Whilst critics have perpetually zoned in on Akerman's vacillation between strong maternal attachment and an impulse to transcend this primary relation — or, in Mateus Araujo's formulation, her 'pivot' between mother and the world[13] — little has been offered in the way of Natalia's own relation to her daughter, which was also subject to the sometimes painful turbulence of ambivalence. For Klein, in her seminal reclaiming of the mother as a figure of contingency, 'ambivalence' denotes not facile indifference, but a constant dialectical shuttling between affective poles of hate and love.[14] Whilst Nelly's adoration of her daughter is fiercely impressed upon the viewer in *News from Home,* in interview with Nicole Brenez Akerman suggests that this love was pressurized by latent frustration and a constant need for space to manage the fierce residues of trauma — 'She didn't get the life she wanted'; 'When

I was little, I was always put in the background so my mother could have her own life and room to herself.'[15]

As ventilating practice, reaffirming links between the body and the vital life-force of the breath, smoking in this context might be theorized as a mode of auto-poesis and of self-fabulation, becoming a gesture that literally ex-presses agency but also, when exercised by mothers, a delineation of a space of pause and of contemplation in which visions of the self independent of maternity can begin to be ignited and emerge. Whilst freighted both by self-destructive and collectively traumatic impulses, it is, across Akerman's corpus, simultaneously and complexly rendered as what Penny Tinkler calls a 'safety-valve',[16] or, following Giorgio Agamben's work on gesture, a means of retrafficking symbolic burdens. Agamben uses the term 'gag',[17] broadly suggesting that objects which are put into the mouth, in particular, make up for an impossibility of speaking and give subjects at a loss for language'[18] — though not unproblematically — other obstacles and other material realities to cathect. In Akerman, this gagging appears both something imposed but also voluntary. The cigarette is taken into the mother's body and her mouth both as a means of taking time for the self and extracting pleasure from inoperativity, but also — precisely via smoking's substitutional, 'gagging' economies — of avoiding 'having to give an account of oneself', in Elena Gorfinkel's words.[19]

In *Jeanne Dielman,* a three and a half hour excavation of the role ritual and meticulous domestic repetition play in safeguarding the mental hygiene of the traumatized post-Auschwitz subject, Akerman's account of her childhood 'in the background' translates formally into a strict policy of set camera choreography, which refuses to intrude into her protagonist's regimented labour of daily life. For Ivone Margulies, this austere, almost painterly composition can be read canonically as a measure of the abstract *froideur* assimilated by new waves of minimalist film-making in the 1970s.[20] For her part, Akerman insists that 'For me, the way I looked at what was going on was a look of love and respect... I let [Jeanne Dielman] live her life in the middle of the frame.'[21] The result is a portrait of a woman — whom Akerman has said is a fictionalized avatar for her mother, and her mother's generation[22] — islanded by her elaborate domestic tics and allergic to all forms of sensuality. When, indeed, in her day job as a prostitute to visiting male clients, Jeanne unintentionally orgasms with a customer, the result is chronic and murderous; a supreme act of violence rectifying the unsettling irruptive force of pleasure which drives cracks into the suppressing surface of routine.

A reading of the film's time-consuming choreographies as a shield designed to tamp down greater appetites, and of smoking in this context as both a rebellious act of willfulness and gag against the unspeakable is encapsulated in a scene in which Jeanne takes vigil over a neighbour's infant. The mother of the child, who we do not see, but whose voice we hear from behind a slightly ajar door, starts to thank Jeanne as she is about to hand over the baby, dilating the exchange by embarking on a long, phatic monologue in which Jeanne, clearly uncomfortable, mumbling consenting noises, barely partakes. At one point, musing on what she might cook for dinner, the unnamed mother ventures 'Now that I smoke, I've lost my appetite...

I would have been fine with a tartine, but the kids need meat.' Mirroring Jeanne's own dependency on ritual as a means of insulation against fleshier consumptions, here smoking is explicitly summed up as a mode of displacement and substitution. The mother smokes, exhumes her carnophilic appetite, in order to be able to prioritize the child, rehearsing typically maternal sacrificial economies. At the same time, some agential preference and capacity for the discriminating judgments of taste is latent in the 'fine with a tartine', which evokes the faculties of choice, or the measure of one whose hunger for the world is selective. In this hierarchy of desires, smoking is privileged, yet is also clearly a way of muffling other forms of nourishment. Without the pacifying, stopping-up or gagging capabilities of an active cigarette, the maternal voice rambles and digresses, which provokes in Jeanne tangible discomfort. Speaking to its complex constellation of intent in Akerman's film corpus, the cigarette becomes in this scene a placeholder for the polarizing impulses to make the self visible, or to light it up, and to, via a deliberate effacement, make it disappear.

In 1982's *Toute une nuit*, a fragmentary, episodic feature organized around singular vignettes which have little in common other than their shared nocturnal setting in the city of Brussels, the mother who smokes as means of both stoking and deferring deeper hungers reappears in the form of a younger Natalia Akerman herself. Twenty-two minutes into the feature, she is portrayed leaning against a wall outside a house, smoking, whilst the voice of a child who again is heard but not seen calls in plaintive fashion from inside, 'Maman, Maman'. In her *Autoportrait*, Akerman recalls this micro-scene, which lasts barely for a minute, as follows: 'Natalia Leibel épouse Akerman, dans *Toute une nuit*, fume devant la porte de sa maison à Strombeck. Quelques instants plus tard, une petite voix l'appelle — Maman, Maman — elle écrase sa cigarette et rentre chez elle.'[23] In tone this caption, underwriting a still image of the film, passes the act off as a prosaic, platitudinous event, yet on screen it is tumultous with the energy of the inexpressible. In not responding to the child's calls immediately, one senses that Natalia as on-screen mother is attempting to cling on to this transitory moment in her day that is not devoted to the ceaseless reproduction of domestic life, and to frame a moment of 'pur plaisir auto-affectif',[24] as Jacques Derrida has characterized smoking. For Agamben, ritualized gestures carry slightly more weight in their ability not only to dispense pleasure but to fashion subjectivity. In *The Use of Bodies* he writes that habit, whilst often written off as an addictive, thoughtless mode of operating, proffers man a space 'to contemplate himself and his potential for acting.'[25] In its inhabitation of the threshold between pure *potential* and what Agamben calls being-at-work, or between desire for action and that action's fulfilment, in other words, habit makes crucial room for the self to emerge and come into existence. ('Only through the contemplation of potential... does something like the experience of an 'own' and of a 'self' become possible.')[26] In *Toute une nuit*, a glimpse of this nascent space is offered to the viewer and Natalia, but is ultimately narrowed by the child's prompts for attention. The positioning of Nelly's stance between two white painted doors, which enact a kind of 'closing in' effect, scenographically rehearses this curtailment. Within the maternal framework, then, gesture as a 'pointing-in towards the self', in Hannah Mowat's terms,[27] can only momentarily endure, before it must be re-directed towards others. In this fragment of a sensual collusion with the self there is, nonetheless, potential for a form of reparation. In holding on to the empty packet and meticulously placing her no-longer needed lighter carefully within its contours before going back inside, smoking for Natalia in this scene, indeed, transcends any status as an idle, throwaway endeavour to become a brief structural support for the evanescences of dispersed subjectivity.

Chantal Akerman herself was a dedicated and prolific smoker: rarely seen unflanked by an accompanying cigarette; regularly interrupting screenings and panel events to nurture her addiction; and even, during filming for the documentary *Chantal Akerman: From Here*, smoking inside when building regulations forbade it. *Ma mère rit*, published in the wake of her mother's struggle with, and eventual defeat by, chronic illness, records the inflections and itinerancies of her habit: placing emphasis not on maternal, but daughterly nicotine transgressions. Up against the claustophobic *huis clos* of Natalia's exhaustively tidied central Brussels flat, and the pressure of having to care for someone on the fragile cusp of dying, the regular act of going out to smoke a cigarette, or walking to the shops to procure a packet, she writes, becomes an act of parallel release and, in the Agambian sense, self-regard in the vein of stimulating a degree of personhood:

> Ce que j'aime, le moment de la journée où je sens que j'ai une vie, c'est quand je marche d'un bon pas pour aller acheter des cigarettes. Tout d'un coup je suis une personne. Une personne libre, une personne qui a quelque chose à faire.[28]

Here, the act of smoking is invested with resuscitating powers. Rather than inscribing Akerman in the stultifying matrix of addiction, it becomes, instead, a conduit, re-connecting her to a wider, more expanded apprehension of the world. Later in the same text, ever harnessing the power of the 'minor' gesture or, in her own words, 'la petite chose à côté'[29] able to inflect larger institutions and modalities, Akerman will more explicitly announce 'Il n'y a que ça qui me sauve, fumer une cigarette sur la terrasse.'[30] The phenomenological coordinates of the act are equally as striking as the act itself, since to smoke a cigarette obligates stepping outside, being in the world, interfacing with exteriority. In excess of the organizing capabilities of habit, or Agamben's gestural economies of contemplation, it becomes a mode of rapturous relationality, close to what Judith Butler conceives as 'enthrallment'. Arguing that it is better to be caught in an attachment complex — even if the attachment is to an ordained 'bad object' — rather than to be above any form of attachment or dependency at all, Butler writes in *Precarious Life* that

> What is prematurely, or belatedly, called the 'I' is, at the outset, enthralled, even if it is to a violence, an abandonment, a mechanism; doubtless it seems better at that point to be enthralled with what is impoverished or abusive than not to be enthralled at all and so to lose the condition of one's being and becoming.[31]

In keeping with Butler's template for living and existing in the world, smoking as conceived in *Ma mère rit* is indeed, a mobilizing and propulsive act: marshalling the subject onwards towards modes of engagement with exterior materiality; allowing her a window of exemption (formally performed by its frequent taking-place on the ledge of the *terrasse*) from the world of daily tasks and minutely orchestrated gestures that comprise caring for the dying.

In a poem chronicling her late father's cigar-habit on his death-bed, 'The Cigars', Sharon Olds notes that this form of daily, measured 'drawing in' amounted to 'his only song'. ('It was his only song, that drawing in,/It was that song or none.')[32] Whilst his cancer, Olds recalls, 'came from smoking and drinking',[33] the ritualized act of wetting and lighting these cinnamon-hued tubes unfolded a reliable moment of reprieve amidst the clinical hospice environment, a moment of conspiracy 'with the soul that he was born with.'[34] In Akerman's film works, and especially her films about mothers, smoking is envisaged similarly as a generative mode of self-absorption, a form of temporal 'drag'[35] that reverses or at least momentarily suspends maternal and domestic temporal economies, and a means of reconnecting with the sensory world. Whilst my reading has prioritized it as primarily a space-making mechanism, smoking in these films casts uncertain shadows, nonetheless, in its intermittent functioning as stop-gap, as gag, 'something put in someone's mouth to keep him from speaking',[36] in an attempt to staunch a voicing of the atrocious unrepresentable. In *Femmes d'Anvers en novembre,* a silent, multi-screen installation piece first exhibited in Antwerp in 2007, the cigarette as placeholder for the unexpressed points to and illuminates the outsider-status of women in public. Yet it also, in the defiant posture that smoking a cigarette in urban space assumes, takes shape as a visible reclaiming, a form of feminised *flânerie* that can be enacted standing still.

FIG. 3.1. Chantal Akerman, *Femmes d'Anvers en novembre* (2008)

Femmes d'Anvers en novembre: Webs of Relation

> Tenir au présent, c'est faire des gestes fragiles, simples, pauvres, répétés, pour vivre jour après jour.
>
> Corinne Rondeau[37]

Having previously experimented with modes of cinematic presentation outside of the projection theatre in works such as *D'Est,* which looped footage from her film of the same name on twenty-five video monitors between two rooms at the Walker Art Center in 1995, *Femmes d'Anvers en novembre* advances this trend in Akerman's late work, splitting twenty vignettes organised around the theme of women smoking at night in Antwerp across a frieze of five moving-image screens. The installation was first exhibited in collaboration with the artist Jan Fabre as part of his multimedial performance *I'm a mistake,* in 2007. Akerman in interviews suggests that her motivation behind crafting the collage lay in a desire to think laterally about 'presence — movement and shape', or 'how you can express different things with the same or similar images.'[38] Beyond abstract interest in the spatializations of routine or repeated choreography, the piece further manifests as a pointillistic meditation on shared social practices of which women can partake and take solace in together when otherwise choked by repressive patriarchal institutions. In rehearsing the fugitive pleasures of an ultimately transient activity, *Femmes* resists, at the same time, any logic of the fetish, linking smoking to the similar ephemerality of the exhibition space,[39] which relieves somewhat the indelible indexicality of the filmic signifier.

Formally, the piece 'undoes' the fixity of the dense wall of the unifying cinematic screen by making the borders between its five windows permeable and porous. Scheduled to be played on continual rotation, yet screened in simultaneity, so that the spectator's attention is perennially divided, it is almost impossible to feel as if one has seen every narrative in full. In addition to this simultaneous, as opposed to sequential approach, the vignettes often migrate across different screens, in non-linear fashion, starting in the middle but concluding on the far right, for example, with actresses also often employed more than once for different stories and scenarios. For Terrie Sultan, 'viewing these interconnected images is like watching a shifting, complex flipbook. Our attention flickers from left to right and back again, as the sudden juxtapositions present new contexts every few minutes.'[40] The effect is to create a contagious, suffused and suffusing web of relation; a sense that these stories are unmistakeably bound up in one another; opposing the smoking act as portrayed in *Jeanne Dielman, Toute une nuit,* and *Ma mère rit* as an individualised gesture, or a means of haloing the self's distinction.

Whilst Laura Marks has famously argued that video is a more erotic, haptic medium than conventional film for its electronic textures of surface density,[41] *Femmes d'Anvers en novembre* strikingly departs from standardised presentations of the smoking act as a portal to eroticism, or seduction signal. Marks writes that video 'invites a kind of vision that spreads out over the surface of the image instead of penetrating into depth'[42] and if *Femmes,* indeed, enacts a gauzy praxis of contagion in its structural horizontality, Akerman's habitual fixed distance and pro-filmic estrangement from her smoking subjects resists proffering this surface as an object we might *touch*. Rather than the spectator's bond with the image, communion between women intra-diegetically takes precedence. Only a handful of portraits seem to concentrate on women smoking in isolation; otherwise tableaus of eponymous *femmes* smoking in concert prevail. In one vignette, two women seated in interior space side by side flick ash into a shared ashtray on a table, never communicating or looking directly at each other, but communing in their parallel processes of self-collection. In another, Hopper-esque framed scene, a group of women huddle together on a porch and smoke, occasionally putting lighters to each other's mouths to ignite new cigarettes, without nonetheless breaking the front-facing, steadfast thrust of their planar gazes tuned to the horizon of the night. The common thread in both instances (as well as in a third vignette, where a collection of women smoke outside an office building, linked only by the force of their habit which requires them to go outside) is that they don't speak to one another, but, still, they smoke. If such terse muteness can find parallels throughout Akerman's oeuvre, where homosocial dynamics between women are often more corporeal than verbal (as in *Je, tu, il, elle*, where the kinetic final sex scene unravels with not a single word uttered) or, as we have already seen, fraught with maternal residues, smoking nonetheless introduces a tertiary dimensionality, a membrane between fractious bodies that invites them to find communality in the reassuring continuity of a recognisable, repeatable act.

In her research into the 'feminization' of smoking in the latter half of the twentieth century, Penny Tinkler notes how the extroverted gesticulation of wielding a cigarette helped women to construct a more active, assertive persona in public: especially enabling them, in photographic portraits, to transition from the 'downcast' posture of early twentieth-century feminized representation into more frontal and defiant bodily positionalities.[43] This evolution dovetails with Akerman's rigorously 'face-à-face' cinematic compositions, designed to avoid fetishism and idolatry, and to meet the profilmic object on its own, ethical terms.[44] In *Femmes d'Anvers*, an apprehension of the cigarette as an index of self-fashioning appears latent in Akerman's attention to the other objects that her featured women sheath around their persons: lurex tracksuits, fur stoles, silk dresses and long coats. At the same time, the cigarette is deployed as a baton to apportion time; or to attenuate the act of waiting. Akerman impresses such an act on the spectator too. Contemplating the length of time it takes to prepare and smoke a cigarette down to its last tarry entrails (which, without any ambient noise as galvanising stimulus, registers as surprisingly extensive) one approaches her general aim to make the spectator 'feel time' rather than 'pass time' via her work.[45] This space of waiting, Akerman suggests, is rich in communal potential. As Jonathan Crary has observed, writing on *D'Est*, 'it is a time in which encounters can occur', in opposition to neoliberalism's '24/7' temporality, which 'presents the delusion of a time *without* waiting, of an on-demand instantaneity, of having and getting insulated from the presence of others.'[46] Crary derives his concept from Deleuze's recognition of the shift, under late capitalism, from what he calls, furthering Foucauldian ideas, 'disciplinary societies' where there were clear demarcations between work and leisure, and 'control societies', which offer no interruption to the ceaseless, obligated flow of hyper-productivity.[47] In the former, characterized by punctuation, breaks, and regular excursions from the loci of industry such as the factory or school, smoking could flourish. In the latter, where the careful measurement of labouring time has collapsed into an infinitely profitable 'now', its capacity as discriminating, segmenting activity atrophies. Under such a lens, *Femmes d'Anvers en novembre* feels sporadically suffused with the melancholy of anachronism; proffered as an ode to a strangely antiquated pastime, coextensive with Agamben's thesis that contemporary life has surrendered its main repertoire of gestures to the unilateralism of technology.[48]

Femmes d'Anvers ventures that this dissipation of the gesture can materially, nonetheless, be participated in and witnessed by the ambling spectator; in the process building an affective archive in excess of Giuliana Bruno's reading of the work as an 'architecture of displacement.'[49] Just as its featured frieze of women pick up and discard cigarettes, we can walk away from the images on screen, but often do not, remaining magnetised, suspended and compelled by this elemental 'arithmetic',[50] in Butler's terms, of simply breathing smoke in and out.

In contrast to the filmmaker's earlier, more-narrative-based use of smoking as a mode of necessary self-absorption, *Femmes d'Anvers* ultimately ventures smoking as a vital, inter-subjective act, which takes place across collective and individual histories. An acknowledgment of inter-subjectivity, the piece suggests, despite late capitalist society's decline of gestural activity, can be applied as salve against the otherwise atomization of Deleuze's prescribed control society and fashion smoking to be more than just a 'symbolization of the symbolic.'[51] In such a context, limiting qualifiers such as 'habit' and 'addiction' recede. In the words of the poet and critic Maggie Nelson, smoking as mode of attachment instead enables that 'in place of an exhausting autonomy, there is the blunt admittance of dependence, and its subsequent relief.'[52] To depend on things — mothers, cigarettes, other bodies, other works of art — is not, in Akerman's oeuvre, something to shrink back from, but to lean towards, with appetite, and curiosity. In this leaning there is structural support underfoot, which might offer a foundation to the threat of the ephemeral, and of subsequent extinction. In Nelson's words, such gestural economies indeed illuminate that 'the web of relation is everywhere, even in our flights of freedom',[53] even perhaps, in Chantal's own flight from the shadows of this world.

Notes to Chapter 3

1. Lesley Stern, *The Smoking Book* (Chicago: University of Chicago Press, 2008), p. 108.
2. 'Ritual had disappeared with my grandfather. With ritual, one knew what one had to do', Chantal Akerman, *Autoportrait en cinéaste* (Paris: Editions du Centre Georges Pompidou/ Editions Cahiers du cinéma, 2004), p. 23.
3. 'I'll smoke this cigarette, then I'll make the bed'.
4. When asked by Brenez to annotate her past filmography, Akerman summarised *Portrait d'une paresseuse* as follows: 'Sonia [Wieder-Atherton] works, I stay in bed.' (Nicole Brenez, 'Chantal Akerman: The Pyjama Interview', <http://www.lolajournal.com/2/pajama.html> Accessed 29 October 2017.)

5. John Berger, *Smoke* (London: Notting Hill Editions, 2017).
6. See Tiago de Luca (ed.), *Slow Cinema* (Edinburgh: Edinburgh University Press, 2016).
7. Mary Ann Doane, *The Emergence of Cinematic Time: Modernity, Contingency, the Archive* (Cambridge: Harvard University Press, 2002), p. 227.
8. In 'Notes on some Schizoid Mechanisms', a seminal essay from 1952, Melanie Klein radically undercut any notion of symbiotic fusion between the infant and the mother, reading the child, from early psychic life, to be rather besieged by primitive aggressive wishes towards the maternal subject that are never fully overcome. Such desires — to destroy, possess, control the mother — in a radical contribution, were appointed 'paranoid-schizoid', whereas an acceptance of the mother as a separate other, a 'whole object' independent of fulfilling the child's every need, was classified as a 'depressive position'. While Klein's interest was not aligned with mothers per se, but with the internal *maternal imago* organising the attendant traffic of the subject's psychic drives, her student, Donald Winnicott, mapped her thinking onto mothers in the world, introducing the concept of 'the good enough mother' to appoint a mother who, while holding space for the infant, adjudicates the right balance of love and loss and slowly 'disappoints' the child so as to cultivate in her a separate sense of self and thus a capacity to relate non-narcissistically to the world ('The Capacity to be Alone', 1958).
9. Lesley Stern, 'Paths Through the Thicket of Things,' *Critical Inquiry*, 28.1, *Things* (Autumn 2001), 317–35 (p. 320).
10. Chantal Akerman cited in Ivone Margulies, *Nothing Happens: Chantal Akerman's Hyperrealist Everyday* (London: Duke University Press, 1996), p. 4.
11. Kate Rennebohm, 'La Ressasseuse: Chantal Akerman, 1950–2015', <http://cinema-scope.com/columns/deaths-of-cinema/> Accessed 29 October 2017.
12. Akerman, *Autoportrait en cinéaste*, p. 30.
13. See Mateus Araujo, trans. by Mark Cohen, 'Chantal Akerman, between the mother and the world', *Film Quarterly*, 70.1 (Fall 2016), 32–38.
14. See Melanie Klein, 'Mourning and Its Relation to Manic-Depressive States', in *Contributions to Psychoanalysis 1921–1945* (London: Hogarth Press, 1940).
15. Nicole Brenez, 'Chantal Akerman: The Pyjama Interview'.
16. Penny Tinkler, *Smoke Signals: Women, Smoking and Visual Culture* (London: Berg, 2006), p. 205.
17. See Giorgio Agamben, 'Notes on Gesture', in *Means Without Ends: Notes on Politics*, trans. Vincenzo Binetti and Cesare Casarino, (Minneapolis: University of Minnesota Press, 2000), pp. 49–63, p. 59.
18. 'The gesture is essentially always a gesture of not being able to figure something out in language; it is always a gag in the proper meaning of the term', p. 59.
19. Elena Gorfinkel, '*Wanda*, Loden, lodestone', Paper written for the ICA London, available at <https://www.ica.art/sites/default/files/downloads/ICA%20Wanda_%20Loden_%20lodestone_v2.pdf>. Accessed 8 May 2018.
20. Margulies, *Nothing Happens: Chantal Akerman's Hyperrealist Everyday*, p. 6.
21. Chantal Akerman, 'Chantal Akerman on Jeanne Dielman', *Camera Obscura 2* (Fall 1977), p. 119.
22. Akerman called *Jeanne Dielman*, for example, 'a love film for my mother' (cited in *Identity and Memory: The Films of Chantal Akerman*, ed. by Gwendolyn Audrey Foster (Trowbridge: Flicks Books, 1996), p. 78).
23. 'Natalia Akerman, nee Leibel, in *Toute une nuit*, smokes a cigarette in front of the door to her house in Strombeck. A few moments later, a little voice calls — Maman, Maman — she stubs out her cigarette and goes back inside', Akerman, *Autoportrait en cinéaste*, p. 25.
24. 'Pure auto-affective pleasure', Jacques Derrida, *Donner le temps: la fausse monnaie* (Paris: Galilée, 1991), p. 134.
25. Giorgio Agamben, *The Use of Bodies* (Stanford: Stanford University Press, 2016), p. 63.
26. Ibid.
27. Hannah Mowat, *Gesture and the cinéaste: Akerman/Agamben, Varda/Warburg* (doctoral thesis). Available at <https://doi.org/10.17863/CAM.6333> Accessed 8 May 2018.

28. Chantal Akerman, *Ma mère rit* (Paris: Mercure de France, 2013), p. 32: ('What I like, is the moment in the day where I sense I have a life; when I walk at a good pace to go and buy cigarettes. Suddenly I am a person. A person at liberty, a person who has something to do.')
29. Chantal Akerman cited in Jean-Luc Godard, 1980, 'Entretien sur un projet: 1. Avec Chantal Akerman', *Ça cinéma*, 19, 5–16 (p. 13): 'Au lieu de montrer un événement "public" parce que sensationnel ou avec plein de choses, je raconterai juste la petite chose à côté.' ('Instead of showing an event which is "public" because it is sensational or has a lot happening, I will narrate just the little thing going on on the side').
30. Akerman, *Ma mère rit*, p. 44.
31. Judith Butler, *Precarious Life: The Powers of Mourning and Violence* (London: Verso, 2006), p. 45.
32. Sharon Olds, 'The Cigars,' in *The Father* (New York: Cape, 2009), pp. 19–20.
33. Ibid.
34. Ibid.
35. I am indebted here to Elizabeth Freeman's work on 'drag' in cinema as a mode of temporal stoppage, dilation, and delay.
36. Agamben, 'Notes on Gesture', p. 62.
37. 'To keep a hold of the present is to make fragile, simple, poor, repeated gestures in order to live day after day', Corinne Rondeau, *Chantal Akerman: Passer la nuit* (Paris, Editions Eclat, 2017), p. 30.
38. Cited in Terrie Sultan (ed.), *Chantal Akerman: Moving Through Time and Space,* (Seattle: Marquand Books, 2008), p. 51.
39. For more on Akerman's 'phenomenologies of the ephemeral' in the installation space, see Jenny Chamarette, 'The Disappearing Work: Chantal Akerman's Phenomenologies of the Ephemeral', *Contemporary French and Francophone Studies*, 17.3 (2013), 347–56.
40. Sultan, *Moving Through Time and Space*, p. 52.
41. See Laura Marks, 'Video Haptics and Erotics', *Screen*, 39.4 (Winter 1998), 331–48.
42. Ibid.
43. Tinkler, *Smoke Signals: Women, Smoking and Visual Culture*, 'the physical act of smoking was in itself a radical departure from feminine standards of appearance and gesticulation', p. 159.
44. In interview with Nicole Brenez Akerman notes how 'les images littérales finissent par ne plus émouvoir, il faut passer par un autre chemin, pour que les gens en face puissent exister et ressentir, dans un vrai face-à-face avec l'image.' 'literal images end up no longer being moving, you need to take a different route so that the people in front of them can exist and feel, in a true face to face encounter with the image.' (Nicole Brenez, 'Chantal Akerman: The Pyjama Interview, <http://www.lolajournal.com/2/pajama.html> Accessed 28 October 2017.
45. See Chris Dercon, 'An Interview with Chantal Akerman About Too Much and Not Enough Cinema': 'I want the spectator to have a physical experience, for him or her to feel time. Films are generally made to literally and metaphorically pass the time. But I want you to experience the time of a character. I don't want you to just go through an emotional experience, but also another kind of experience, like with music, that is unique because it is purely physical. *Contour*, <http://www.contour2005.be/UK/ca.htm> Accessed 28 October 2017.
46. Jonathan Crary, *24:7: Late Capitalism and the End of Sleep* (London: Verso, 2013), pp. 123–24 (emphasis my own).
47. Gilles Deleuze, 'Postscript on the Societies of Control', *October*, 59 (Winter 1992) 3–7.
48. See Agamben, 'Notes on Gesture, pp. 49–63: 'by the end of the nineteenth century the Western bourgeoisie had definitely lost its gestures', p. 49.
49. Giuliana Bruno, 'Projection: On Chantal Akerman's Screens, from Cinema to the Art Gallery', *Senses of Cinema*, December 2015, <http://sensesofcinema.com/2015/chantal-akerman/projection/>. Accessed 28 October 2017.
50. See Judith Butler, *Frames of War: When is Life Grievable?* (London: Verso, 2009), p. 169.
51. I am paraphrasing here Derrida's review of smoking in *Donner le temps* as 'une dépense inutile, une dépense de luxe, une pure consommation.' ('a useless expense, a luxury expense, pure consumption.')
52. Maggie Nelson, *The Argonauts* (Minneapolis: Graywolf Press, 2015), p. 102.

53. Maggie Nelson, 'A Sort of Leaning Against', in *The Writers' Notebook II: Craft Essays from Tin House*, ed. by Christopher Beha (Portland: Tin House Press, 2012), p. 92.

CHAPTER 4

Ageless: Akerman's Avatars

Jenny Chamarette

Chantal Akerman was only 18 when she made her first short film, *Saute ma ville*. The figure of the young woman, played by Akerman, radically and violently disrupts the domestic space of her apartment, transgressing all of the domestic meticulousness later portrayed in elongated detail in *Jeanne Dielman, 23, quai du Commerce, 1080 Bruxelles* from 1975. Of all the films of Akerman that I have watched, this angry, young, singing woman returns to me over and over again. In this vision, there is so much farcical, explosive, rabid anger: a mercurial state of self-rebellion that burns under the surface of many of Akerman's other images. *Saute ma ville*'s English title is *Blow Up My Town*. But in fact, the film does not portray an act of mass urban destruction. It is instead a small, radical act of self-annihilation by a young woman whose gestures still betray a little of her gauche, awkward adolescent body. In the black leader of the end of the film, the young woman's last self-destructive act isn't even visible. The sound of an explosion is all that is left, followed by her triumphant, out-of-tune singing. Akerman kills off the figure of the young woman aged 18, in 1968. The very first film she ever makes is a shadow of her own death. It is a significant overstep to make any comparison between this baroque, rebellious, raging representation in *Saute ma ville*, and the circumstances of her actual death, aged 65, in October 2015, when she took the decision to end her own life. But perhaps there is another way of seeing it. The figure-avatar of the young woman floats through very many of Akerman's films. This ageless figure stands in, over and again, for Akerman, whose own body will now age no further, since to age one must be alive, still changing, still moving. Ageing is a sign of life, even though at the same time it portends mortality. Ageing is, in a sense, the opposite of death, even as it draws death nearer. Agelessness, as an ambivalent form of cinematic resistance, is what I see in Akerman's work, which flies from and is drawn to forms of selfhood.

    Throughout her life, Chantal Akerman was a writer, photographer and installation artist. She also made films, for which she is most widely celebrated and commonly known. There is a particular temptation to claim only one type of creative space for women artists, to deny their polymorphic creative pursuits. As Rozsika Parker and Griselda Pollock pointed out in 1981, Art History (and its compatriot discipline, Film Studies) has an overwhelming tendency to categorize, deflect and narrow the production of art by women. This in itself is more a result of the ideological structures of knowledge production than a definition of those women making art.[1] As a scholar of women artists, I have found it tempting and confusing in equal measure to describe Akerman as a filmmaker like Agnès Varda (except that they are both photographers, writers, documentarists, installation artists); Shirin Neshat as an installation artist (though she too is a painter, photographer and filmmaker) and Marina Abramović as a performance artist (though she is also a filmmaker, transmedia star and latent celebrity). The works these artists leave behind are more complex than a singular summary of their parts: they are multiple, transmedial, interpersonal. They blur lines between self and subject, suffused with emotion and a sense of corporeality. And writing about women artists itself is a precarious double act: their writing, per se, becomes part of their creative complexity, and it intertwines with mine as a writer-scholar. That creative complexity is what I work with and respond to: adding my own voice to theirs, I seek out patterns that may or may not become lines of thought for me, a woman writer, to follow. For me, writing is not an act of literature, but an act of art. Artmaking is therefore polyvalent, refractory, and resistant.

The question of ageing, and agelessness, is both self-evident and difficult to reconcile with the figure of Akerman, given her early passing. It is also surprisingly difficult to resolve with my own work. Two of the figures whom I most admire, Agnès Varda and Louise Bourgeois, one living, one dead, are and were active into their ninth and tenth decades. Their meditations on ageing are different too: Varda considers her own body as a site of auto-ethnographic interrogation, particularly in her well-known film, *Les Glaneurs et la glaneuse* (*The Gleaners and I*, 2000), and most recently the limitations of her vision and memory come to the fore in her collaboration with the global street artist and photographer JR in *Visages Villages* (*Faces Places*, 2017). Bourgeois' 'late' period, after the death of her husband, Robert Goldwater, in 1973, is undoubtedly the one for which she has received the widest critical acclaim. Her political and creative activity flourished while she was in her sixties and beyond: ageing for her gave an emotional force that propelled her to analyze and thereby to survive the rage she felt for her own familial relations. And familial relations are at the heart of this chapter, but not, as has so often been explored with relation to Akerman, with regard to the figure of the mother, whose ageing body and sudden decline are depicted with such painful clarity in Akerman's last film, *No Home Movie* (2015). This chapter instead turns to issues of daughterhood, intersubjectivity and the refusal of ageing, which resonate throughout Akerman's films and writing, whether or not Akerman herself is visible within the frame.

Simone de Beauvoir's existential feminist phenomenology examines ageing as another lived experience that differentiates the expressions of power between men and women. For Beauvoir, old age is a diminishment of power in as much as it is also a phenomenon that brings to the surface the instability of life, and which therefore challenges the assumption that ageing is a slow-moving form of death:

> La vieillesse n'est pas un fait statique c'est l'aboutissement et le prolongement d'un processus. En quoi celui-ci consiste-t-il? Autrement dit, qu'est-ce que vieillir? Cette idée est liée à celle de changement. Mais la vie de l'embryon,

> du nouveau-né, de l'enfant est un changement continu. Faut-il en conclure
> comme l'ont fait certains que notre existence est une mort lente? Assurément
> non. Un tel paradoxe méconnait l'essentielle vérité de la vie; elle est un système
> instable où à chaque instant l'équilibre se perd et se reconquiert: c'est l'inertie
> qui est synonyme de mort. La loi de la vie, c'est de changer. C'est un certain
> type de changement qui caractérise le vieillissement; irréversible et défavorable,
> un déclin.[2]

Unceasing change, then, is also part of age and ageing, as much as it is part of every day that is lived: the difference is the power differential which asserts that ageing is a process of decline. Perhaps it is a fault in my own thinking that I see ageing as a cumulative source of critical reflection among many others, inseparable from other cultural, social and embodied indicators of change. If I try to isolate ageing as a mechanism for thinking about Akerman's films, it becomes a multi-faceted lens through which I can see many other issues at stake: self-production, affect, embodiment, gender, visibility, intergenerational relationships, maternity (or its absence), daughterhood, mortality.

At the very least, I want to suggest that, throughout Akerman's prolific filmmaking career, *ageing* is something refused, denied, exchanged in an oddly permanent and strangely replaceable relation between generations of on-screen women. *Agelessness*, a suspension of life and death, refuses the indexical links between ageing, vivacity and mortality. And that suspension is closely linked to a space of intimacy and displacement in Akerman's work. The films I mention in this chapter, *Saute ma ville* (1968), *Les Rendez-vous d'Anna* (1978), *Aujourd'hui, dis-moi* (1980), *Demain on déménage* (2004), *La Folie Almayer* (2011), and *No Home Movie* (2015), all refuse, suspend or otherwise do battle with age, mortality and the passage of time, using diverse but mutually resonant tactics. Resistance to domesticity and transit through the depiction of exterior urban topographies go hand in hand with an intimate attention to interior space, and the space of relations between mothers and daughters. In each case, there is a resistance to ageing so powerful that the young women of each film become interchangeable avatars — interchangeable for each other, and interchangeable, in a more diffuse sense, for the autobiographically-infused subjectivity in Akerman's films. While the term 'avatar' is more commonly associated with virtual reality and gaming, its broader meaning pertains to bodily incarnations, deriving from the Hindu Sanskrit term for descent.[3] An older sense of the avatar relates to its iconic value as a manifestation of a particular person. It therefore seems particularly relevant to use such a term to describe the interchangeable replacements of one young female figure for another, across almost the entirety of Akerman's filmmaking. Descent, in the form of a queer genealogy of female avatars, becomes a means of evading the 'decline' that Beauvoir identifies as the inimicable change of ageing. The older figures are not done away with — as becomes apparent in both *Aujourd'hui dis-moi* and *No Home Movie* — but they seamlessly shift position in relation to their younger selves. This quality of resistance to the passage of time, and its affective implications, is what I think through in this chapter.

Resisting Age

I have in earlier writing referred to Akerman's work as offering a kind of 'resistant cinema': resistant to categories of nationhood, medium, generic conventions of documentary and feature-length fiction films.[4] Akerman made multi-channel installations and musicals, epistolary autobiographical films and testimonials. Her work slips in-between different ways of thinking about film, and about selfhood, memory, family, sexuality, gender, identity, displacement. This 'resistance' is also to do with contesting a singular subjective position: refusing a consistent 'I' voice in Akerman's work, and thereby challenging autobiography as a means of delineating selfhood and subjectivity, in as much as her work also embraces it. Ros Murray has thoughtfully extended this idea of resistance to a positive and radically queer feminist temporality. She writes of resistance as the exercise of power through gendered and sexual difference, depicted in Akerman's *Je tu il elle* (1975): 'it is through bodily sexual acts rather than subjective identities that the film operates its queer resistance.'[5] In this film, the bodily sexual acts are between two young women — acts which, as Murray and Ivone Margulies have noticed, elide difference between the position of 'elle' that the title seems to work so hard to delineate.[6] This is problematic insomuch as it creates an almost suffocating proximity between the possibility of an 'I' and the possibility of a 'you' in Akerman's work. This intoxicating proximity of self to other manifests itself elsewhere in Akerman's films, outside sexual relations, and in other relational forms. Alisa Lebow gives a compelling argument for Akerman's lifelong concern, obsession even, with her mother, Natalia Akerman, also known as Nelly, and the combination of stifling proximity and heretical distance that plays out in her films. She suggests that Akerman effectively creates a slippage between the 'I' voice of herself, and the 'I' voice of other selves, the most significant one being her mother, a woman who retains the living memory of Akerman's past. Lebow describes this as 'a complete and thoroughgoing slippage of subject-object relations, wherein there can be no subject, no articulated "I" on its own, no boundary between the "I" and the "m/other"'.[7] Akerman both becomes and is not quite different from her own mother. But perhaps this sense is broader: the 'I' subject of Akerman's films and writing both becomes and is yet somehow not equivalent to other 'I's, other selves. Suffocatingly close and yet not quite identical.

The slippery resistance to categorizations and delineations in Akerman's work seems to work in two ways. There is a resistance to genre classification, to medium, certainly to narrative convention, resistance to direct autobiographical account, and resistance to heteronormative frameworks of sexuality. But that resistance to boundaries also produces slippage and elision, not knowing, or not showing, where one person begins and another ends. This becomes a resistance to the distinctions between you and I, self and other, individual and context. When Akerman's young 18-year-old avatar blows herself up, she also blows up her town. There is no meaningful distinction between the one individual and the many. Perhaps this is a way of understanding the figure of the young woman, as she appears and reappears across Akerman's fiction films. Akerman as a young woman on-screen in *Saute ma ville* and *Je tu il elle*, is replaced by Aurore Clément in *Les Rendez-vous d'Anna*. Aurore

Clément is replaced by Sylvie Testud in *Demain on déménage*. And the figure of the white, metropolitan French/Belgian young woman is displaced in altogether more complex ways in Akerman's adaptation of Joseph Conrad's novel, *Almayer's Folly*, by the Belgian-Rwandan-Greek actor Aurora Marion. This retinue of young female figures retains ghostly elements of individuality. They are all played by prodigiously talented performers, who each bring distinctive physical and emotional qualities to their roles. Nonetheless, the slippage between young, female performers and Akerman's resistance to individual subjective positions in her films seems more than coincidental.

Daughters, Transit, and Time

While some women become mothers, many (but not all) women begin as or become daughters. And while I myself am not defined solely by my daughterhood, my position as a daughter forms part of the relational compact that makes up the notion of myself as a woman in the world. Daughterhood is a powerfully dominant (but by no means exclusive) characteristic of femininity, far more common than motherhood. But while motherhood often implies a certain reproductive age, daughterhood does not. The temporality of these two relations is different. The figure of the young woman is implicitly that of a daughter, particularly so in many of Akerman's films. Each young female figure in her films is childless, wandering, often connected but even more often displaced. Women — mothers and daughters — wander in many of Akerman's films of the 70s: even Jeanne Dielman, the famous mother of Akerman's eponymous film whose range of movement is so strangled by the limits of Brussels and her apartment, wanders from time to time: to the haberdashers where she seeks a match for a lost button. To the market to buy potatoes. To the cobblers to repair shoes. The letters from Jeanne's sister decry her singledom, her apparent inability to move forward with her life after the death of her husband. They bind her to her wifehood and her status as an adult daughter and sibling, which Jeanne resists, first by degrees, then by an avalanche. In one of Akerman's semi-autobiographical novellas, *Une famille à Bruxelles*, she writes about women who stay close and women who go far away, from a perspective that slips between that of a mother left behind in Brussels, and that of a daughter, affirmatively elsewhere:

> Chacun a sa vie. Surtout quand on est loin. Et même quand on est près mais quand on est près ça se sent au téléphone et on peut se dire à bientôt et parfois on se voit. On dit aussi à bientôt à ceux qui sont loin au téléphone mais on sait qu'on ne se verra pas bientôt et parfois ceux qui sont loin on ne les appelle pas ou presque jamais même quand c'est de la famille proche.[8]

Nearness and farness, the impression of proximity and the facticity of distance, these are concerns of mothers and daughters. But the daughters are always far away. I recognize in Akerman's writing a duality: the transparency of writing in the close third person — so close that it is almost impossible to distinguish between third and first; between *she* and *me*. But there is also the sadness, reserve and frustration of a

Fig. 4.1. Aurore Clément in Paris, *Les Rendez-vous d'Anna* (dir. Chantal Akerman, 1978)

Fig. 4.2. Church of the Madeleine in *Les Rendez-vous d'Anna* (dir. Chantal Akerman, 1978)

Fig. 4.3. Sex Shops in Pigalle, *Les Rendez-vous d'Anna* (dir. Chantal Akerman, 1978)

dispersed family. The impression of distance through proximity, and of intimacy through distance, is a consistent paradox in Akerman's filmmaking too. Like in *Les Rendez-vous d'Anna*, where the young woman, Anna (Aurore Clément), operates at a distance from the temporal reminder of where she came from that is her mother. On tour to promote her new film, Anna waits on trains, endlessly shuttling between European cities. She is alone, but connected, by the telephone, to her mother, and also to her male lovers. Even her female partner, who she never quite reaches, is part of that network of wired media and train tracks. Her wandering, and her paradoxical disconnectedness within a nexus of European connections, place her in a strange sort of hang-time. For the time that she is travelling, she is ageless: her temporality is halted. This agelessness is written in her face, a kind of miserable inertia in the midst of movement.

What I see in Anna's young, unlined face is quiet, absorbed misery. I search for the signs of sadness in her face, for the prick of tears in her shining eyes, the slight adjustment of her jaw and opened mouth as if to exhale pain, just as I search for identifying landmarks in the city that are implicitly the objects of Anna's looking. The matching dashboard shot that follows the extended, silent portrait of Anna, reveals a dehumanized, barely illuminated Paris, populated by the rear lights and bumpers of endless streams of cars. Almost nothing of human shape or size is observable within the frame: vehicles and buildings, street lamps and street furniture dance before the screen and emanate light in a human darkness, reflected occasionally in an otherwise invisibly present windscreen. Both the camera, and the implied vision of Anna, demonstrate a desolate absorption in the movement through the city of Paris, where the church of the Madeleine and the sex shops of Pigalle intermingle with car headlamps and wet streets. She looks, she listens, she waits, as she travels. But as she looks outwards, beyond the frame, she is also looking inwards; her apparent misery is as impenetrable as the barely distinguishable outlines of a city in movement.

Giuliana Bruno has described this commingling of interior and exterior space as a means of tracking 'an intimate journey'. For Bruno, technologies of travel and communication are deeply entwined with intimacy: 'A family or personal history can only be displayed in a virtual place of transit — the railway or the hotel at that time, the smart phone or the laptop now — a site inhabited each "night and day" by different stories'.[9] Bruno describes transit as a space of affective intensity, but this is somehow combined in Akerman's films, and even more so in her moving image installations, with a sense of slowed time, a kind of *intemporality*, that runs against the grain of any possibility of fluid, seamless connection. This quality of hang-time or dead time she identifies particularly in one of Akerman's last multi-channel installations, *Femmes d'Anvers en novembre* (2008), which for her 'renews Akerman's filmic sense of inhabiting a city, dwelling especially on those instants of pause and transition, reflection and anxiety, when women are on their own, ambling, walking in the rain, lingering, caught in an intermediate zone. The work is suspended between a before and an after, in the unsettling time of a transitory moment.'[10]

Transit and transition seem to be intimately linked for the young female avatars of Akerman's films. But what if this intermediate zone — whether a zone of wandering, or a zone of domestic space — were the zone of processing, where things happen psychically, particularly related to the emotions and embodiment of subjectivity? What if the quotidian zone of laboured or professional activity were the place where that embodied life is halted? Where stopping and doing nothing much at all is not so much a means of resisting ageing, as a different form of change? Intermediate zones — of wandering and of stillness — might offer a way of rethinking the relationships between ageing, human temporality, and resistant subjectivity, which persist in the female protagonists of Akerman's films.

Intergenerational Akerman

A rarely discussed mid-length film for television that Akerman made in 1980, aged 30, called *Aujourd'hui, dis-moi*, brings together wandering and domestic stillness, and the intergenerational relations between young and older women. At the time of writing, the film is digitized and available in its entirety via the Institut National de l'Audiovisuel website, and is a kind of fictionalized documentary tracing a series of interviews with female Holocaust survivors living in Paris about their family lives, while sitting in their homes eating cake and drinking tea or coffee. The interviews given by these women are impeccably articulated: they tell their stories with such grace that it seems difficult to imagine that the images and sounds are anything other than formally scripted and choreographed. And yet, the domestic settings, and the direct honesty, tenderness and emotion with which these women speak give a powerful sense of augmented authenticity. Whereas for Walter Benjamin 'the presence of the original is the pre-requisite to the concept of authenticity',[11] both performance studies and documentary theory have had frequent recourse to other ways of understanding authenticity, particularly where any notion of the 'original' is ontologically unstable. In the case of the moving image, where performance and self-presentation overlap closely, the temporality of 'authentic' performances falls out of joint, as Rebecca Schneider highlights:

> The explicit replay of a time-based art troubles the prerogatives of singular artists, the assumptions of forward-marching time [...] Touching time against itself, by bringing time *again and again* out of joint into theatrical, even anamorphic, relief presents the real, the actual, the raw and the true as, precisely, the zigzagging, diagonal, and crookedly imprecise returns of time.[12]

In *Aujourd'hui, dis-moi*, the positioning and design of each interior shot is carefully designed so as to maximize screen space and attention on the older women as they tell their stories. The means by which these accounts are manufactured on screen gives rise to layers of artifice as well as layers of authenticity; layers which bring their personal storytelling as elderly witnesses into theatrical relief within an imprecise temporality, as Schneider so aptly describes.

Akerman, as listener-protagonist, says very little in these encounters, occasionally nodding with encouragement. The presence of the on-screen Akerman evidently gives pleasure to the women, but there is also the reassurance of storytelling and a form of oral history in these encounters — a speaker, and a listener. Even though their stories are of death, genocide, disappearance, there is also a quality of calm joy in the intergenerational exchange between a younger and an older woman. In between each visit to an older woman, the film segments shots of Akerman moving through Paris, via the Métro, while the voiceover, spoken by Akerman's mother, Nelly, describes her own history of post-Holocaust survival. The account that Nelly gives at intervals where Akerman is depicted walking from apartment building to apartment building, is disarming: honest, authoritative, deep, quick and intelligent. It is distinctively, heartrendingly different from the quality of Nelly's voice, as captured in Akerman's' last film, *No Home Movie*.

The title of the film *Aujourd'hui, dis-moi* implicates both the present moment, and storytelling, as means of preserving intergenerational connection—intergenerational temporality, even. Storytelling as a means of connecting at a distance; the present as a means of accessing the process of storytelling. The tellers of those stories are human vessels, and with each unique and precious vessel, the story changes. And on that process of change, there is also a mode of quiet pleasure. I don't know quite what to do with this notion of the pleasure of intergenerational ageing and of witnessing that ageing process, other than to return, as if on an eternal loop, to Beauvoir's assertion that the ideologies of ageing bear infinitely close resemblance to the continual change that is life. This kind of pleasure is linked to resistance, to queering the temporality of female ageing — not as a period of decline and stasis, but rather as avatarial descent: a marker of the constant change which, as Beauvoir reminds us, is a condition of life. If there is pleasure in ageing through intergenerational contact, as much as there is a refusal on Akerman's part to experience or represent this decline through herself, then perhaps this is what is mirrored both in *Aujourd'hui, dis-moi*, and in Akerman's last film, *No Home Movie*.

Viewing these two films in close proximity, there is a shock in the dramatic change to the quality and timbre of Nelly's voice — from the fullness of pleasure, to the thinness of pain. In *No Home Movie,* her voice broadcasts age in a viscerally distinctive way: its pace and volume gradually diminish to a trickle, and then a grunt, and then a gurgling, visceral cough. In comparison to Nelly's voiceover from *Aujourd'hui, dis-moi* it constitutes a more poignant indicator of ageing through sound than comparative portraiture might do through vision. It is possible to trace ageing in Akerman's films, but it is the ageing of others, the gradual transition of those who constitute the memories and testimonies of domestic life, from living material into celluloid stock or digital images, that becomes visible (or indeed audible) and contextualized on screen.

No Home Movie is littered with long sequences in Nelly Akerman's apartment where she moves back and forth in front of the camera, aimlessly wandering. Each sequence reveals so much about Akerman's elderly mother's bodily comportment and health. In the second sequence of the film, the camera is stood at table height, thus revealing most of Nelly's body as she passes to and fro in front of it. Her left arm is held tensely against her body, protectively, while her right arm swings loosely akimbo. The imbalance of these two sides of her body immediately draws attention to immobility, and also to pain: I could see in Nelly's body, before any speech or voiceover informed me of this, that her slightly shuffling, imbalanced gait and trapped arm indicated injury.

The intermediate zone of waiting, preparing, doing nothing much, is exactly where Nelly's bodily subjectivity becomes visible, just as it does for Akerman's fictional avatar-protagonists. The pleasure and pain of embodying memory in Nelly's ageing body seem to come to the fore, just as her position as mother, as keeper of memories, seems to hold Akerman in the same pattern of nearly-invisible daughterhood, the same ageless moment. Now ageless in the mortal sense, since this is the last record of both Nelly and Chantal, speaking, breathing, and living together. Perhaps it is not surprising then, that we barely see Chantal Akerman at all in *No Home Movie*. She is sometimes captured crossing the field of vision of the camera she has placed in Nelly Akerman's Brussels apartment. But in other locations, in hotel rooms and apartments as Akerman travels, she is behind the camera, filming the sickly-sweet Skype conversations she has with her mother. Then again, human bodies are almost completely obliterated in segments of the film, where, for instance, the screen becomes pixelated and defocuses her mother's face. Or where the exposure of the video camera is deliberately stopped so low that her mother's ailing body is barely visible. Or where Akerman records the barren landscape of the desert in Israel, or the emptiness of her mother's apartment in the last, mute sequences of the film.

I appreciate that there is a slippage in my own thoughts here, between the female figures on-screen in Akerman's films. I have slipped, from talking about the apparently ageless, apparently replaceable but nonetheless consistent figure of the young woman in Akerman's films, to talking about an intimate portrait of Akerman's mother, Natalia — Nelly. I'm aware that by doing this I may be missing the point of talking about ageing — that it is essential to point out the social, cultural, physical, aesthetic and formal difference between the depictions of young women and depictions of ageing women. But I keep returning to the initial words of Simone de Beauvoir: that ageing is not a determinate point, but rather an extension of a process of constant change. Constant change is nonetheless potentially alarming, and brings with it social signals of the diminishment of power. At the same time, I want to suggest that this slippage in Akerman's own films — between female protagonists especially — is a means of *resisting* the designations of ageing as decline. To call this perverse is probably *not* missing the point at all: Akerman's work has long been lauded as an example of queer and resistant filmmaking. If she queers the temporalities of daughterhood, and indeed the temporalities of motherhood, then she is also queering the temporalities of ageing, particularly and specifically female ageing.

It is obvious to say that ageing and temporality are intimately linked. But if this is true, then other kinds of temporality are also called into play. Hang-time in domestic space and hang-time through transit seem, rather paradoxically, to bring together the emotional intensities of adult mother-daughter relationships. Perhaps the central question I am asking here, is how the interchangeability of young (and old) female protagonists in Akerman's films connects to, or descends from, the transitional emotional topographies that they experience in the films' narrative structures? These are recurring patterns across Akerman's fiction and non-fiction films, which emerge in the young female avatars' contact between exterior spaces of transit, and interior spaces of domestic, emotional and intergenerational contemplation. When considering the films in relation to one another, across a span of nearly fifty years, the persistence of these forms creates a pattern of meaning across an oeuvre. What is the temporality of this pattern? How do the spaces which frame and are inhabited by Akerman's avatars indicate the temporal relations of subjectivity, such as ageing, and daughterhood? Perhaps *indicate* is the wrong word, given the emphasis I have placed on the slippery resistance of Akerman's work. The films do not *indicate* the place of daughterhood, or of ageing, or indeed of subjectivity, so much as refuse to indicate or locate intergenerational relations — or any kind of subjective relation — in a distinct or exclusive form: not as gradual decline, but as tumbling, transformative descent. Rather than considering the slippage between the 'I' form and the 'you' form of address, or the interchangeable avatars of the films, as a kind of cinematic psychopathology, I wonder whether it might be possible instead to consider these slippages and resistances as something other: a different form of queer kinship, where the distance between the feminine 'I' and the feminine 'you' is forever changing, overlapping, defiant, and indeed, ageless.

Notes to Chapter 4

1. Rozsika Parker and Griselda Pollock, *Old Mistresses: Women, Art and Ideology* (London: Tauris, 2013 [1981]), pp. xxvi–xxviii, pp. 1–14, pp. 169–70.
2. Simone de Beauvoir, *La Vieillesse* (Paris: Gallimard, 1970), p. 22. 'Old age is not a mere statistical fact; it is the prolongation and the last stage of a certain process. What does this process consist of? In other words, what does growing old mean? The notion is bound up with that of change. Yet the life of the foetus, of the new-born baby and of the child is one of continuous change. Must we therefore say, as some have said, that our life is a gradual death? Certainly not. A paradox of this kind disregards the basic truth of life — life is an unstable system in which balance is continually lost and continually recovered: it is inertia that is synonymous with death.' Translation in Simone de Beauvoir, *The Coming of Age*, trans. by Patrick O' Brien (New York: Putnam, 1972), p. 11.
3. 'avatar, n.'. 2017. *OED Online*. Oxford University Press. <http://www.oed.com/view/Entry/13624> (accessed 5 January 2018).
4. Jenny Chamarette, *Phenomenology and the Future of Film: Rethinking Subjectivity Beyond French Cinema* (Basingstoke: Palgrave Macmillan, 2012), pp. 151–56.
5. Ros Murray, 'The Radical Politics of Possibility: Towards a Queer Existential Phenomenology Through Chantal Akerman's Je tu il elle (1975)', *Feral Feminisms*, 5 (2016), 44–56 (p. 52).
6. Ivone Margulies, *Nothing Happens: Chantal Akerman's Hyperrealist Everyday* (Durham, NC: Duke University Press, 1996), p. 1. Cited in Murray, 'Radical Politics', p. 52.
7. Alisa Lebow, 'Identity Slips: The Autobiographical Register in the Work of Chantal Akerman', *Film Quarterly*, 70.1 (2016), 54–60 (p. 56).
8. 'Everyone's got their own life. Especially when you are far away. And even when you're close by but when you're close by you can feel it on the telephone and you can say see you soon and sometimes you see each other. You also say see you soon on the phone to those who are far away but you know that you won't see each other soon, and sometimes the ones who are far away you don't call them or hardly ever even when it's close family' (translation mine). Chantal Akerman, *Une famille à Bruxelles* (Paris: L'Arche: 1998), p. 9.

9. Giuliana Bruno, 'Projection: On Akerman's Screen', in *Chantal Akerman: Too Far, Too Close*, ed. by Anders Kreuger (Antwerp: Ludion/MHKA, 2012), pp. 15–34 (pp. 16–17).
10. Bruno, 'Projection', p. 18.
11. Walter Benjamin, 'The Work of Art in the Age of Mechanical Reproduction', in *Illuminations: Essays and Reflections,* ed. by Hannah Arendt, trans. by Harry Zohn (New York: Schocken Books, 1968 [1936]), pp. 217–51 (p. 220).
12. Rebecca Schneider, *Performing Remains: Art and War in Times of Theatrical Reenactment* (London: Routledge, 2011), p. 16.

CHAPTER 5

Real Estates:
The Comedy of Spaces and Things in Chantal Akerman's *Demain on déménage*

Hilde D'haeyere and Steven Jacobs

A Couch in Ménilmontant

Demain on déménage is a 2004 film comedy directed by Chantal Akerman and written in collaboration with Eric de Kuyper, who had also worked on the screenplay of *Je, tu, il, elle* (1975) and *La Captive* (1999). A tale about moving and settling, it tells the story of Charlotte Weinstein (Sylvie Testud), a restless, chain-smoking writer who is trying to compose erotic prose. At the beginning of the film, her mother Catherine (Aurore Clément), a cheerful piano teacher who was widowed after being married for 41 years, moves in with her. They start living together in an apartment divided over two floors, interconnected by means of a hatch and open stairs. Charlotte's floor, the one on top, has a front door that connects to the streets of Ménilmontant, a neighbourhood situated on a hill overlooking Paris. The constellation with two apartments, one above the other, is inspired by the way Chantal Akerman herself lived in Ménilmontant's rue Henri Chevreau with her life partner, cello player Sonia Wieder-Atherton. Most scenes of the film are situated in this double-decker apartment designed by Christian Marti (Production Design), Régine Constant (Art Direction), and Marie-Laure Valla (Set Decoration). Its remarkable spatial layout contributes largely to the relations between the characters, the development of the episodic narrative, and the construction of comedy. A dynamic interplay between drifting and dwelling, the loose plot revolves around the ways Charlotte and Catherine try to settle into their new apartment, quite quickly realizing that they are not feeling at home and that they need to find another place. While Charlotte and Catherine search for real estate, a series of potential buyers, most of them middle-aged couples struggling in one way or another with their relationships, visit the apartment. Eventually, the mother moves out while the daughter remains, teaming up with one of the visitors in a new constellation of family life.

With an emphasis on enclosed spaces, rooms, domestic interiors, and the notion of dwelling, *Demain on déménage* joins many other films by Akerman.[1] The very titles of films such as *La Chambre* (1972), *Hotel Monterey* (1972), *News from Home* (1976), *Letters Home* (1986), *Le Déménagement* (1992), *Un Divan à New York* (1996), *La Captive*, and *No Home Movie* (2015) evoke houses, hotels, and rooms as focal points of Akerman's explorations of domesticity and seclusion — topics that were already apparent in many of her early films. By means of her characteristically static camera and extended long takes, Akerman meticulously explored secluded rooms in *La Chambre*, *Hotel Monterey*, and the first part of *Je, tu, il, elle*, inspired by Structural Cinema's phenomenological preoccupation with spaces. The title of *Demain on déménage* echoes an earlier Akerman film that shared these concerns in its theme and visual style. In *Le Déménagement* (*Moving in*, 1992), the main character (Sami Frey) walks the length and breadth of his apartment from wall to wall. Reminiscent of the spatial trajectory in Michael Snow's *Wavelength* (1967), each new shot moves in a little closer to Sami Frey, who is sitting in a chair facing the spectator amidst the unpacked boxes of his life, until the final camera movement frames his face in an extreme close-up. The rigorous and formal investigation of rooms, corridors, doors, windows, pieces of furniture, and household utensils also marks other Akerman films of the 1970s, most particularly *Jeanne Dielman, 23 Quai du Commerce, 1080 Bruxelles* (1975). In all these films, Akerman composes cinematic spaces like dollhouse universes, evoking interiors constructed by an ingenious system of visual axes reminiscent of Dutch seventeenth-century genre painting, which was the product of an emergent bourgeois society and its cult of domesticity. Like Johannes Vermeer or Pieter De Hooch, Akerman presents her spaces as complex configurations of domestic rooms and corridors, offering well-balanced vistas. Her emphatic attention to the stability of the frame and the frames-within-the-film-frame presents the interior as a viewing device or optical instrument. Rooms become spaces enclosed within straight lines and pictured with a frontal symmetry. Open windows or doors merely suggest an exterior world that is not, or is only partially, visible. In these spaces, composed characters find themselves in a state of absorption, turning the interior into a place of isolation, silence, introspection, and meditation.

Cramped Loft

Demain on déménage, too, focuses mostly on interiors while their connection to and situation in the exterior world remains conspicuously off-screen. The few exterior street views evoke a certain local atmosphere but hardly establish an urban context. The house, clearly, is a space completely separated from the hustle and bustle of the city. The mother's apartment is not even directly connected to the outside world, but sunken deep into the entrails of the apartment building. (Used only at the very end of the film, the door on that floor opens to let a couple of potential buyers leave the building with their newly born baby.) Visitors repeatedly notice the calm and quiet, and it is only with the opening of a single small window that a disproportionate amount of city noise pours in. In doing this, *Demain on déménage* seems to present the house as a space of seclusion and protection, in line with the traditional notions of the house as a place of safety and domestic bliss. As Walter

Benjamin famously demonstrated, in the nineteenth century the domestic interior became the ultimate domain of the private individual, serving to sustain individuals in a cocoon of peace and comfort, amidst the brutal forces of the industrial metropolis.[2] The domestic interior thus became the innermost core of bourgeois cosiness, a place where individuals left the mark of their private existence on the rooms they inhabited, through the extensive use of cushioning materials, such as curtains, wallpaper, upholstery, carpets, table cloths, bric-a-brac, and the like.

Akerman, however, distorts the idea of domestic protection to add a sense of confinement. Although often situated in bourgeois houses and apartments, Akerman's films do not evoke the house as a shelter that offers a sense of security. The interiors in *Saute ma ville* (1968), *Jeanne Dielman*, *La Captive*, and *Là-bas* (2006) do not conjure up feelings of domestic bliss; they rather seem to keep the characters imprisoned. Akerman's rooms invariably have a claustrophobic feel; her camera locks up the spaces in the strict rectangle of the film frame, much as her characters are contained within the spaces they occupy.

Remarkably, in *Demain on déménage*, this enclosure is completely at odds with the architectural form of the living spaces. The loft-like apartment of *Demain on déménage*, the former gloves atelier of the deceased father, does not show the traditional configuration of separate spaces of bourgeois homes that are characterized by complex floor plans with numerous rooms and corridors; it rather is an industrial duplex, a spacious workspace that spreads out over two floors. Potential buyers are informed that there are 'no load-bearing walls, so to change the layout, everything is possible — with a little imagination.'[3] (Ici, il n'y a aucun mur porteur, donc si vous voulez changer quelque chose dans la distribution des pièces, c'est possible. Tout est possible, avec un peu d'imagination.) Nonetheless, the apartment never evokes the open, airy, flexible spaces favoured by modernist architects and today's life-style industry. On the contrary, throughout the entire film, the apartment remains a cramped space, filled with old-fashioned, time-worn, and handed-down furniture. Both floors are packed with stacked armchairs, bookcases, flowerpots, lampshades, and piles of unopened boxes. The air is heavy with smoke and dust. The wide open space is even partitioned into impenetrable segments using blankets as curtains to separate sleeping areas, their walls clumsily covered with textiles as means of decoration and insulation. Paradoxically, this act of decoration creates cosy bedroom areas that answer to the conventions of a family house, the very image of the warm, upholstered bedroom pictured in the colourful painting that is frequently visible throughout the film.

Family Shrine

Akerman presents the private house as a site of clutter and things, in line with Benjamin's nineteenth-century 'phantasmagoria of the interior'.[4] First and foremost through objects (and not by means of a 'genius loci') the home is transformed into a shrine to family, a space in which the memory of loved ones and ancestors is kept alive. *Demain on déménage* presents the house as a place where a diary of a

Fig. 5.1. Chantal Akerman, *Demain on déménage* (2004).

deceased family member resides in the wardrobe, an armchair harbours a yarmulke, and the mother sleeps with a suitcase that is as old as the daughter. The contents of the suitcase — a hat, a shirt, a tie, a pair of gloves, underpants, aftershave, an electric razor, a pair of trousers — assemble as the empty shell of the absent father figure, confirming the home as a pre-eminently feminine space. This house clearly safeguards the female lineage of the family, from the grandmother, present through the read-out words from her diary, to mother and daughter, and later, the new partner with a baby girl. Indeed, more than merely a space secluded from the outside world, nineteenth-century bourgeois culture presented the house as a shelter for women, to protect them against the dangers of public space that was first and foremost claimed by men.[5] Akerman's interest in the interior, then, follows directly from the female and family themes she pictures, hence her association with a feminine and feminist film praxis. Various scenes in *Saute ma ville*, *Jeanne Dielman*, *L'Homme à la valise* (1983), and *No Home Movie* (2015) evoke the established tradition of showing domestic interiors in order to represent the habitat of women, more particularly the habitat of mothers.

In this aspect, *Demain on déménage* is closely related to *Aujourd'hui, dis-moi* (1982), an interview film made by Akerman for the French television channel INA that was part of a series on grandmothers. In *Aujourd'hui, dis-moi*, Akerman records her visits to three elderly ladies who welcome her with coffee and cakes in the living room of their homes. These 'grandmothers' share stories about ancestors and family history in memories that hand down, from (grand)mother to (grand)daughter, the habits, principles, and morals of Jewish culture. The domestic interior, then, is not simply the habitat of women and mothers, but also the space where history is re-imagined from a female point of view and the manual of life is handed down the maternal line of descent — since the paternal line was so brutally disrupted by the Holocaust.

In *Demain on déménage*, mother and daughter do not only live under the same roof, they occasionally also share a bed. The duplex apartment's layout with the floor of the mother situated under the level of the daughter, suggests the impact of a maternal subconscious in Charlotte's life. The familiar metaphor of the house as a womb-like space is further developed by the opening and closing of the hatch connecting both flats, and the opening and closing of the curtains that envelop the sleeping areas. Furthermore, the apartment also becomes the chosen place for childbirth when a pregnant buyer comes back to deliver her baby. At the end of the film, Charlotte raises this baby together with the biological mother, thereby starting the next episode of generational family life among mothers and daughters.

Domestic Blisters

Despite the fact that domestic rooms are predominant in Akerman's oeuvre, dwelling in them is often problematic. Only rarely do Akerman's characters feel at home in the household spaces that her camera so extensively and meticulously records. Only the pregnant woman really likes the apartment: 'I feel at home nowhere, but here I feel good. I've never felt so good in an apartment', she says. (Je ne me sens nulle part chez moi, mais ici, je suis bien. Je ne me suis jamais sentie aussi bien dans un appartement.) 'Me too, I feel at home nowhere', (Moi non plus, je ne me sens nulle part chez moi) is Charlotte's reply.

Likewise, although being in each other's proximity, mother and daughter do not really live together in *Demain on déménage*. Like other Akerman films that depict the themes of living together and cohabitation, such as *L'Homme à la valise*, *Nuit et jour* (1991), *Un Divan à New York*, or *Là-bas*, *Demain on déménage* pictures situations in which people stay over at other people's homes or share a house, voluntarily or forcedly. Also, sharing a living space is not reserved for relatives or lovers, Akerman characters simply distribute their personal needs over different places. Charlotte does not only share a house with her mother, she also decides to share a studio apartment with a woman who already has a house with a husband, kids, and a maid but who also needs a place for herself. While Charlotte just needs 'a table, a chair and a lamp so as to write' (besoin d'une table, d'une chaise et d'une lampe et je pourrais me mettre à écrire), the other woman needs 'an armchair, a coffee table, and a coffee maker' to be 'in peace' (besoin d'un fauteuil, d'une table basse et d'une cafetière, et là je serais tranquille). Evoking the narrative of *Nuit et jour*, they decide to rent the place together, Charlotte using it in the mornings, the other woman in the afternoons. Not only their time of day is zoned, so is the space of the room, with an area on the front-right for Charlotte's writing desk and a sitting zone back-left for the roommate.

Living, for Akerman, in short, is just staying over, passing by, swapping or zoning spaces. Instead of being dwellings, Akerman's houses are platforms for lodging, temporary and partial living. Instead of places with psychological significance for the people that occupy them, Akerman's houses are rather what Marc Augé described as 'non-places' — spaces that are primarily zones of transience and that do not have a special meaning for their users.[6] The title of *Demain on déménage*, in fact, contains a double promise: 'tomorrow, we move' expresses the longing both for another place and a different time. The film does not so much deal with houses and rooms to live in, as with being in between spaces and in between directions to use those spaces: between moving in and moving out, between up and down, between interior and exterior. This halfway position is a trope of all Akerman films. It is visualized in her emphasis on doors, windows, stairs, and

Fig. 5.2. Chantal Akerman, *Demain on déménage* (2004)

passages, from the corridors in *Hotel Monterey* and the hotel rooms in *Les Rendez-vous d'Anna* (1978) to the bay window in *Là-bas* and the hallway in *No Home Movie*, conveying Akerman's interest in the spaces in-between: between the personal and the public, the past and the present, the living and the dead.[7] For Akerman, living and dwelling are inherently connected to the themes of migration and exile that, as many commentators have noted, mark her entire oeuvre. In *Demain on déménage*, the characters do not really live on the sixth and seventh floors of the apartment block, they rather have created a transitory campsite, nestling between unpacked boxes in a tent constructed with blankets.

Comedy of Moving

In *Demain on déménage* Akerman's fundamental preoccupation with unhomeliness, rootlessness, and loss of direction is also a major source of comedy. Great examples are the scenes in which Charlotte, trying to create space in the claustrophobic apartment, dumps pieces of furniture on the street at night. First she puts one chair on the sidewalk but soon adds two armchairs, where she calmly smokes a cigarette, undisturbed by the pouring rain. In so doing, Charlotte transforms the street into a drawing room that is no less sparsely decorated than her shared writing studio. Akerman's inversion of interior and exterior brings to mind the Surrealist scenario that Henri Storck published in *L'Âge du cinéma* in 1951.[8] (Incidentally, Henri Storck plays the first client of the titular character in *Jeanne Dielman*.) Storck's film script *La Rue, scénario* describes a situation in which people leave the interiors of their houses, placing all their furniture on the street to live there. As in Storck's unrealized film, Akerman's scene of wandering furniture perfectly illustrates the transitory nature of dwelling — the French, Italian, German, and Dutch words for furniture (respectively *meubles*, *mobili*, *Möbel*, *meubilair*) still evoke the mobility of the way of life of the upper classes, moving from one castle to another taking their portable furnishings along with them. This mobile aspect of furniture is frequently spoofed in early French film comedies where objects are animated into movement to haunt the residents, like in Georges Méliès' *L'Auberge du bon repos* (1903), Segundo de Chomon's *L'Hôtel hanté* (1909), or Romeo Bosetti's *Rosalie et ses meubles fidèles* (1911). The very struggle of people to put cumbersome furniture into movement recalls also many American slapstick comedies. Particularly Catherine and Charlotte's idea of dragging the furniture one street higher up the hilly site of Ménilmontant pays homage to films like *The Music Box* (1932), in which Stan Laurel and Oliver Hardy attempt to move a piano upon a huge flight of stairs.

Two shots of a piano bookend *Demain on déménage*. The entire film is framed between two almost surreal images of a grand piano dangling on ropes against a blue sky. Again, the piano hovers between spaces and functions: it is not only a very heavy and bulky object that has to be moved by professional movers, it is also a musical instrument that serves as a piece of furniture. An emblem of the bourgeois home, the piano is an object that gathers family members for music and songs, thus connecting high culture with family values. Such a valuable object is, in slapstick comedies such as *The Music Box*, *One Week* (Buster Keaton, 1921), *Sold at Auction* (Charley Chase, 1923), and *Wrong Again* (Leo McCarey, 1929) among many others, very likely to be the target of destructive gags. Yet in *Demain on déménage* the grand piano is as restless as the humans. Moving in and out of homes and hanging down from a crane animated by the heavy breathing of its owner, the piano's location in between places, types of usage, and states of aliveness, exemplifies the comic situation noted by Henri Bergson in his famous theory on *Laughter*, namely the situation which gives us 'in a single combination, the illusion of life and the distinct impression of a mechanical arrangement.'[9]

Comedy of Cleaning

In *Demain on déménage*, boxes are kept closed and pieces of furniture remain stacked instead of being used. Even having a meal, the ultimate domestic activity and a form of family gathering with ritual connotations, occurs between unpacked boxes and empty cupboards. Several scenes that focus on objects of furniture, infrastructure, or household utensils, such as a crystal chandelier, a fridge, or bathroom plumbing, emphasize the stained nature of Akerman's conception of the home. Even in the new places Charlotte and Catherine consider moving to, objects and places are haunted by the tangible presence of the past. The country house they visit in the company of a real estate agent is vacated, devoid of its residents, yet still containing all the items of family life. Places smell of disinfectant, fumigation, or damp. The peculiar odour of empty fridges evokes the former presence of inhabitants, in houses where nobody has been living for longer periods of time.

Importantly, the motif of the empty fridge is connected to the theme of cleanliness that runs throughout the film. While the phantasmagoria of the interior, as Benjamin demonstrated, involves marking the space with traces of the inhabitant, moving into a house, implies cleaning it to remove all traces of earlier occupants. 'It'd calm me to tidy the kitchen', both mother and daughter state when unable to sleep (Si je me lève et je vais ranger la cuisine, ça me calmera). The charming and melancholic real estate agent Samuel Popernick (Jean-Pierre Marielle), who brings Charlotte and Catherine to other houses, denotes both a transitory form of dwelling and the need to clean in *Demain on déménage*. As Holocaust survivor,

Popernick links the film's story to the tragedy of the camps as Marion Schmid has extensively demonstrated.[10] Yet, the characters' inability to find a home not only connects to the themes of migration and exile, but also to the sanitization of the past. As in earlier Akerman films, most famously *Saute ma ville* that also pictures obsessive cleaning, Akerman utilizes slapstick comedy to dedramatize the deeply felt conditions of her personal life as a second generation Holocaust survivor and wandering woman of Jewish descent. Aside from the many references to cremation in the smoking oven and vacuum cleaner in *Demain on déménage* that have been detailed elsewhere, we here focus on instances of comedy that ensue from cleaning operations with an architectural aspect.[11]

Centrally located in the duplex apartment is the bathroom. Usually the most secluded room of a home, the washroom here is completely exposed, only separated from the living room by a glass wall. It draws immediate attention from the visitors who show a remarkable interest in the capacity of the hot water tank and the state of the pipes. In another apartment Popernick explicitly mentions the 'bathroom with a separate toilet. This is rare in France.' (Voici la salle de bain, avec les toilettes séparées. C'est rare en France.) Since bathroom activities include cleansing the body, the transparency of toilets and bathrooms ties into the inside-out logics of slapstick comedy, directing attention to the usually hidden activities of the lower stratum of the human body to flout the norms of prudish and proper society.[12] Therefore, bathrooms and plumbing abound in slapstick comedy: from Buster Keaton's *One Week* (1920) and Chaplin's *Pay Day* (Charlie Chaplin, 1922) to several Mack Sennett productions with titles such as *The Plumber* (two versions, one in 1914, another in 1925), *The Plumber's Daughter* (1927), *Peaches and Plumbers* (1927), *The Singing Plumber* (1932), and *The Plumber and the Lady* (1933).[13] In line with these slapstick comedies with incompetent plumbers and failing bathroom fittings, the bathroom facilities in *Demain on déménage* are entirely lacking: the water pressure is too low to take showers, the piping does not meet legal standards, all the joints are limed-up, and the bathtub is too small for an adult. The dysfunctionality of the equipment confirms the inadequate architecture that is unable to provide comfort or intimacy. The centrality of bathing and cleaning in *Demain on déménage*, then, displays the comic, yet painfully vain attempts to wipe out the dirt traces of the past.

Dirty Talk

A commissioned writer who is working on a pornographic novel, Charlotte finds inspiration for erotic situations not in the intimacy of bath- or bedrooms, but in family furniture and real estate. In her imagination, the old armchair in the corridor hosts the naked, intertwined bodies of her characters Claudia and Pierre, a bucket of cleaning water raises the idea of juicy sex, and double curtains are a matter of love and eroticism. In other instances she conflates places with people engaged in erotic talks. Listening in to café conversations, Charlotte mistakes the real estate-clichés 'very charming', 'attractive', and 'well-proportioned' for erotic appraisals of people. She hears the walls of her shared studio come alive with voices that whisper sexual

Fig. 5.3. Chantal Akerman, *Demain on déménage* (2004)

encouragements, like 'Continue, Yves, continue', and 'More, Daniel, more'. As Charlotte jots down poetic observations of household situations, she translates her immediate surroundings into shorthand for eroticism. In so doing, the vernacular transforms into the pornographic, while precisely the banal origins secure the comedic effect. In such a context, a domestic communication like 'Les plombs ont sauté' (the fuses have blown) comically transmits the idea of a sexual climax. The pornographic novel unintentionally turns into a farce — 'pas porno, mais rigolo' (not porn, but comedy) — much as moving and cleaning become sources of comedy, by associating the acts of sex, and moving and cleaning with household objects that are as unsexy, immobile, and dirty as unwashed curtains, cluttered living spaces, dysfunctional bathrooms, and defective vacuum cleaners.

Triple Return to Origins

Both Marion Schmid and Jenny Chamarette, in their analyses of *Demain on déménage*, describe Akerman's engagement with slapstick comedy as a 'double return to origins' that references both the early days of cinema and the films from Akerman's own early career, particularly her debut *Saute ma ville*.[14] We would like to take this argument one step further, pointing out a third return to origins embodied in the references to slapstick comedy in *Demain on déménage*: the Akerman trope of doing things *as if for the first time*.

In the silent comedies of the 1910s and 1920s, the discovery of and the confrontation with the novel features of modern technology was an important topic. Struggling with machines, motorized traffic, skyscrapers, indoor plumbing and other paraphernalia of industrial modernity, slapstick comedians explored ways to cope with the dangerous tensions caused by the mechanizations that massively emerged in the first decades of the twentieth century. By interiorizing the logistics of the machine in their biomechanical way of acting and by treating mechanical movement and mechanized behaviour as comedy material, they neutralized the frightening aspects of modern technology.[15] When confronted with mechanical devices, Akerman's protagonists, like slapstick characters, display an elegant, choreographed, yet destructive clumsiness. Even the simple chore of making coffee with a percolator turns out to be a difficult task for Charlotte whose name evokes, according to Akerman herself, Charlie Chaplin, who was lovingly called Charlot in France. In line with Chaplin's skirmishes with a murphy bed and other household objects in *One A.M.* (1916), the characters in *Demain on déménage* are constantly moving, replacing, and battling with objects, manhandling electrical household appliances and pieces of furniture. Even the aforementioned scene with Charlotte sitting deadpan outside in the rain echoes Buster Keaton's sitting in front of his mechanical house in *One Week* (1920) after the torrent.

One important trait, however, distinguishes slapstick comedy from Akerman's comic choreography of disorder: while the historical slapstick comedians are exploring the novel gadgets of a developing machine technology, *Demain on déménage* equips its protagonists with old and trite tools, finding ridicule in the struggle with commonplace household machinery, like vacuum cleaners and kitchen ovens. This emphasizes Akerman's home as a warehouse of everyday, yet obsolete, malfunctioning, and time-worn memorabilia that make it a shrine for family souvenirs.

Key to transforming the familiar into comedy is to make sure every common object and situation is handled as if it were the first time one encountered it, thereby making it novel each time again. Charlotte learns by doing that the dishwasher is not for storing food and that an empty fridge can be filled. Like Catherine's piano pupils who need to keep on practising the same music scales, Charlotte apprehends by repeating: phrases she is first told, she later passes on like acquired knowledge. Mastering the skills of writing by naming and repeating everyday activities, the pattern of repetition with variation is the basic rhythm that structures the entire narrative. That beat is underscored by the noises made by the manhandled objects: a soundtrack of piano music, typewriter tapping, stumbling footsteps, doorbells, and telephone calls accompanies Charlotte's clumsy explorations. Gypsy music is repeated in her out-of-tune humming, household communications are rephrased as pillow talk. Speaking and walking happens in jumpy rhythms that compose a stop-and-start pattern of storytelling that defines slapstick comedies as well as *Demain on déménage*.

Fundamentally, all Akerman films are battles with time, told in narratives that are not fluent or logical, but episodic and fragmentary, filled with blanks and repeats. Her entire oeuvre demonstrates the struggle for ways to inhabit and exist, and brings to the fore quintessential characters that are ideally suited for such a venture: the amateurs, who accost the world through direct and physical explorations, their clumsy process of learning transmitting both a loving engagement and a natural ineptitude. This embodied absentmindedness is a fundamental trait that Akerman characters share with slapstick comedians — a much more essential quality than slapstick's speed, violence, or destruction. *Demain on déménage* owes its flavour of loss, failure, and rediscovery to Akerman's comedic handling of things and spaces as if she encountered and handled them anew — each time again, in each film again.

Gradually, as the narrative of *Demain on déménage* unfolds, the duplex loft starts looking more organized, less cluttered, dusty, or polluted. Also Charlotte becomes more professional, discovering her writing skills and a talent for living. Finally the departure of Catherine lets in some air, light, and calm into the premises, preparing the place for a new episode of family life among mothers and daughters.

Notes to Chapter 5

1. See Steven Jacobs, 'Semiotics of the Living Room: Domestic Interiors in Chantal Akerman's Cinema', in *Chantal Akerman: Too Far, Too Close* (Amsterdam: Ludion, 2012), pp. 73–87.
2. Walter Benjamin's meditations on the bourgeois interior can be found in several of his writings included in the *Gesammelte Schriften* (7 vols, Frankfurt a/M: Suhrkamp, 1974–1989), particularly 'Das Paris des Second Empire', 'Erfahrung und Armut', and the chapter 'Das Interieur, die Spur' in *Das Passagen-Werk*.
3. All French dialogue lines are taken from the film. English translations were transcribed from the subtitles in the 2005 Kimstim DVD-edition.
4. Walter Benjamin, 'Das Passagenwerk', *Gesammelte Schriften* V (Frankfurt a/M: Suhrkamp, 1982), fragment I3a.
5. On the metropolis as a masculine space versus the Victorian home as a feminine realm, see Janet Wolff, 'The Invisible Flâneuse: Women and the Literature of Modernity', in *Feminine Sentences: Essays on Women and Culture* (Berkeley: University of California Press, 1990); Suzanne Nash (ed.), *Home and Its Dislocations in 19th-Century France* (Albany: State University Press of New York, 1993); Dolores Hayden, *The Grand Domestic Revolution: A History of Feminist Designs for American Homes, Neighborhoods and Cities* (Cambridge, MA: MIT Press, 1982); and Dolores Hayden, *Redesigning the American Dream: The Future of Housing, Work and Family Life* (New York: W. W. Norton & Company, 2002).
6. Marc Augé, *Non-Places: Introduction to an Anthropology of Supermodernity* (London: Verso, 1992).
7. Elias Grootaers, 'Prisma #11', *Filmmagie* (5 October 2017), published online in Dutch on < http://www.sabzian.be/prisma/prisma-11>.
8. Henri Storck, 'La Rue, scénario', *L'Âge du cinéma* 4–5 (August-November 1951), 61–62.
9. Henri Bergson, *Laughter: An Essay on the Meaning of the Comic* [1900] (Whitefish: Kessinger, 2004), p. 30.
10. Marion Schmid, *Chantal Akerman* (Manchester: Manchester University Press, 2010), pp. 159–71. On *Demain on déménage* as a Jewish film, see also Jacques Mandelbaum, 'Demain on déménage (2003)', in *Chantal Akerman: Autoportrait en cinéaste* (Paris: Cahiers du cinéma/Centre Pompidou, 2004), p. 214. (Originally published in *Le Monde*).
11. Marion Schmid, *Chantal Akerman*, pp. 159–71; and Jenny Chamarette, 'Sight Gags and Split Terrains: Burlesque Comedy, Gesture and Fragmented Intersubjectivities', in *Phenomenology and the Future of Film: Rethinking Subjectivity beyond French Cinema* (London: Palgrave MacMillan, 2012), pp. 158–67.
12. See Rabelais on the meaning of the lower stratum of the body in carnival and grotesque realism, in Mikhail Bakhtin, *Rabelais and His World* (Bloomington: Indiana University Press, 1984), p. 81.
13. See Steven Jacobs, 'Slapstick Homes: Architecture in Slapstick Cinema and the Avant-Garde', *Journal of Architecture*, 23.2 (2018), 225–48.
14. Marion Schmid, *Chantal Akerman*, p. 163; and Jenny Chamarette, 'Sight Gags and Split Terrains: Burlesque Comedy, Gesture and Fragmented Intersubjectivities', p. 159.
15. On slapstick cinema and its fascination with the machine, see Michael North, *Machine Age Comedy* (Oxford: Oxford University Press, 2008); Owen Hatherley, *The Chaplin Machine: Slapstick, Fordism and the International Communist Avant-Garde* (London: Pluto Press, 2016); and Steven Jacobs and Hilde D'haeyere, 'Frankfurter Slapstick: Benjamin, Kracauer, and Adorno on American Screen Comedy', *October*, 160 (Spring 2017), 30–50.

CHAPTER 6

Diaries, Thresholds and Gazes as Anamnesis in Chantal Akerman's Cinema

Anat Zanger

Memory is always reinvented but with a story full of holes.
CHANTAL AKERMAN[1]

In the opening sequence of Chantal Akerman's 2004 film *Demain on déménage*, we see a black grand piano being hoisted up to an upper storey of a Parisian building. The mother (Aurore Clément), clutching a battered suitcase under her arm, intently follows the piano suspended in mid-air with her gaze. A group of people stand beside her on the pavement, urging the piano on with shouts of encouragement, groans, and murmurs. 'Il est passé!',[2] the mother informs her daughter. The piano comes to rest on the lower level of the apartment, and the mother plays it while movers pile up her belongings around her. At the same time, on the upper level, her daughter Charlotte (Sylvie Testud) asks one of the movers to help her hang a crystal chandelier. The mover sneezes in response to the musty air in the room, and she says 'Attention! ... ça vient de Bohème, c'est du cristal pur',[3] adding that her father used to tan hides in that room. He sneezes again, passing the chandelier back to Charlotte, but it slips out of her hands and smashes on the floor. 'C'était de mon grand-père de Kazimiez [...] en Pologne',[4] she laments.

The Jewish Belgian film director Chantal Akerman is renowned for her avant-garde cinematic work and video installations, such as *Saute ma ville* (1968), *Jeanne Dielman, 23, quai du Commerce, 1080 Bruxelles* (1975), *Les Rendez-vous d'Anna* (1978), *D'Est: au bord de la fiction* (1995), *De l'autre côté* (2002), and *No Home Movie* (2015). Akerman was of Polish descent and a second-generation Holocaust survivor. In this chapter, I would like to introduce and analyze the cinematic devices in her oeuvre, especially two of her major films, *Demain on déménage* and *D'Est* (1993), and her video installation *Marcher à côté de ses lacets dans un frigidaire vide* (2004). I will show how movement — between past and present, as well as between fiction and history — in these works is employed to reveal traces of her past.

Critics and scholars have identified Akerman's film *D'Est* and the subsequent video installation *D'Est: au bord de la fiction* as her first works to be understood in the context of the Holocaust. Kristine Butler notes that '[f]ew, if any, critiques

Fig. 6.1. Suitcase and gazes following the piano in *Demain on déménage* (dir. Chantal Akerman, 2004)

have adequately dealt with the importance of [Akerman's] own social and cultural position: the fact that she is not only a woman and European, but also a Belgian and a Jew of Polish ancestry'.[5] Moreover, Ivone Margulies and Alisa Lebow, in their studies of *D'Est*, observe that the film's underlying motif might be a gaze at the traces of history shared by Akerman's parents, who moved from Poland to Belgium.[6] I argue, however, that Akerman's involvement with Holocaust memory began in an earlier work — her 1982 documentary *Dis-moi* — in which she filmed testimonial interviews with her own mother as well as with several other women Holocaust survivors. She recorded testimony regarding these women's experiences in Eastern Europe during the Holocaust five years before Claude Lanzmann created his monumental project, *Shoah* (1985).[7] The presence of Holocaust traces in this early film attests to the centrality of the Holocaust and post-memory in Akerman's work.

I would like to suggest a textual reading of Chantal Akerman's work in the context of the debate, opened by Giorgio Agamben and Georges Didi-Huberman, around the notion of the image as trace and as truth. As observed by Emma Wilson, both Agamben's discussion in *Remnants of Auschwitz* of the film shot in Bergen-Belsen immediately after the camp was liberated, and Didi-Huberman's *Images malgré tout* put forward the differences between films such as Alain Resnais's *Nuit et brouillard* (*Night and Fog*, 1955) and Lanzmann's *Shoah*.[8] Whereas Resnais seeks to visually articulate the daily experiences and routines of being in a concentration camp through archival materials, Lanzmann rejects the possibility to portray the 'unimaginable'. Hence, he uses instead numerous, diverse and even contradictory testimonies as 'micro histories' instead of 'images without imagination', such as archival photographs. Within the context of this debate, Akerman's films offer a third possibility — they comprise within them the narrative of both personal and collective histories of first-and second-generation Holocaust survivors. Therefore, they do not attempt to portray the past or to reveal the indexicality of it, but to allow traces of the past to be present as a 'secret' from one generation to another.

This chapter will identify the cinematic elements that enable Akerman to tell a story that comprises a layer of daily events alongside a parallel sphere of traumatic 'postmemory'.[9] As I intend to show, Akerman deploys a number of tropes and rhetorical devices that recur in her work and enable her to embed another story within her plots and characters: that of the trauma of the second generation of Holocaust survivors. In both her fiction and non-fiction films, Akerman consistently uses events and objects as a pretext to trace the inner world of her characters, thereby providing expression for an emerging post-memory. To decipher the intrinsic code defining Akerman's work as post-memory, I will discuss the way Akerman creates an alternative means of telling history: an *anamnesis*. Throughout this chapter, I will analyze the interactions between the audio and visual channels within the text, as a vehicle for signification, while inter-textually relating to the way these channels convey cultural and cinematic memory.

Analyzing the scene I described in the opening of the chapter, for example, we can note that both the piano (as an audio channel) and the chandelier (as a visual one) play significant roles in the inner lives of the mother and daughter. Textually, the efforts accompanying the act of placing these objects reflect the mother and daughter's difficulties in finding their own place. As a cultural intertext, this sequence draws attention — amongst the many objects the apartment overflows with — to the piano and the chandelier as clear signifiers of the nineteenth-century European bourgeoisie.[10] As a cinematic intertext, the tension between 'here' and 'there' is encapsulated in both the piano and the chandelier, which function as a driving force in Akerman's other films as well, including *Dis-moi*, *D'Est*, and *Un Divan à New York* (1996).

Citing Walter Benjamin, Didi-Huberman notes that '[a]n image ... is that in which the "Then" encounters the "Now" in a flash to form a constellation'.[11] Marianne Hirsch defines the work of post-memory as striving 'to reactivate and re-embody more distant political and cultural memorial structures by reinvesting them with resonant individual and familial forms of meditation and aesthetic expression'.[12] As I intend to show, Akerman's moving images and penetrating sounds delineate a constant dialogue between the recorded materials and elided ones. I will focus on certain recurring figures that facilitate this oscillation between the two worlds of then and now and elaborate on familial forms and aesthetic expression of post-memory via four main categories: thresholds, objects and remains from the past, a diary, and an anxious gaze.

Thresholds

The spatial topography of Akerman's films includes many sites of transition such as railway stations, airports, and border crossings. Unlike these 'non-places', (in Marc Augé's terminology),[13] the home, as the sheltered, private sphere of its inhabitants, traditionally functions as the 'place' of the human subject. Yet in Akerman's *Demain on déménage* and *Un Divan à New York*, the intensive movement of the films' protagonists to and from home divests the domestic sphere of its traditional function and transforms it into a site of transition as well. Not only is the spatial topography of Akerman's films in constant movement, so are her characters, which seem to operate according to a similar principle. They are forever caught in a liminal, in-between state — dragging furniture about in the middle of the night; wandering around in pyjamas during the day; exchanging their apartment for someone else's; waiting at a train station; wandering restlessly from place to place in an attempt to find the 'right' place.

In the documentary film *D'Est* that Akerman filmed during three trips to Russia via Germany and Poland, the camera focuses on passers-by waiting at a train station, waiting on line for a tram, people walking through the streets, or on figures undertaking various daily activities in their homes. In this film, Akerman documents Eastern Europe during the early 1990s, before it became westernized. Her camera accompanies anonymous faces and passers-by moving through open expanses of landscape and through snow-covered city streets. The sound track comprises a combination of sounds: footsteps in the snow and voices coming from a television set in the background. Akerman's camera creates several types of cinematic memories. First, there are intertextual cinematic allusions to the vast expanses featured in John Ford's Westerns and the Siberian tundra seen in the Russian films of Alexander Dovzhenko. Second, there are textual references as Akerman is flooded by memories related to her own Jewish family. She testifies:

> My parents are from Poland. Since the thirties they've been living in Belgium, where they feel very much at home. For a long time — my whole childhood — I believed that their way of life, the way they ate, talked, and thought, was the way all Belgians lived. It was only much later, as an adolescent, that I understood the differences: between them and other parents and even between me and other young girls in my class.[14]

In the fictional film *Demain on déménage* introduced above, a mother and her grown-up daughter who have been living together since the mother was widowed, put their apartment up for sale. A stream of potential buyers visits the apartment, which is cluttered with the mother's furniture: a piano, endless armchairs, tables and cabinets. In order to show it they are forced to remove some of the furniture, which they do at night in their pyjamas. The mother and daughter in turn look at a number of apartments together, but ultimately the mother moves in with her real-estate agent.

Throughout the film, the mother and daughter wait (for a buyer, for a lover, for inspiration), search (for an apartment, for a job) and yearn for change. All of their actions are motivated by events and memories from their past, while on a threshold: they are trying to find their way into their future. These feelings are recurrent themes in Akerman's films that generate a space of memory in which the present exists as a trace of the past or as a form of longing for the future. Thus, instead of a state of stability, the films suggest displacements and dislocations.

Objects and Remains of the Past

Objects inscribed in these films, like in Proust's madeleine cake, play the role of evoking a lost past. For Akerman, everything in Eastern Europe appeared at once alien and familiar; the sights and smells were 'almost like home', the language and the way people lived were foreign, yet the sound of the language was familiar. She felt as though she had lost her memory and it had suddenly returned. In the personal journal she kept during her travels in Eastern Europe, Akerman writes: 'It was winter and I was far from home in a strange land, where I didn't speak the language. It was a strange language, to be sure, but one whose musicality and resonance were so familiar that words and even whole sentences came back to me'.[15] Indeed, Akerman's personal memories are intertwined with collective ones. When Akerman focuses on the faces and bodies of figures crowding the platform and waiting with their bundles, they evoke images belonging to the same place at another time — the Second World War and the Holocaust. In this context, Akerman's text may be considered a collection of personal testimonies mediated and remediated through video art and films that add yet another layer to the cultural memory. These texts contribute to the constant reshaping and redrafting of the lexicon and grammar of 'cultural memory' through the personal, mediated memory of film and television.[16] As Marita Sturken defined it, cultural memory is 'produced through objects, images and representations. These are technologies of memory not vessels of memory in which memory passively resides.'[17]

In this film, Akerman develops a visual language characterized by static long shots and long travelling shots in which her camera accompanies random groups of standing, waiting, or moving people. As Marion Schmid remarks in the context of Akerman's documentary *Sud* (1999),

> Akerman has always insisted that long takes are necessary to stir the spectator from a state of passivity and to divest the quotidian of its familiarity [...]. If the camera allows spectators to hover long enough on a tree for example, they might remember that not so long ago, African-American men and women were brutally lynched [...]. The long take, in other words, renders visible the invisible and allows the past to inscribe itself in the present.[18]

The space in which the travelling of both the film's director and figures takes place has no concrete boundaries. A distinction may seem to exist between the filmed material and the filmmaker's gaze. However, Akerman's cinematic language undoes these traditional boundaries, creating an identity shared by the cinematic writing and the film's internal world. In this sense, the film's a-linearity, fragmentation, non-synchronous sound, repetitive modes, and metonymic symbolism evoke post-traumatic experience.[19] Thus, following Hirsch, we may consider *D'Est* as a work based not on personal memories, but rather on postmemory inherent collectively to those who experienced an event, albeit transmuted by personal postmemory.[20]

Akerman says that she only found out what the film was about once it was made:

> People who were waiting there, packed together to be killed, beaten or starved or who walk without knowing where they are going, in groups or alone. There

is nothing to do. It is obsessive and I am obsessed. Despite the cello, despite cinema. Once the film is finished I said to myself: so that's what it was *that again*.[21]

As Griselda Pollock notes: those two words '*that*' and '*again*' tell the story of intergenerational transmission of trauma.[22] Handed down from her parents and from cultural memory, Akerman's memories of Jewish life in the East are not personal but rather 'prosthetic memories'.[23] Prosthetic memories are defined as memory that emerges at the interface of a person and historical narration of the past. Thus, the post-memory experienced by Akerman through her mother embeds a broader Jewish post-memory of events she herself has not experienced. This memory constitutes an ephemeral autobiography of a past experienced via the mother's memories and indirectly revealed through reflection in other people's faces. Dominick LaCapra addresses the question of collective representation via the voice of testimony, and the authenticity of that testimony.[24] He notes the historiographic tendency to rely verbatim on testimony about trauma and to reproduce it as is, instead of regarding it with a degree of skepticism. In this sense, the voices and images in *D'Est* produce filmed testimonies of the present haunted by the past, while simultaneously making present the interaction between the two.

Reading one film set against the other, we may notice that while the plot of *Demain on déménage* takes place in Paris, the material dimension of the present gives way to the presence of Eastern Europe — more precisely Jewish Eastern Europe — in a manner reminiscent of the earlier film *D'Est*. The mother and her daughter Charlotte are of Jewish-Polish origin, as is their real-estate agent. During the first meeting between them, the lingering smell in the apartment the agent is showing them reminds them of the terrible odour pervading the camps in Poland. Later in their new apartment, their kitchen is often swathed in smoke rising from the toaster and thick, dark smoke belches from the vacuum cleaner the mother uses, smothering the cinematic image. Popernick (Jean-Pierre Marielle), the real-estate agent, notes while visiting them that the smell in this apartment too, is the smell of 'there'. Smell and smoke evoke elusive traces of a materiality that no longer exists and produces memory through oblivion.

The mother carries a worn brown suitcase that once belonged to her husband with her everywhere. The suitcase contains the husband and father's clothes, alongside some personal effects. In order to feel 'at home', the mother adopted the habit of sleeping with the suitcase in her bed beside her. The suitcase constitutes a central object in the film, containing items and memories from the past. Unlike the piano, which symbolizes nineteenth-century bourgeois domesticity, the suitcase incorporates the possibility of wandering between past and present, between home and outside it. When a potential buyer of their apartment is left homeless, Charlotte urges her mother to lend him the suitcase with all its contents. Reluctantly and with great difficulty, she relents and allows him to use it for a few days. This becomes a turning point for her, after which she is able to release some of her memories and move forward.

Indeed, the piano and the suitcase function in the film as symbolic metonymies for feminine and masculine desire. It is through the piano that the mother expresses

Fig. 6.2. Black smoke as a trace of the past in *Demain on déménage*
(dir. Chantal Akerman, 2004)

her sexual desire: she teaches her new lover to stroke the keys of her piano before she succumbs to his advances, and she dances with him to its music. The suitcase, filled with her dead husband's most intimate objects, including his shaving gear, pyjamas, and underwear, functions throughout the film as a substitute for her husband. Thus, towards the dénouement of the film, as the mother leaves the apartment to start a new life with Popernick, the real-estate agent, the returned suitcase finds its way into the boot of his car.

The Diary

Régine-Mihal Friedman adopts, albeit critically, Vincent Colonna and Jacques Lecarme's insights on the diary genre in cinema and television.[25] On the one hand, the proximity of the media to the diary requires 'simultaneous narration', while, on the other, diaries enable the 'fictionalization of lived experience'. This can be seen also in the film *Demain on déménage*, in which the diary suggests a mélange between fictionalization and lived experience, narrated in numerous voices.

A potential buyer who visits the apartment in the film finds a diary written by Charlotte's grandmother in one of the closets:

> MÈRE. Qu'est-ce que c'est, Charlotte?
> FILLE. Je ne sais pas. Madame Declore l'a trouvé dans l'armoire.
> MÈRE. Mais c'est le journal de ma mère, de ta grand-mère. [...] Je ne savais pas qu'il existait. Tout a été perdu. Tout. Elle, là-bas, enfin, tout.
> FILLE. Mais toi, tu es là. [...]
> MÈRE. C'est un miracle que je suis là, et que tu es là, tu sais.[26]

FIG. 6.3. *Objet trouvé*: the diary in *Demain on déménage* (dir. Chantal Akerman, 2004)

Interestingly, the film maintains a cinematic intertextual dialogue with Akerman's video installation *Marcher à côté de ses lacets dans un frigidaire vide*. In *Demain on déménage*, an empty refrigerator opens on several occasions to represent hunger and emptiness, a theme reflected as well in the title of the video installation, in which Akerman herself is talking with her mother Nelly. In it, they discuss, among other things, the diary discovered by chance in a cupboard in Akerman's parents' apartment. The grandmother wrote the diary as a young woman; later, in 1942, she was murdered in Auschwitz. As in the fictional film that followed, three generations of women are represented in the installation through their voices in different modes. The grandmother writes in Polish, the mother reads and translates the diary into French, and the daughter, Akerman herself, listens and asks questions.

The video installation consists of a flat screen on which samples of all three women's writing are projected simultaneously and a spiral roll of white, transparent material into which one can walk to read words and phrases from the diary and quotes from Akerman herself. In her description of the installation, Giuliana Bruno emphasizes the multi-layered inscription of the diary in the video installation and the inter-relation between the three generations.[27]

Was a diary in fact found in Chantal Akerman's parent's apartment, or is it a fiction?

As Hirsch observes, the post-memory of second-generation Holocaust survivors emerges from experiences from their childhood. These impressions can be so powerful that they constitute memories in their own right, and thus, put into question the validity of an actual diary.[28] The diary serves as an object linking past and present in Akerman's cinematic and video art. In the installation, Chantal

Akerman's mother, Natalia (Nelly) Akerman, does not realize that certain descriptions were written by her mother in her youth, until she encounters a remark that she herself had written on the margin of her dead mother's text.[29] In addition, there are two other notes alongside the mother's, added by Chantal Akerman and her sister as words of comfort to her.

In both the video installation and the film, the mother kisses her daughter but we do not know why. Akerman remarks:

> I know why, she has just discovered what I and my sister added. First, what she had written following her mother's last words. She did not remember it. She no longer remembered what she had written.[30]

The film *Demain on déménage* involves two diaries — a conventional one and another, which consists of Charlotte's written impressions and notes for a pornographic novel she has undertaken to write. I argue that the film plays with the convention of the diary genre from the start by presenting both apparently incompatible types of diary: the one Charlotte is writing and the grandmother's diary discovered in a cupboard. Throughout the film, we see Charlotte pulling out from her pocket a notebook, in which she remarks on the day's events and records random conversations and phrases she hears from her mother, in a café, in a film, or on television. Initially, the viewer is tempted to view Charlotte's jottings as a journal in what Anna Jackson suggests to be a 'formless genre', which scripts itself 'by chance upon quality' and embodies a 'spirit of newness'.[31] As the film progresses, however, it becomes clear that Charlotte's notes mostly comprise of remarks and experiences of a sexual nature, all second hand, gathered ostensibly for her book. This diary is contrasted with the one found in the cupboard — the same diary which is mentioned in the installation. Nevertheless, when Charlotte's random jottings become more personal towards the end of the film, they too serve as a vehicle for self-examination.

Akerman toys with the concept of diary when she implies to the viewers that what they see as Charlotte's diary is in fact a series of random quotes and impressions. Autobiography, as defined by Sidonie Smith, is a written or verbal communication that takes the speaking self as the topic of the narrative and transforms it into both subject and object — including letters, diaries, and oral history under this rubric.[32] However, Charlotte's diary-in-the-making contributes to the formation of her sexual identity and thus provides a subjective and subversive alternative to the film's 'formal' and conventional diary.

A passage in the grandmother's diary reads: 'Je suis une femme. Il ne faut donc pas dire mes pensées à voix haute.'[33] This can be explained in light of Anna Jackson's observation that '[f]eminist interest in the diary as a women's genre has also emphasized the importance of privacy, often making a connection between privacy and resistance'.[34] In the privacy of her diary, the grandmother expresses her resistance. As the film's plot evolves, both Charlotte and her mother dare to fulfil the grandmother's spiritual will: to express their desires and thoughts out loud and act upon them. Thus, Charlotte's informal journal helps her to define her sexual preference for another woman, and her mother to begin a new life with Popernick.

Both through the kiss passed on from mother to daughter, and the grandmother's unfulfilled desires transmitted to the mother and daughter, we may identify the diary as an 'inter-generational transport-station'.[35]

Gazes

The potential journey in Akerman's films is always fraught with difficulties and often never materializes at all. It is an inner voyage no less than a geographical one. Akerman's journeys combine existing landscapes, objects, and figures with her own gaze. In her camera work, she contrasts interior and exterior, silence and sound, and static and travelling shots. Thereby, she renders the spectator conscious of the act of looking. Thus, for example, in *D'Est*, when Akerman's static camera lingers for a long period on a country road — waiting for the passage of a single car, alighting on treetops or on figures working in a field — she underscores the way in which the space is framed and filmed.

According to Roland Barthes, the gaze may be interpreted scientifically in three related ways: 'in terms of information (the gaze informs), in terms of relation (the gazes are exchanged), in terms of possession (by the gaze, I touch, I attain, I seize, I am seized): three functions: optical, linguistic, haptic.'[36] Yet the gaze, Barthes argues, also functions as a signifier of anxiety, always searching for something or someone.

This anxious, searching gaze is omnipresent in Akerman's films. It reveals itself in the marginal, seemingly incidental moments in which the film's narrative loses control and focuses on areas of uncertainty. In *D'Est*, for example, the camera travels across snow-covered streets at night, and lingers on the faces and bodies of passengers waiting to enter the hall of an East European train station, their silhouettes sparsely lit by the street lamps. The camera accompanies figures bundled up in heavy coats and hats, carrying bags and briefcases on their way to work or back. The camera pauses on the interiors of modestly furnished crowded residential apartments, and the figures, which are performing their daily activities inside: sitting at their dining tables, watching television, playing the piano, cooking in the kitchen — but not looking at the camera. The lens captures these figures many times through an open window or a partially open door. The camera's gaze follows the figures' movements at times, at others it waits for them to approach or distance themselves from it. The journey of the camera, the figures, and the spectator is a plotless, unexplained journey, which as such, emphasizes its own aimlessness. Restlessness is conveyed by the camera's movement as it stubbornly clings on to anonymous figures and deserted streets, waiting for something to happen, endlessly searching.

An anxious gaze is also present in *Demain on déménage* as can be seen in the opening sequence previously described. Catherine the mother closely follows the movers — will they be able to overcome the difficulties and hoist the piano into the house? Their actions are accompanied by her guiding words ('plus à gauche'),[37] by her sighs, and by the sighs and gaze of the crowd that has gathered around to watch the drama. Towards the end of the film, the piano is lowered out of the apartment, and again a crowd gathers round as Catherine anxiously watches and guides the movers. Thus, the film is framed by two anxious gazes, which accompany the raising and lowering of the piano. Between the two gazes the mother and daughter move from one apartment to another, their furniture is replaced, a pornographic novel and a romance are initiated but get stuck. Between the two pianos lies the post-traumatic discourse that conveys the 'transgenerational phantom',[38] which encapsulates the buried secrets. This 'crypt' is transmitted from one generation to the next and continues to haunt even those that are not directly connected to the trauma, which is unconsciously expressed in their speech and behaviour. 'What haunts are not the dead, but the gaps left within us by the secrets of others.'[39]

The intensity of looks and gazes in Akerman's work, which serve to reveal post-trauma and post-memory, is amplified by the combination of long travelling shots with static ones to produce searching anxious gazes.[40]

Anamnesis: Towards a Conclusion

Through the tropes and figures of thresholds, objects and remains of the past, diaries, anxious gazes, journeys lacking a destination, odours of gas and smoke, exilic discourse, and testimonies, Akerman creates a palimpsestic text that relates to both the 'there and then' and the 'here and now'. Rather than decoding, she makes present; instead of history, she offers a form of memory — an *anamnesis,* which according to Jean-François Lyotard functions to process a given event.[41] In his discussion of the manner in which trauma is processed, Lyotard notes that both anamnesis and history preserve the presence of what has been doomed to oblivion. Yet while history attempts to adhere faithfully to what actually happened, anamnesis allows the unexpected and the unknown to emerge and to guide it. While history reconstructs the lost object, in anamnesis, the surviving vestiges of the lost object 'present' within it are paramount. Anamnesis, thus, comprises a continual process of forgetting and remembering. Its goal is to locate, by means of free association, the recurrent appearance of a meaningful signifier.

By underscoring the permeable quality of the present, Akerman's act of filming becomes a series of gestures towards the past. Her films portray the permeable membrane of the relations between mother and daughter, and more generally those between first- and second-generation Holocaust victims. Unlike Alain Resnais in *Nuit et brouillard*, Akerman does not deploy the cinematic image as document; nor does she reject it altogether, as Claude Lanzmann in *Shoah* does. Instead, she consistently traces the presence of memory and post-memory between event and picture and between the first and second generation of Holocaust survivors. In keeping with LaCapra's view of the contested function of testimonial historiography, Chantal Akerman creates Holocaust testimonies that are not always necessarily an 'accurate reconstruction',[42] but rather provoke a measure of doubt when contaminated by the present perspective.[43]

Notes to Chapter 6

1. Quoted in Griselda Pollock, 'The Long Journey: Maternal Trauma, Tears and Kisses in a Work by Chantal Akerman', *Studies in the Maternal*, 2.1, (2010), 1–32 (p. 1). The Jewish Belgian director Chantal Akerman died in 2015 at the age of 65; hence, her latest film *No Home Movie* (2015) became her last. This chapter is dedicated to her memory.
2. 'It made it through.'
3. 'Be careful... it's pure Bohemian crystal.'
4. 'It belonged to my grandfather in Kazimierz, in Poland.'
5. Kristine Butler, 'Bordering on Fiction: Chantal Akerman's *From the East*', in *Identity and Memory: The Films of Chantal Akerman*, ed. by Gwendolyn Audrey Foster (Carbondale: Southern Illinois University Press, 2003), pp. 162–78 (p. 168).
6. See Ivone Margulies, *Nothing Happens: Chantal Akerman's Hyperrealist Everyday* (Durham: Duke University Press, 1996), p. 202; Alisa Lebow, 'Memory Once Removed: Indirect Memory and Transitive Autobiography in Chantal Akerman's *D'Est*', *Camera Obscura*, 18.1 (2003), 35–82 (p. 46).
7. See also Griselda Pollock's discussion of *Jeanne Dielman*, noting that it might also be read as a text that contains traces of a Holocaust survivor's inner life, in 'The Long Journey'.
8. Emma Wilson, 'Material Remains: Night and Fog', *October* 112 (2005), 89–110 (p. 89).
9. For the concept of postmemory see Marianne Hirsch, *The Generation of Postmemory: Writing and Visual Culture After the Holocaust* (New York: Columbia University Press, 2012).
10. Professor Israel Bartal, private communication, Philadelphia, April 2016.
11. Georges Didi-Huberman, *Phasmes: essais sur l'apparition* (Paris: Minuit, 1998), pp. 240–41.
12. Hirsch, *The Generation of Postmemory*, p. 33.
13. Marc Augé, *Non Places: Introduction to an Anthropology of Supermodernity* (London: Verso, 1995).
14. Quoted in Butler, 'Bordering on Fiction', p. 168.
15. Quoted in Butler, 'Bordering on Fiction', pp. 168–69.
16. For a discussion of cultural memory see Astrid Erll, *Memory in Culture*, trans. by Sara B. Young (New York: Palgrave Macmillan, 2011); for memory in the age of reproduction, see Anton Kaes, 'History and Film: Public Memory in the Age of Electronic Dissemination', *History and Memory*, 2.1 (2009), 111–29.
17. Marita Sturken, *Tangled Memories: The Vietnam War, the AIDS Epidemic, and the Politics of Remembrance* (Berkley: University of California Press, 1997), p. 9.
18. Marion Schmid, *Chantal Akerman* (Manchester: Manchester University Press, 2010), p. 112.
19. Janet Walker identified the characteristics of cinematic post-trauma in *Trauma Cinema: Documenting Incest and the Holocaust* (Berkeley: University of California Press, 2005).
20. See Marianne Hirsch, *Family Frames: Photography, Narrative, and Postmemory* (Cambridge: Harvard University Press, 1997) and Lebow, 'Memory Once Removed'.
21. Quoted in Pollock, 'The Long Journey', p. 7.
22. Ibid.
23. Alison Landsberg, *Prosthetic Memory: The Transformation of American Remembrance in the Age of Mass Culture* (New York: Columbia University Press, 2004), p. 2.
24. Dominick LaCapra, *Writing History, Writing Trauma* (Baltimore: Johns Hopkins University Press, 2001).
25. Régine-Mihal Friedman, 'Autobiography and Postmemory', in *Zwischen-Bilanz: Eine Festschrift zum 60. Geburtstag von Joachim Paech,* (2002), <http://www.uni-konstanz.de/paech2002/zdk/beitrag/Friedman.htm> (accessed 22 August 2016); Vincent Colonna, *Autofiction et autres mythomanies littéraires* (Auch: Tristram, 2004); Jacques Lecarme, 'La Légitimation du genre', *Cahiers de sémiotique textuelle*, 12 (1988), 21–79.
26. MOTHER. What's that, Charlotte?
    DAUGHTER. Madame Declore found it in the cupboard.
    MOTHER. It's your grandmother's journal. I didn't know it existed. [...] Everything has been lost. Everything. She, there, everything.
    DAUGHTER. But you're here.
    MOTHER. It's a miracle that I'm here, and that you're here, you know.

27. Giuliana Bruno, 'Projection: On Chantal Akerman's Screens, from Cinema to the Art Gallery', *Senses of Cinema*, 77 (2015), 1–15 (p. 9).
28. See Edna Moshenson's discussion of *Jeanne Dielman* in 'Chantal Akerman: A Spiral Autobiography', in *Chantal Akerman: A Spiral Autobiography*, ed. by Edna Moshenson (Tel Aviv Museum of Art, 2006), pp. 13–35.
29. See Griselda Pollock, 'Art as Transport-Station of Trauma? Haunting Objects in the Works of Bracha Ettinger, Sarah Kofman and Chantal Akerman', in *Representing Auschwitz: At the Margins of Testimony*, ed. by Nicholas Chare and Dominic Williams (New York: Palgrave Macmillan, 2013), pp. 194–221 (p. 218).
30. Quoted in Pollock, 'The Long Journey', p. 17.
31. Anna Jackson, *Diary Poetics: Form and Style in Writers' Diaries, 1915–1962* (New York: Routledge, 2010), p. 10.
32. Sidonie Smith, *A Poetics of Women's Autobiography: Marginality and the Fictions of Self-Representation* (Bloomington: Indiana University Press, 1987), p. 19.
33. 'I am a woman and therefore cannot express all my desires and thoughts out loud.'
34. Jackson, *Diary Poetics*, p. 11. As observed by Marion Schmid in her analysis of the film, this phrase cited from the grandmother's diary 'lucidly expresses the limitations of the female condition filtered through the mind of an adolescent.' (Schmid, *Akerman*, p. 165).
35. As defined by Bracha Lichtenberg-Ettinger, quoted in Pollock, 'Art as Transport-Station of Trauma?', p. 198.
36. Quoted in Martin Jay, *Downcast Eyes: the Denigration of Vision in Twentieth-Century French Thought* (Berkeley: University of California Press, 1994), p. 441.
37. 'a little to the left'.
38. Nicholas Abraham and Maria Torok, *The Shell and the Kernel*, vol. 1: *Renewals of Psychoanalysis*, trans. and intro. by Nicholas T. Rand (Chicago: University of Chicago Press, 1994).
39. Abraham and Torok, *The Shell and the Kernel*, p. 171.
40. For a discussion of Akerman's cinematic language, see Michael Tarantino, 'The Moving Eye: Notes on the Films of Chantal Akerman', in *Bordering on Fiction: Chantal Akerman's D'Est*, ed. by Kathy Halbreich, Bruce Jenkins and Janet Jenkins, (Minneapolis: Walker Art Center, 1995), pp. 50–54.
41. Jean-François Lyotard, 'Anamnesis of the Visible' [in Hebrew], *Studio*, 99 (December-January 1998–99), 28–35. See also Jean-François Lyotard, *The Differend: Phrases in Dispute* (Minneapolis: University of Minnesota Press, 1988).
42. LaCapra, *Writing History*, p. 108.
43. This chapter was first delivered as a paper at the Hubert D. Katz Center for Advanced Judaic Studies in Philadelphia (2016) and at an international conference of the Tisch School at Tel Aviv University. I would like to thank colleagues at these two conferences, as well as the editors of this volume.

CHAPTER 7

❖

Unknown Deaths in *La Captive*

Emma Wilson

Black milk of daybreak we drink it at evening.[1]
PAUL CELAN

FIG. 7.1. Chantal Akerman, *La Captive* (1999) © Fondation Chantal Akerman — collection Cinémathèque royale

Between 1953 and 1969 Austrian poet Ingeborg Bachmann wrote essays to be delivered on the radio about the writers and philosophers Robert Musil, Ludwig Wittgenstein, Simone Weil, and Marcel Proust.[2] In speaking about Proust, she focuses on the later volumes of *A la recherche du temps perdu*, and on the conception of love. For Bachmann, Proust conceives love as tragic. She finds in his work, 'l'amour comme catastrophe et destin'.[3] She details this further: 'Tout amour est malheureux et les amants, soumis à cette effroyable loi, tombent dans un engrenage de peur, de jalousie et de mensonge, ils sont la proie d'une souffrance que la mort et l'absence ne peuvent apaiser.'[4]

I take Bachmann's reading of Proust as a point of departure for a discussion of Chantal Akerman's 1999 film, *La Captive*. This film is a free, melancholy adaptation of one volume of the *Recherche*, *La Prisonnière*.[5] It shows Akerman developing a somber, shadowy, nocturnal late style that is pursued in her still more claustrophobic adaptation of Conrad, *La Folie Almayer* (2011).[6] These works on madness and elation seem to foreshadow also her eventually unrealized project to adapt Dostoyevsky's *The Idiot*.

Bachmann, appraising Proust, writes: 'Les moments de bonheur, de plaisir et de satisfaction rendent l'âme dans l'analyse et la décomposition minutieuse qu'on en produit.'[7] She sees Proust showing fleeting happiness, pleasure, sexual or not, destroyed by excess analysis. She continues: 'Les seules exceptions sont les instants de contemplation et d'abandon mystique.'[8] This leads her to explain: 'Le fameux passage par lequel commence le volume *La Prisonnière*, lorsque le narrateur est plongé dans l'observation d'Albertine endormie, coïncide avec l'arrêt du cours des événements, de l'action et du mouvement.'[9] This is a moment when agitation and mental noise stop, as Albertine's sleep permits the narrator to rest psychically, appeased by stillness. This is a moment of contemplation, of spiritual repose. Bachmann shows that in Proust it is short-lived. She gives voice to the grief and madness in the text:

> Aussitôt après, le réveil fera revenir la douleur, et l'enfer sera de nouveau présent; la trame des mensonges dans laquelle les deux personnages intriquent savamment leur fils va reprendre son tissage. Les secrets entourant Albertine vont redevenir agissants, les ombres de Gomorrhe vont tomber sur elle et les dialogues qui auront lieu seront une unique torture.[10]

Bachmann's hyperacuity opens reflections on the pleasure of those scenes in *La Prisonnière* where the narrator enjoys Albertine, his lover, while she is apparently asleep.[11] Bachmann responds to the rhythms of these areas in Proust, the reprieve from the spiral of thought, before the return of infant, infernal terrors of abandonment and estrangement. She feels the force, and tranquility, of these moments of peace, and also their brevity. Her language pushes towards the extreme, as she speaks of fear, catastrophe, hell, and torture. She also reckons intriguingly with uses of the agony of doubt and questioning that returns. The lesson she takes from Proust is stark: 'seule la douleur nous permet de comprendre et de reconnaître les autres, de discerner les différences et de produire l'art.'[12] In Bachmann's argument this pain is part of relation, part of art, and it does not end. This is my point of departure for Akerman, as this discussion moves in two stages, first looking at sleep, then at death.

La Captive has been read, justly, as a film of the sexual relation between men and women, and as a film of jealousy and obsession.[13] Bachmann, a poet reading Proust after the Shoah, inspires further, more labile visions of the pain in *La Captive*. I see the film exposing all but unfathomable areas of psychic life in scenarios which are hard to make sense of fully, and sometimes literally hard to see. Akerman herself writes in her *Autoportrait en cinéaste*:

> *La Captive*, je ne savais pas. Je me suis dit, que cela allait se révéler après, le film fini. Mais ce qui s'est révélé, c'est l'opacité même. Et je l'ai accepté.
> Opaque. Oui.[14]

Sleep

Akerman shares Bachmann's fascination with Proust's moments of stillness and contemplation. The first sleeping sequence in La Captive begins about twenty minutes into the film. The second full love scene occurs after one hour and a quarter.[15] In interview with Frédéric Bonnaud, Akerman recounts:

> Pour les relations sexuelles entre le Narrateur et Albertine [...] j'ai repris quasiment point par point ce que Proust écrit, comment il se tient derrière elle, comment il la frôle, comment il l'appelle dans sa chambre, ou va dans la sienne, comment il la caresse quand elle dort, ou fait semblant de dormir, comment elle dit 'Andrée' dans son sommeil, mais c'est sa main à lui qu'elle tient, et comment les deux jouissent.[16]

This emphasis on *jouissance*, pleasure, for Albertine, is important in Akerman's account.[17] She continues in the interview to explain this pleasure, saying: 'C'est une des choses les plus fortes pour montrer combien au fond c'est toujours l'imaginaire qui te fait jouir.'[18] Her insistence on the imaginary, the imagination, is in line with moments in the film where her male protagonist Simon (Stanislas Merhar) questions two female lovers about whether they imagine another loved one while they make love. They do. This slippage in the mind to other lovers is apt for the polymorphous approach to sexuality in Akerman's films.[19]

True to her thoughts about *jouissance*, Akerman specifies further about La Captive:

> C'est une situation qui fait fonctionner leur imaginaire à tous les deux: il n'y a pas de pénétration, c'est une jouissance provoquée par leur imaginaire, un cérémonial très au point entre eux deux, jusqu'à ce que sa jalousie à lui et son questionnement permanent deviennent plus pesants que le plaisir partagé.[20]

Akerman sees the relation between Simon and his lover, renamed Ariane (Sylvie Testud), as consensual and even contractual, as implied in the language of ceremony or ritual. In discussion with Dominique Païni, she lends weight to this point, arguing 'ils ont trouvé tous les deux un dispositif qui leur convient'.[21] She explains that Ariane can take pleasure in not thinking about Simon, while Simon's obsession is satisfied by Ariane's escaping him. The latter point brings the film very close to La Prisonnière and its examination of jealousy as a motor of desire. But Ariane's pleasure in this schema is more peculiar. Païni speaks of Simon's wish to find a way to enter into Ariane's body, his onanism, his rubbing against her. He and Akerman agree that this wish for fusion fails. He goes on to speak of viewers' shock at Ariane's apparent 'soumission' and 'disponibilité'.[22] Akerman argues that Ariane is submissive only within this schema. The ritual, like an s/m contract, allows Ariane to find pleasure in submission. Akerman implies that, as with s/m, this submission does not touch other ways of acting in other social circumstances.[23] She aligns her film's take on sexuality, the imaginary and ritual, with Kubrick's *Eyes Wide Shut* (1999), and also with Genet. Her position on finding pleasure in submission is open — 'trouver son plaisir comme on peut', she says.[24]

For Akerman, as she explains to Païni, Ariane takes pleasure in submission until the ritual no longer works, and at this point she runs away. The film moves on from the enclosure of the Parisian apartment where much of it is set, to the highway, to glimpsed stretches of France, and finally to the open sea where Ariane dies.[25] It shows the working of the ritual and its faltering and breakdown. It shows a repetition that moves towards dysfunction. Allowing Ariane's consent and pleasure in the first iteration of this ritual offers an open understanding of what makes pleasure work. The dissolving of that relation as the film ensues lets the fragility of the schema be revealed, and leaves exposed the impossible traction it creates. The film moves meticulously through these stages, imagining Ariane's pleasure in these scenes of stillness, and then contemplating its disappearance.

Akerman tells Païni that she does not want to tell her viewers what to think. She herself does not feel in control of the meanings and feelings aroused in her films. And so the sleeping sequences are incomprehensible, opaque, as their affective charge remains open. They are scenes about pleasure, consent, stillness, and about threat, narcolepsy, necrophilia. They are scenes about the sexual relation and the imagination, but they also bear traces of other attachments and offer a stage for thinking relation, the impossibility of fusion, *tout court*. Here indeed they are amply Proustian. As Christopher Prendergast argues: 'Albertine is the novel's outstanding instance of what Deleuze says of Proustian love in general: "the reasons for loving never inhere in the person loved but refer to ghosts"'.[26]

For Gérard Lefort, *La Captive* recalls 'Fragonard pour son érotisme des lits défaits'.[27] Raymond Bellour conjures an image of Ariane as reclining nude, or nymph, or the classical Ariadne abandoned: 'Elle dort dans son lit à rideaux, dans un mélange de tissus aux tons vifs et profonds, abandonée comme dans un tableau.'[28] In hyacinth-blue sheets, embroidered in white, Ariane lies naked singing under her breath. Flowered satin curtains are around her. A thick gold bracelet clasps her wrist. She is somnambulistic, trance-like in her expressions. She asks Simon, in words which seem to trigger the ritual and to seal its power: 'Voulez-vous que je vienne?'[29] He says no and she returns to her *rêverie*, her song seeming to lull her into the state of passivity that is apparently erotic for them both. The camera stays with her for a while as she stays absorbed. Simon returns to his room and in a strange play of distance and proximity, and peculiar propriety, he calls her on an internal phone, asking her now to come. He invites her passage from her bed to his — Ariane's illicit transit between the rooms of the apartment is one of the idiosyncrasies of the film and recalls interruptions and moments of undress in eighteenth-century French art.

She comes down the corridor in a silk gown. He closes her in his arms. But the couple are awkward and polite, finding nothing to do until they settle on listening to music. With Schubert's support, Simon starts kissing Ariane, before beginning to question her about where she has been. He goes to fetch water and speaks to his grandmother whose coughs have echoed through the walls. When he returns Ariane has apparently fallen asleep. She is seen from Simon's point of view lying back. Simon contemplates her. His relief echoes Bachmann's sense of the scenes in Proust. Simon's face shows pleasure, the indulgence of a parent seeing a child sleeping, and the glee of a seducer. He sits beside her and his moves are precise. He touches her feet and runs his hand up her leg. He moves her still hand. If she is inanimate these moves are creepy. If she is feigning sleep their charge increases as she lets herself be touched and moved. The long take is tenser as it continues, his moves more frenetic as he risks waking her, kissing a hollow in her neck while she still does not respond. Her lack of response enables his desire. He touches her with his fingertips. Her moves seem involuntary. He climbs on her and comes behind her, the darkness and formality of his pyjamas striking. Ariane is fragile, silky.[30] Her sex is revealed in her gown. It is visible in the shot as he rubs against her, their bodies closer and in more accord than they have been anywhere else in the film. Her visible sex, her moves, let the sequence show her pleasure, until she seems to awake saying 'Andrée', the name of her girlfriend. The scene shows the schema as it works, and as Ariane, unentered, touched, moved, comes.[31] They talk and then he dismisses her and she goes to her room.

The second scene shows Simon arriving in the apartment while Ariane is already apparently asleep in her curtained bed. He crouches beside her, in his overcoat, and speaks to her as she lies with her eyes closed on the blue pillow. Her sleep here verges on indifference. He whispers to her and she makes no response. Her recumbent head fills the frame, making visible an artery that jumps in her neck. Having failed to wake her, Simon climbs on her like a nightmare animal and his face is inclined into her neck and he moves against her. The ritual is disturbed because he is here on her, in her bed. He clutches her. Her body tends to move with his but his arm is entrapping her and she is murmuring in her sleep. She moves away from him. He questions her. She says that she has said nothing, 'rien'. Returning to the schema she says, 'Vous voulez que je vienne?' but the words have lost their lulling power, the ritual falters, its mechanisms revealed. Neither of them reaches pleasure now. His demonic questioning absorbs him. Ariane's stillness seems glacial, anhedonic, indifferent. She stays in bed. He returns alone to darkness. If the two scenes are played simultaneously, the scenario shifts painfully. Close in action, remote in affect, they shadow each other.

When they are driving, towards the end of the film, Simon asks Ariane what she thinks about when they make love. She replies, 'à rien', nothing. She repeats, 'je pense à rien'.[32] 'A rien', which nearly, but not quite, echoes in the name 'Ariane', of course has a mnemonic valence in Akerman's work.[33] In her *Autoportrait en cinéaste*, recalling her childhood, and thinking about its relation to her corpus, she says: 'il n'y a rien à ressasser disait mon père, il n'y a rien à dire, disait ma mère. Et c'est à ce rien que je travaille'.[34] She continues to speak of her relation to her mother's past: 'Les cauchemars, elle les garde pour elle. Bien enfouis, en elle. Mais moi, je les devine. Je crois les deviner. En fait, je ne sais rien ou très peu, ni de ses cauchemars, ni de son passé, alors je les imagine et les cauchemars et le passé'.[35] Her lack of access to her mother's past returns as she speaks about her connection to Proust. She says she feels close to an imaginary Marcel who exists inside her. She notes: 'Lui, il voulait que sa mère lui lise des histoires. Moi je voulais connaître l'histoire de ma mère'.[36]

The sleeping sequences in *La Captive* recall the scene in *Les Rendez-vous d'Anna* (1978) where Anna (Aurore Clément) spends the night in a hotel room with her mother, played with fragility and awe by Lea Massari.[37] The darkness of the scenes is comparable. The scenes also resemble one another affectively in their opacity. There is an asking of questions. Anna asks 'on se couche?' and, as her mother watches her undress, 'on ne se déshabille pas?'[38] Her mother replies: 'Laisse-moi te regarder un peu'.[39] As they lie in bed, Anna asks, 'tu veux que j'éteigne?'[40] In the darkness Anna speaks to her mother about an encounter with a woman. Anna says that she thought of her mother. She asks if her mother has ever loved a woman. A small interruption of time seems to carry the sense that she has. She has loved Anna, who has been missing. Anna speaks now, like an imaginary Marcel, of remembering her mother's perfume when she was a child on the evenings her mother would go out. On the railway platform the next morning her mother says: 'Anna, dis-moi que tu m'aimes'.[41] Anna replies, impassive, 'Je t'aime', and walks out of the frame.

In her *Autoportrait en cinéaste*, Akerman writes: '**Ma mère...** J'en ai tant parlé en parlant de mes films. Ai-je vraiment travaillé tant d'années pour elle, autour d'elle, en rapport à elle?'[42] This stays open. In the *Recherche*, love for the mother ghosts the narrator's love for Albertine. This inheritance is also honoured in Akerman's work in the relay of scenes between *Les Rendez-vous d'Anna* and *La Captive*. The alignment is not straightforward. Ariane interposes a maternal 'rien', a refusal to speak, to Simon's questioning, recalling Akerman's accounts of her own mother. Ariane's delicate pearls recall Léa Massari's jewelry in *Les Rendez-vous d'Anna*. Ariane is an impassive, blank mother to Simon's anxious child. Yet Simon also wants to look at Ariane, his relentless attention maternal in this respect, melancholy, as she tries to shake him off. Akerman lets the sleeping sequences become more unknown, more opaque. The agony of a relationship, the love between Simon and Ariane, is also here about illicit tenderness, and implacability, the unknown, 'rien'.

If the two sleeping sequences show the breakdown of a ritual, the last part of the film takes this malfunction to its nightmare end. Akerman departs from Proust in her different imagining of the death of Ariane.

Death

As the film nears its close, at the sea, Ariane pauses for a long moment to look out at the waves, a sublime wild surface. In the hotel room with Simon, somnambulistic, she walks out onto the balcony to see the sea in the darkness. The sound of the sea from the open doors engulfs the room, lashing next to Simon's manic suggestions of places they might visit. The electric energy is painful, echoed in the music from Rachmaninov's *The Isle of the Dead*. Simon says, like Anna's mother, 'Laisse-moi te regarder'. He kisses Ariane. Stifling, she glances towards the open doors and says she wants to swim. He detains her and orders them a meal. The room is so dark, the roaring of the waves seems present inside.

Simon walks onto the balcony. He now realizes Ariane is in the sea. He runs naked into the waves, roiling, surfy water. His pale limbs are just visible at the right of the frame as he swims. The film cuts to a closer image in the water. Ariane is swimming backstroke. She is moving blindly, but she is afloat and strongly alive in the water.[43] The frame is taken over with the dynamic churning of the water around her. Simon is near her and is heard repeating 'doucement', gently. The shots have the rapidity and commotion of real events. She cries out as if in alarm. They struggle in the water. The music is somber and the shots almost completely dark. It is very hard to see what happens. Recollected, the shots seem to bear fantasmatic traces, where Simon holds Ariane under, his arms pushing her down.[44] At dawn he is rescued alone, in desolation.[45]

Ariane has suffocated in the room. She goes to swim alone at night in the wild sea. Her impulse to do this presses down in the scene. She expresses her liberty, the film leaving it impossible to know if her moves are simply determined and hedonistic, insane in the mania of the situation, or suicidal. The scene shows her need to escape Simon, and the decisiveness of her departure, after their prevaricating through the afternoon about whether to split or remain together. She takes up none of his offers and instead swims alone. There is release, pleasure, in her liberty before her death. It remains unknown whether she might have survived, swimming, without Simon's intervention. She is vulnerable in the sea, but more so surely in the vehemence of Simon's love.

Simon realizes she has gone in the dark emptiness of the room. The film carries his disorientation. His impulse is to follow her into the sea, to reach her. The urgency of his moves, his natal, dreamlike stripping naked and entering the waves, belie his wish to fuse with her. He moves to save her and fails, as she cries out at his closeness. His presence in the water disturbs her. As she repels him, a live, moving organism fleeing from him, he seems to seek to make her still, to hold her down. The scene plays out so fast that these remain instinctual, unfathomable feelings, their effect radiating as they are recalled.

This melee of feelings is part of the rarity of the scene. In love, trialing fusion, there is also the wish to kill the other, to curb her liberty, to hold her intact, still. The film shows this horror. Her failure to survive allows the film to come close to issues of partner violence. One of the disorientations of the film, seen next to *Les Rendez-vous d'Anna*, is the only very small degree of difference between scenarios of tenderness and of criminality. The same words return as the sense flips.

Akerman's late filmmaking goes into this agony, a place of wanting to kill, and wanting to die, of consuming love, impulses let out with grief. Her films are tender, coruscating and enervated all at once. They achieve rarefied honesty, lament, and levity. They let opacity exist. For Bachmann, Proust reveals that pain in love does not end in death. Bachmann is reading the novel after the Shoah, in the wake of this void, this 'rien' and its unknown deaths. In *La Captive*, beyond love, night and opacity become spaces for feeling the failure of knowledge, the threat of alterity, the impossibility of afterlives.

Schmid describes the moments at the start of *La Captive* where Simon watches home movie footage of Ariane and her friends on the seashore.[46] She observes:

> Drawn by the filmic image, Simon abandons his position next to the projector

and sits down in front of the screen, his dark silhouette engulfing the figure of his lover, who, at this precise moment, turns her back to the camera and disappears into the waves.[47]

At the very start of the film the drama of attempted fusion, escape and suppression of the other is already played out geometrically, in the briefest moments of footage. Already here Akerman is playing with the falling of shadows, a motif that returns in her work. Its motivation is found in Proust, where the narrator talks about his pleasure in the fusion of his shadow with Albertine's.[48] Later in *La Captive* Akerman films Proust's scene faithfully in the Bois de Boulogne, seeing Simon and Ariane's shadows in the grass. This scene looks forwards to other light effects in the film, darker still, of trees against the night sky. Akerman works similarly with shadows in her two more recent installations *Maniac Summer* (2009) and *Maniac Shadows* (2013).

In *Maniac Summer*, the shadows have a historical point of reference in the cataclysmic moment in Hiroshima. In conversation with Elisabeth Lebovici, Akerman says:

> I had heard someone talking about Hiroshima, and it had made a great impression on me. The intense radiation of the blast left afterimages on walls, shadows of the bodies of people who were standing there, in the instant before they died.[49]

The shadows hold the instant before death. Silhouettes, in the installation images, take on diabolic lability, paper thin and menacing as afterimages, blinding floaters.

In *Maniac Shadows* Akerman shows her own shadow falling in shallows. The milky water threatens to engulf the image. She stands still so the shadow is motionless with the waves moving over and over the projected image. The shadow creates an eclipse in the sandy, sunlit, liquid image. Further in, Akerman returns to the touching of shadows of two loved ones, the overlapping shapes continuous, dipping towards one another. Speechless images of Akerman and M. walking are seen, their shadows tending towards one another. The light is warmer on the sand. The image migrates from channel to channel, in the three-stream installation, and idle humming is heard, the words of 'The Way You Look Tonight', and the sound of the wind. Akerman places a still of the same image at the very close of her late text *Ma mère rit* and writes:

> On s'est aimées, on s'est séparées je ne sais plus pourquoi, et on s'aime.
> Même nos ombres s'aiment quand on marche.[50]

In Bellour's reading of *La Captive*, Simon comes to a brutal sense that he is speaking in vain to Ariane as she sleeps. Bellour writes: 'Il sait alors, comme le spectateur l'a vu, ou cru voir, ou senti dans l'image, qu'il est vraiment l'autre de l'autre, et que c'est sans remède, sinon dans la mort peut-être.'[51] Bellour conjures death as a remedy, but tempers this.[52] *La Captive* is still more measured. Akerman admits in her film the desire to destroy a loved one. She takes us into this nightmare while showing its horror. Making her own version of *Vertigo* in *La Captive*, she repeats a narrative of dizziness and murder, but stretches it out, and makes it opaque, impeding any move to closure and relief. For Bachmann, reading Proust, even death and absence do not alleviate suffering. There is no remedy. This seems the case in *La Captive* where the opening of the film, where Simon views and questions Ariane in home movie footage, is generally read as a scene that takes place chronologically after the rest of the drama.

For Bachmann, pain, 'la douleur', is what allows us to know and recognize others. Akerman is less ready to ascribe utility to pain. But in these late films, in *Sud* (1999), in *La Folie Almayer*, and in *La Captive*, she returns to crimes that repeat the brutal annihilation of the other, individually and systematically. Her films look closely and slowly at situations where the other is endangered. In the pain of these representations, there is recognition and knowledge, however opaque.

If she focuses on pain, Bachmann responds too to the scenes of contemplation in *La Prisonnière*, moments of repose where pleasure is held. Akerman likewise lets the first sleeping scene exist as idyllic, illicit, outside time, as the echoing of *Les Rendez-vous d'Anna*, the strange love scene with the mother, also indicates. In all the melancholy of her work, and its sensitivity to pain, Akerman also allows moments of sunlit happiness, of ambient feeling. This resting from anguish is held in the shadow picture at the end of *Ma mère rit*. These moments are not a remedy to the agony she shows. The nightmare with its unknown deaths continues. But this pleasure is also there, perverse, beautiful, suddenly untouched by pain.

Notes to Chapter 7

1. This epigraph is taken from Paul Celan's poem 'Deathfugue', Paul Celan, *Selected Poems and Prose of Paul Celan*, translated by John Felstiner (New York: W.W. Norton, 2001), p. 31. The poem was first published in Romanian translation with a title meaning 'Tango of Death'.
2. I refer here to the French edition, Ingeborg Bachmann, *Le Dicible et l'indicible: Essais radiophoniques — Robert Musil, Ludwig Wittgenstein, Simone Weil, Marcel Proust*, translated and with an introduction by Michèle Cohen-Halimi (Paris: Ypsilon, 2016 [originally published in German in 1978]).
3. 'love as catastrophe and destiny', ibid., p. 84. Translations from the French are my own unless otherwise stated.
4. 'Every love is unhappy and lovers, under this terrifying law, fall into a spiral of fear, jealousy and lies, they are victims of a form of suffering that death and absence can't calm', ibid., p. 84.
5. In her *Autoportrait en cinéaste*, Akerman details the circumstance of her chance to make *La Captive*. She was in bed listening to the radio and heard Paulo Branco speak about producing *Le Temps retrouvé* (1999). She continues: 'je me dis je devrais l'appeler, cela faisait au moins 20 ans que j'avais envie d'adapter *Albertine prisonnière*' ['I told myself I should call him since I had wanted to adapt *Albertine prisoner* for at least 20 years'], (Paris: Editions du Centre Georges Pompidou/ Editions Cahiers du cinéma, 2004), p. 16. She didn't call him, but saw him in the Café de Flore a few months later and spoke to him then. She pursues the narrative in an interview included in the France Culture radio programme 'Proust à l'écran: "La Captive" de Chantal Akerman', broadcast in 2009 (see <https://www.franceculture.fr/emissions/les-nuits-de-france-culture/proust-a-lecran-35-la-captive-de-chantal-akerman>). For further discussion of *La Captive* as adaptation of *La Prisonnière*, see Martine Beugnet and Marion Schmid, *Proust at the Movies* (London: Routledge, 2005) and Peter Kravanja, *Proust à l'écran* (Brussels: Ante Post, 2003).
6. For Corinne Rondeau, night, darkness and opacity become the matter of Akerman's work from *D'Est* forwards, see *Chantal Akerman passer la nuit* (Paris: Editions de l'éclat, 2017), p. 61.

7. 'Moments of happiness, pleasure and satisfaction are destroyed in the analysis and painstaking undoing one does of them', Ingeborg Bachmann, *Le Dicible et l'indicible*, p. 84.
8. 'The only exceptions are instants of contemplation and mystic abandonment', ibid., p. 84.
9. 'The famous passage with which the volume *La Prisonnière* begins, when the narrator is deep in observation of Albertine asleep, coincides with a stopping of the course of events, of action and movement', ibid., p. 84.
10. 'Immediately after, awakening will bring back the pain, and hell will be present again; the web of lies in which the two characters knowingly interweave their threads will be woven again. The secrets surrounding Albertine will take on power again, the shadows of Gomorrah will fall on her and the dialogues which will take place will be a unique torture', ibid., p. 84.
11. There are two major scenes in *La Prisonnière* (Paris: Gallimard, Bibliothèque de la Pléiade, 1988), vol. 3. In the first (pp. 578–82), the narrator compares the sleeping Albertine to a plant, and takes pleasure against her dormant body, and in the second (pp. 620–23) he hears her murmur in her sleep. The novel returns to an image of Albertine asleep (p. 888) where the narrator contemplates how her consciousness will always escape his grasp.
12. 'only pain allows us to understand and recognize others, to make out differences and produce art', ibid., p. 86. Ingeborg Bachmann's love for Paul Celan and its painfulness are expressed in their letters. She writes to him from Vienna on 10 November 1951: 'Your absence makes everything easier and harder for me at the same time. I yearn for you in a painful way, yet I am sometimes glad that I do not currently have the opportunity to go to you', Ingeborg Bachmann and Paul Celan, *Correspondence*, translated by Wieland Hoban (London: Seagull Books, 2010).
13. See Raymond Bellour's essay 'Ces images d'un malheur sans partage' ['These images of an unsharable distress'], *Trafic*, 35 (Autumn 2000), 20–24, where he compares the film to Antonioni as he looks at the breakdown of the couple. Jean-François Rauger mentions Antonioni, Godard and Duras in this regard, 'Scènes de couple dans la prison des mots', *Le Monde*, 17/05/2000 (accessed in BIFI dossier de presse). Frédéric Bonnaud references Maurice Pialat, describing *La Captive* as 'le grand film contemporain consacré au couple, le *Nous ne vieillirons pas ensemble* d'aujourd'hui', 'Librement inspiré', *Les Inrockuptibles*, 27/09/2000. Martine Beugnet and Marion Schmid look at the ways in which Akerman makes use of the 'elusive nature of the cinematic image' to explore 'the destructive mechanisms of a jealousy that has become pathological', 'Filming Jealousy: Chantal Akerman's *La Captive* (2000)', *Studies in French Cinema*, 2–3 (2002), 157–63 (p. 158).
14. Chantal Akerman, *Autoportrait en cinéaste*, pp. 128–30.
15. In an intervening sequence Ariane seems to fall asleep in the car in which the lovers are driving through the Bois de Boulogne.
16. 'For the sexual relations between the narrator and Albertine [...] I practically repeated point by point what Proust wrote, how he places himself behind her, how he brushes against her, how he calls her into his room, or goes into hers, how he caresses her while she is sleeping, how she says "Andrée" in her sleep, but it's his hand she is holding, and how they both come', Frédéric Bonnaud, 'Tutoyer Proust', interview with Chantal Akerman, *Les Inrockuptibles*, 27/09/2000 (accessed in BIFI dossier de presse).
17. George Rafael comments differently on Ariane: 'When she's with him, she's not there; she seems remote, passive to the point of narcolepsy, even when they make love, which is a one-sided affair of frottage', 'La Captive', *Cineaste*, 27.1 (Winter 2001), 33–34 (p. 34).
18. 'It's one of the strongest things to show how in the end it is always the imaginary that makes you come', Frédéric Bonnaud, 'Tutoyer Proust'.
19. Akerman tells Bonnaud that reading Proust as an adolescent she was captivated because 'ça touchait à ma sexualité de jeune fille' ['it related to my girlhood sexuality'], ibid..
20. 'It's a situation that makes each one's imaginary work: there is no penetration, it's sexual pleasure conjured by their imaginary, a ritual which works very well between them, until his jealousy and continual questioning become heavier than the shared pleasure', ibid.. In interview with Jean-Michel Frodon and Jacques Mandelbaum, Akerman says: 'je n'ai cessé de me demander pourquoi Ariane restait avec Simon. J'avais trouvé une réponse, fausse: parce qu'elle l'aime. Je n'ai compris qu'après qu'elle reste avec lui parce que le dispositif la fait jouir' ('I haven't stopped

asking myself why Ariane stayed with Simon. I had found a reply, which was wrong: because she loves him. I only understood afterwards that she stays with him because the schema makes her come'), 'Chantal Akerman traverse les songes d'Albertine', *Le Monde*, 27/09/2000 (accessed in BIFI dossier de presse).

21. 'they have both found a schema that works for them', 'Chantal Akerman et Dominique Païni, Conversation', bonus material included on Gemini films DVD of *La Captive* (2001). Akerman says more bluntly to Nick James: 'That's their way of having sex. And it's very close to Proust's description. They both take pleasure, but it's a separate pleasure, fantasmique. I think everyone needs fantasy to make their sexuality work', Nick James, 'Magnificent Obsession', *Sight and Sound*, 11.5 (May 2001), 20–21 (p. 21).
22. 'submission', 'availability', 'Chantal Akerman et Dominique Païni, Conversation'.
23. In a short piece in *Autoportrait en cinéaste*, Sylvie Testud speaks about her conception of Ariane:
    — N'as-tu pas peur de la passivité d'Ariane? me demande Chantal.
    Je suis surprise.
    — Je ne sais pas exactement qui elle est. Je ne l'imaginais pas passive. Je l'imaginais libre ('Aren't you afraid of Ariane's passivity?', Chantal asks me. I am surprised. I don't know exactly who she is. I imagined her as free'),
    'La Captive — J'ai faim, j'ai froid', Chantal Akerman, *Autoportrait en cinéaste*, p. 212.
24. 'find your pleasure as one can', 'Chantal Akerman et Dominique Païni, Conversation'. Marion Schmid speaks aptly of the couple's 'idiosyncratic love-making', *Chantal Akerman* (Manchester: Manchester University Press, 2010), p. 156.
25. Its geography, though re-arranged, reminds me of Visconti's *Vaghe stelle dell'orsa* [*Sandra*] (1965).
26. Christopher Prendergast, *Mirages and Mad Beliefs: Proust the Skeptic* (Princeton, NJ: Princeton UP, 2013), p. 171. The quotation from Deleuze is taken from the English edition of *Proust and Signs*, translated by Richard Howard (London: Allen Lane, 1973), p. 30. Akerman was also a reader of Deleuze on Proust. She writes in her *Autoportrait en cinéaste*: 'Deleuze, encore, dit d'Albertine, c'est un être de fuite. Encore une fois, il a raison' ('Deleuze, again, says of Albertine, she is a being of flight. Once again he's right'), p. 82.
27. 'Fragonard for his eroticism of unmade beds', Gérard Lefort, 'Un mâle, des mots', *Libération*, 16/05/2000 (accessed in BIFI dossier de presse). Praising the work of cinematographer Sabine Lancelin, Jean-François Rauger writes: 'La sensualité picturaliste de certains cadres confère une densité inédit aux lieux et aux corps', 'Scènes de couple dans la prison des mots', *Le Monde*, 17/05/2000 (accessed in BIFI dossier de presse). A scene from the set is seen on p. 18 of *Autoportrait en cinéaste*, together with a still of Ariane in bed, and on p. 51 there are two further reclining images of Ariane, with a seated and then prone Simon against her. These latter images are placed against bed scenes in *Les Rendez-vous d'Anna* on the facing page. Further pictures from *La Captive* appear pp. 126–27.
28. 'She sleeps in her curtained bed, in a mix of materials with strong and deep colours, abandoned as in a painting', Raymond Bellour, 'Ces images d'un malheur sans partage', p. 24.
29. 'Do you want me to come?'
30. Her image recalls Nicole Kidman's in *Eyes Wide Shut* where she wears a pale nearly transparent slip and her hair is similarly fair.
31. I follow Bérénice Reynaud's line: 'The originality of Akerman's representation of women is that she shows them as active desiring subjects, even when they seem to be repressed or in a position of passivity', 'These Shoes are Made for Walking', *Afterall: A Journal of Art, Context and Enquiry*, 6 (2002), 42–51 (p. 51).
32. 'I think about nothing'.
33. Peter Kravanja makes reference as well to Bergman's *Persona* (1966) and the return of the word 'ingenting' ('nothing' in Swedish), *Proust à l'écran* (Brussels: Editions de la lettre volée, 2003), p. 116.
34. 'there is nothing to go over said my father, there's nothing to say, said my mother. And I work on that nothing', Chantal Akerman, *Autoportrait en cinéaste*, pp. 12–13. The film is dedicated to her father.
35. 'she keeps her nightmares for herself. Deeply buried inside. But I guess them. I think I guess

them. In fact I know nothing, or very little, either about her nightmares or about her past, so I imagine them, both the nightmares and the past', ibid, p. 13.
36. Ibid, p. 20. Laure Adler writes, in her contribution to *Autoportrait en cinéaste*, 'Letters Home', 'Chantal Akerman qui n'est pour rien une lectrice infatigable de Marcel Proust, tente de capter simultanément ce qui fait du mal et ce qui fait du bien entre une mère et une fille' ['Chantal Akerman who is not for nothing a tireless reader of Marcel Proust, tries to capture simultaneously what hurts and what is good between a mother and a daughter'], p. 197. In interview with Frédéric Bonnaud, Akerman says: 'Le tout début de *La Recherche* [...] m'intéresse beaucoup, tout le rapport avec sa mère, mais j'en ai marre de faire des choses liées à la mère, même si je sais qu'on n'en a jamais fini...' ('The very start of the *Recherche* [...] interests me a lot, all the relation with his mother, but I'm tired of doing things linked to the mother, even if I know that you're never finished with that...'), 'Tutoyer Proust' *Les Inrockuptibles* 27/09/2000 (accessed in BIFI dossier de presse). Eric de Kuyper, who worked on the adaptation with Akerman, writes: 'Adapter un livre c'est l'adopter. Ou se faire adopter par lui' ('Adapting a book is adopting it. Or being adopted by it'), 'Oublier Proust', *Trafic*, 35 (Autumn 2000), 15–19 (p. 19).
37. B. Ruby Rich comments that in *Les Rendez-vous d'Anna*, 'every sex scene ends in coitus interruptus' and 'the hottest moment occurs when Anna gets into bed with her mother to confess her love for another woman', *Chick Flicks: Theories and Memories of the Feminist Film Movement* (Durham: Duke University Press, 1998), p. 172.
38. 'Shall we go to bed?'; 'We're not getting undressed?'
39. 'Let me look at you a little.'
40. 'Shall I put out the light?'
41. 'Anna, tell me that you love me'.
42. 'My mother... I've talked about her so much in talking about my films. Have I really worked so many years for her, around her, in relation to her?' Chantal Akerman, *Autoportrait en cinéaste*, p. 13.
43. It has been said earlier in the film that she swims well.
44. For Jérôme Momcilovic, '*La Captive* se conclut exactement comme *Vertigo*: par un meurtre', *Chantal Akerman: Dieu se reposa mais pas nous* (Paris: Capricci, 2018), p. 77. For Ginette Vincendeau, 'it isn't clear whether she drowns accidentally, commits suicide, or whether he kills her', 'The Captive', *Sight and Sound*, 11.5 (May 2001), p. 45.
45. Gérard Lefort, referencing Nerval, writes, 'il finira veuf et inconsolé', 'he will finish widowed and inconsolate', 'Un mâle, des mots', *Libération*, 16/05/2000 (accessed in BIFI dossier de presse). Bellour offers a magisterial reading of the last shots of the film in 'Ces images d'un malheur sans partage', pp. 21–22.
46. I also look at these in a very different reading, '"Les rendez-vous d'Ariane": Chantal Akerman's *La Captive*', *L'Esprit Créateur*, 42.3 (Fall 2002), 60–69.
47. Marion Schmid, *Chantal Akerman*, p. 155.
48. Marcel Proust, *La Prisonnière*, p. 680.
49. Chantal Akerman in conversation with Elisabeth Lebovici, 'Losing everything that made you a slave', in *Chantal Akerman: Too Far, Too Close*, edited by Dieter Roelstraete and Anders Kreuger ([Ghent: Ludion; Antwerp]: M HKA, 2012), pp. 94–103, p. 101.
50. 'We loved each other, we separated and I no longer know why, and we love each other. Even our shadows love each other when we are walking along.' Chantal Akerman, *Ma mère rit* (Paris: Mercure de France, 2013), p. 197. *Maniac Shadows* can currently be viewed here: <https://vimeo.com/141589708> (accessed 3 August 2018).
51. 'He knows then, as the spectator has seen, or thought she or he has seen, or felt in the image, that he is truly the other of the other, and that this is without remedy, if not in death perhaps', Raymond Bellour, 'Ces images d'un malheur sans partage', p. 24.
52. Tony McKibbin questions, 'must the love object die to maximize the sense of despair', 'La Captive and the power of love', *Studies in French Cinema*, 3.2 (2003), 93–99 (p. 97). For Jean-François Rauger, '*La Captive* est une tragédie. L'auto dissolution d'un être dans le doute et l'angoisse aboutissant à la destruction de l'objet aimé et incompris' ('*La Captive* is a tragedy. The self-dissolution of an individual in doubt and anxiety leading to the destruction of the loved, uncomprehended object'), 'Scènes de couple dans la prison des mots'.

CHAPTER 8

❖

Texas (is not Paris) is Burning: The Drag of Dis/Orientation in Chantal Akerman's *Sud*

So Mayer

> From [Frantz] Fanon we learn about the experience of disorientation, as the experience of being an object among other objects, of being shattered, of being cut into pieces by the hostility of the white gaze. Disorientation can be a bodily feeling of losing one's place, and an effect of the loss of a place; it can be a violent feeling, and a feeling that is affected by violence, or shaped by violence directed toward the body. Disorientation involves failed orientations: bodies inhabit spaces that do not extend their shape, or use objects that do not extend their reach. At this moment of failure, such objects 'point' somewhere else or they make what is 'here' become strange. Bodies that do not follow the line of whiteness, for instance, might be 'stopped' in their tracks, which does not simply stop one from getting somewhere, but changes one's relation to what is 'here'. When lines block rather than enable action they become points that accumulate stress, or stress points. Bodies can even take the shape of such stress, as points of social and physical pressure that can be experienced as a physical press on the surface of the skin.
>
> SARA AHMED[1]

Chantal Akerman's documentary *Sud* (South, 1999) names (its) orientation as its subject in its title. As Marion Schmid writes: 'Inspired by the literature of William Faulkner and James Baldwin... [Akerman] undertook a journey to the South of the United States in preparation for a film focusing on racial violence and exploitation and the traces these have left in the region's landscape.'[2] Having already begun to research the southern states, Akerman was alerted to the murder of James Byrd, Jr., an African American musician, which took place in Jasper, a small town in East Texas, on 7 June 1998. Byrd, Jr. hitched a ride with three white men, all members of white supremacist groups, who chained his body to the back of a pick-up truck and dragged him, alive, over three miles of county road, before leaving what remained of his body in front of a black cemetery. Byrd, Jr.'s death, often referred to by the evocative term 'lynching', is an extreme example of the phenomenon that

Sara Ahmed notes in *Queer Phenomenology*, whereby '[b]odies that do not follow the line of whiteness, for instance, might be "stopped" in their tracks, which does not simply stop one from getting somewhere, but changes one's relation to what is "here".'[3] Akerman's film is precisely an investigation into the way in which race — and specifically, the history of racial hate crime in the southern states of the US — changes one's relation to what is 'here'. Her camera is 'stopped' in its tracks by this disorientation; almost always fixed, even when travelling in a car, it is stopped by the tracks and traces of the hate crime committed against Byrd, Jr., producing a film that inhabits the shocked moment of the murder, with its central section capturing (captured by) Byrd, Jr.'s funeral.

Akerman's film is a concerned and concerted effort to create forms of movement for the body 'stopped' in its tracks by racist violence, predicated on her own changed 'relation to what is "here"', as a white Francophone Belgian Jew who had been making films in North America since the 1970s. *Sud* consists of and proceeds through the encounter, alternating interviews with both white and African-American Jasper-ites with different relationships to the Byrd case, from familial to institutional, with meditative shots of the town, in particular its streets and green spaces. It wrestles with the idea of the essay film and postcard film (would *A Propos de Jasper* be possible?); and with the talking-head documentary, as she will do later, in a more complex and intimate way, in *No Home Movie* (2015). Yet Jasper *is* a home for almost all of her interlocutors, albeit one complicated by endemic and systemic racism — a complication with which Akerman's film struggles, in both senses. The framing of the 'postcard' shots reads a profound and stifling alienation into the landscape that is challenged by some of the African-American interviewees' nuanced and grounded relationship to their home town.

It thus forms a productive contrast, temporally, tonally and aesthetically, with a subsequent observational documentary, *The Two Towns of Jasper* (Whitney Dow and Marco Williams, 2002), which was shot around and during the trials and convictions of all three murderers: Shawn Berry, Lawrence Russell Brewer, and William John King. Dow and Williams, white and African American respectively, have continued to collaborate on films together; Dow also produced the interactive television documentary *The Whiteness Project* for POV. Travelling to Jasper with a white camera crew, to document the white side of town, and a black camera crew, to document the black side of town, Dow and Williams make race the subject of their documentary — but within their observational take on the community's reaction to the trial, they trace race's disorienting effect on the landscape, literalised in a fence that divides the town's major cemetery into 'white' and 'black' burial grounds, and which was removed through the actions of the Ministerial Alliance (who played a crucial role in keeping the peace after the murder).[4]

Both Akerman's and Dow and Williams' films include a strikingly similar shot that mimics, inverts, memorialises, seeking both to remember and to erase, the dragging of Byrd, Jr., by offering a rear view of the road from the back of a moving car. As Schmid points out, Akerman sustains the shot, which closes the film, for seven minutes;[5] Dow and Williams use segments of the shot repeatedly, throughout the film. In *Sud*, it echoes and disorients the repeated use of tracking shots of Jasper taken through the passenger window of a moving car. Apparently still (in relation to the window frame), the camera in these shots has both a slight fish-eye that distorts the framing, and blurs the middle distance where houses and shop fronts appear; and a slight, persistent but not consistent drift toward the rear of the window, a sense of the shot being dragged backwards, which adds a further curvature to the image at the edge of the frame. Akerman seeks an aesthetic and — in the use of *longue durée* — form that drags, both memorializing and analyzing the murder as her closing shot attempts to do. There is a temporal drag at work in relation to African American history, as I analyze later with reference to Elizabeth Freeman's queer theory of the term, that is produced by the camera, whether in its unblinking stillness or its almost imperceptible motion. Shooting in the immediate aftermath of the murder, Akerman's does not have the same temporal distance or framework as Dow and Williams; but, because of the aesthetic stringency, her film does not feel like a report *in medias res*.

Thomas Wicke and Roxane Cohen Silver note that Akerman, Dow and Whitney were not the only people who came to Jasper to try and remediate the crime; in fact, Dow and Whitney's film frequently captures the crowd of reporters, both local and national, around the courthouse, and follows the story of a white male presenter from the local station KJAS, offering an implicit insight into the media's impact on the shape of the unfolding story. As Wicke and Cohen Silver argue in their ecological analysis of the community psychological impact of the murder of Byrd, Jr.:

> The effect of the media transformed what very likely would have been just another local tragedy affecting a few families into an international event that provided a stage for opposing interest groups. The media made the story and placed themselves squarely in the middle of the community trauma; they were active participants. The effect of the media cannot be overstated.[6]

This is particularly significant because Byrd, Jr.'s murder and the subsequent national media coverage led, eventually, to the passing of the Matthew Shepard and James Byrd, Jr. Hate Crimes Act, signed into law by then-President Barack Obama on 28 October, 2009, more than a decade after both of the murders it commemorated; or rather, it commemorated that the convictions of both Shepard's and Byrd, Jr.'s murderers occurred despite the absence of active hate crimes legislation in Wyoming and Texas, respectively.

In her study of the twinning of the cases by the media and the law, Jennifer Petersen notes that the 'politics of public feeling' were qualitatively different between the two cases, despite their temporal, narrative and political yoking, as reflected in their remediations:

> The murders of Byrd and Shepard, however, were the most mediated, circulated, and condensed into various media narratives... Each man's death has echoed through popular culture texts, from music to visual art to commercial media texts. This uptake in popular texts was not equal, however. Several books document the aftermath of the murder of James Byrd Jr. in Jasper.

> Showtime and PBS dramatized and documented the murder and its aftermath...
> [Compared to Shepard's entry into pop music, theatre and narrative television, and web memorials], Byrd's death, while it certainly has not receded from public memory, has not been so visibly memorialized, taken up, circulated and remembered in the media. This fact alone asks us to think about the politics of who we remember, who we are asked to feel for, and how.[7]

While Petersen briefly discusses Dow and Whitney's film, which was broadcast on PBS in 2002, neither she nor Wicke and Cohen Silver appear aware of Akerman's *Sud*, which suggests that it found a primarily international audience. It premiered at Cannes in 1999, in Director's Fortnight, followed by screenings at the Toronto International Film Festival and New York Human Rights Watch International Film Festival in 1999, and the Thessaloniki Documentary Festival, the Argentinean International Festival of Cinema and Video on Human Rights and Melbourne's REAL life on film Festival in 2000. Given Akerman's 'oppositional strategy consistent [across her] oeuvre, where key formal and thematic elements are consistently counterposed',[8] and counterposed additionally to the formal strategies of observational documentary and news media, it is interesting that the film experienced its own dis/orientation and re-orientation, from international festivals where Akerman was highlighted as an auteure (Cannes; Toronto, where, as programmer Kay Armatage describes, she went out of her way to secure invitations for every one of Akerman's films)[9] to human rights (and) documentary festivals.[10]

Thus, despite Akerman's oppositional strategies, the film played some part in the news/realist media conversation around the Byrd, Jr. murder, at the level of international conceptions of human rights, offering a disorienting representation of American racial politics on the international stage. As Schmid argues, this journalistic and documentary imperative is unusually palpable in the film's aesthetics: 'Visually, *Sud* verges on the reportage genre, even though its disjointed syntax and restrictive cinematic vocabulary resolutely signal its status as an experimental work.'[11] For Capp, reviewing the film on its Melbourne screening for *Senses of Cinema*, 'Akerman's formalist obsessions [become] almost a conceit'[12] when the racial politics that the filmmaker encounters 'can be experienced as a physical press on the surface of the skin'.[13] Capp describes the film as possessing an 'oddly unsettling and ultimately compelling effect',[14] one that might derive from this 'press', in Ahmed's terms, of the raw moment of the murder and its immediate aftermath against Akerman's formal strategies of distanciation. The film draws an ambiguous ethical line with this commitment to distanciation, given the distancing and dehumanising use of a chain and truck to drag a body to death. As ever in Akerman's work, the costs and challenges of human intimacy — across or at boundaries of gender, sexuality, ethnicity, religion and class — are felt in her aesthetic choices. For some viewers, as Capp suggests, those choices may not be commensurate with the act and context of Byrd, Jr.'s murder and its aftermath, producing the 'unsettling' effect of the historical event exceeding the filmmaker's frame, as Akerman's closing shot suggests.

Both Akerman's film and *The Two Towns of Jasper* omit any material representation of the crime — something broached in Kirsten Johnson's documentary *Cameraperson*

(2016). Johnson was an additional camera on the white crew for Dow and Williams' film, and in her archival auto-documentary, she includes two outtakes from her time shooting in Jasper, which was focused on the courtroom (which is barely seen in the finished film). In one scene, which Johnson has noted in Q&As was the one she felt most ethically and legally uncertain about including in her composite documentary, the prosecutor Guy James Gray unboxes and holds up the heavy, long rusting chains that were used to drag Byrd, Jr. He flinches at the smell as he removes them from the cardboard evidence box. The chains present both a material connection to the specific murder of James Byrd, Jr., and a compressed yet palpable history of the enslavement of African bodies on which the U.S. was built. Schmid observes that Akerman's long take of bare trees summons Billie Holiday's song 'Strange Fruit' and thus offers a comparably compressed yet palpable history of lynchings, as described by one of her interviewees, Mrs. Callins, who witnessed them in her childhood.[15] But Johnson does not present the chains in isolation, or duration: instead, what is palpable is Gray's intimate and kinaesthetic reaction of physical repulsion, as the disorientation of racism becomes felt (and clearly smelt) in his (white male) body. Akerman's camera hangs back from the trees: we see them, but need historical context to interpret them.

Ahmed continues, in her chapter on disorientation, with the observation (in relation to Countee Cullen's poem 'Tableau', about a white boy and a black boy walking in public together), that 'queer objects support proximity between those who are supposed to live on parallel lines, *as points that should not meet*. A queer object hence makes contact possible. Or, to be more precise, a queer object would have a surface that supports such contact' (emphasis in original).[16] *Sud*, in which a white filmmaker with a white Francophone filmmaking team, enters a small, traumatized community and focuses predominantly on its African-American inhabitants, both is and is not such a queer object. Akerman's talking-head interviews, which focus on a single isolated speaker, convey a lack of social cohesion that is challenged by Ricardo C. Ainslie and Kalina Brabeck, who identify a 'Center Holds Model' operating in Jasper, predicated on a notably well-developed African-American middle class for East Texas, as well as supportive and transparent law enforcement.[17] The relation between Akerman's interviews — and between the interviews and the tracking shots — remains unstated. Schmid argues that '[d]ifferent accounts complete, confront or contradict each other in a complex web of stories that spectators are left to piece together and whose veracity and intent... they must assess for themselves'.[18] Yet there is a sense in which the accounts, particularly by African-American and white speakers, are presented as 'parallel lines... *that should not meet*'.

The Two Towns of Jasper ends with an African-American community funeral (not Byrd, Jr.'s), where a family member notes that the deceased woman was buried on the historically-black side of the cemetery, despite the removal of the fence. In the case of the deeply-embodied nature of racial politics in the deep South, the film suggests, there is no possible queer object that can support proximity; the film both replicates (through its use of two different crews) and attempts to break — through its editing — with tradition. In a particularly striking scene, captured by the white crew following Berry's brother during his trial, members of the Byrd family interrupt a press conference to ask their own plangent and unanswerable questions over the forest of microphones. This direct conversation is one of the very few between African American and white interlocutors captured in the film, and suggests — in a perhaps utopian manner — that observational documentary can 'make contact possible'.

Sud's perhaps deliberate failure to become a surface for proximity is best described by an African American pedestrian captured by the mobile car-window camera. 'No filming, ma'am', he calls out to Akerman. 'Don't do that.' The camera persists in shooting. Drivers and passengers in other cars occasionally wave at the camera, demarcating a clear economic/class line. Byrd, Jr., as white journalist Michael Journee tells Akerman, was known around Jasper as the man who walked everywhere because he did not have a car, a clear marker of either poverty or prior convictions or both in the rural U.S. It was this errant status, in a vehicular culture, which led him to hitch a ride with Berry, who was driving the pick-up truck that belonged to him, and his passengers Brewer and King, both former convicts from outside Jasper. Journee's account of the crime repeatedly disorients Byrd, Jr. from Jasper norms: he walked everywhere; he was driven out of town to a back road six miles away; and his body was dismembered by the dragging.

This errancy lends Byrd, Jr. what Ahmed might describe as a queerness, an effect that persistently disorients and distorts all the accounts of racial and local identity in both films; speakers repeatedly note that Jasper is functional *except for* this one crime. One of Akerman's interviewees, Dereck Mohammed (the interviewees' names are given in the credits only, and not as intertitles or subtitles) comments that the aim of white supremacists, among whom Byrd, Jr.'s murderers were included by their affiliation to Aryan gangs in prison, is 'to stop blacks from becoming real men'. Mohammed is dressed in snappy formal wear, seated on a wooden window seat suggestive of a church or funeral home; he presents his black masculinity with great elegance in defiance of the resurgence of white supremacy that underlies the actions of Berry, Brewer and King. In this small but telling comment an implicit connection between blackness-as-disorientation and queerness comes to the surface, a structural connection between Matthew Shepard and James Byrd, Jr.; between the drag to which Byrd, Jr.'s body was subjected and the drag performed within the queer community. The drag that disarticulated Byrd, Jr.'s head and arms from his torso, when his body struck an exposed culvert, flashes up — in this assertion by Mohammed — a profound embodied proximity to the communitarian re-embodiment and re-articulation of the ball scene in defiance of such racist dismemberings (literal and metaphorical); it thus includes Byrd, Jr. within a larger, multivalent African American national cultural resistance.

There is one scene in *Sud* that hazards this link: at the funeral, Akerman's camera focuses on the female speakers and mourners, foregrounding them in a situation where the legal and social aspects of the crime were dominated (as Petersen notes) by men. Byrd, Jr.'s sisters, dazzlingly dressed, perform a gospel song in tribute to him, captured in close-up; as Capp notes, this centrepiece of the film is '[t]echnically inferior... with poor sound',[19] distorting the electronic organ played by one sister. As throughout the film, particularly in interiors, Akerman and her cinematographer struggle to capture the tonalities of African-American skin, so that subjects' features are often blurred and indistinct. But the vibrancy of the performance and costuming, and its considerable duration, compel the viewer's attention, if only because it offers one of the film's few scenes of verbal and physical interaction between two people, a minor model of solidarity and collaboration that also — in its close-up of the sisters' bright, sequinned outfits — suggests a queer possibility. The line between ethnic fetishization and the queer object is difficult and disorienting, and Akerman's film, like Byrd, Jr., wanders across it. Demarcating a distinction between that which depicts race and that which troubles raced depictions, Alessandra Raengo argues that, '[u]nlike the image *of* race, the racial image, I propose, is not one in which race is present as an intelligibly visible object. Instead, the racial image is where race acts as a form of the articulation of the visual — a template, an epistemology, a map, an affect, a gestalt, a medium' (emphasis in original).[20] It is in the gesture toward making queerness visible and palpable that Akerman comes closest to a 'racial image', in Raengo's terms, where race-as-disorientation can become an articulation of the filmmaker's aesthetics, an affect or medium for her filmmaking rather than that which disorients it.

There is an interesting comparison to be made with Amy Villarejo's account of the 'lesbian impression' in Ulrike Ottinger's *Exile Shanghai* (1997). Villarejo, concerned with the kind of formal strategies for the invisibilization of the lesbian auteure that also marks Akerman's late films, argues that:

> Even if not 'about' lesbians in an obvious way, *Exile Shanghai* nevertheless records a lesbian impression of exile and of history, a lesbian's impression of the world around her... inextricable from the affective politics of the archive associated with the extermination of the Jews and others by the Holocaust in Europe... What *matters* is precisely the difference lesbian might make, however oblique the *presence* of lesbian might be in its making... investigating under what system and according to what principle one consigns the Shanghai [Jewish] exiles specifically to a record of persecution or survival (emphases in original).[21]

Of course, there are strong parallels with Akerman's four late documentaries, compiled as the box set Exilios, in terms of 'find[ing] a subject... that seeks to evade the repetition-compulsion indicative of acting-out' in representation of the Holocaust.[22] As Schmid brings out in her analysis of the film, *Sud* is a companion piece to *D'Est* and both films are haunted by the ideas of Walter Benjamin.[23] Both Raengo and Villarejo suggest a productive effacement of about-ness within the visual in contrast to journalistic or observational documentary, which can only produce images *of* race, or *of* queerness.

Yet in her disorientation in Jasper, including the displacement of herself and her auteurial signature from the frame of the film (in contrast to Villarejo's argument that Ottinger is present in her address to Jewish exile), Akerman comes up against the complexities posed by bell hooks in her account of *Paris is Burning* (Jennie Livingston, 1990), as a white lesbian documenting an African-American community from the outside. hooks notes that 'since [Livingston's] presence as white woman/ lesbian filmmaker is "absent" from *Paris is Burning*, it is easy for viewers to imagine that they are watching an ethnographic film'.[24] While Akerman's stylistic disorientations disrupt any reception of *Sud* as classical ethnographic film, her absence could be said, at its extremes, to assume 'an imperial overseeing position that is in no way progressive or counterhegemonic'.[25] Unlike Gray handling the chains in *Cameraperson*, Akerman does not make her own implication in the racialized politics of embodiment visible or palpable. The difference lesbian makes is slight — all the more so, as it is filled with potential; one amplified, as Villarejo explores in relation to Ottinger, by her Jewishness. The hymn in the church suggests, very implicitly, the parallels drawn by African American Christian communities between the Jews of Exodus, and the historical experience of African slavery in the Americas: of exile and a path to redemption, often denoted by the place of the River Jordan in spirituals. But Akerman's studied absence — for most viewers at human rights film festivals, her auteurial identity would have been far less familiar or palpable in the film than for viewers at a major international festival — does not fully allow this resonance, or its import, to emerge.

Its dormant possibility brings the viewer up against the limits of (white liberal) queer politics for addressing race in the U.S. This is palpable if we consider that Akerman makes a case for the experience of James Byrd, Jr. being a form of what Elizabeth Freeman has called 'temporal drag', which she identifies as a particularly lesbian encoding of temporality.[26] Freeman writes that, for lesbian feminist artists looking to recuperate second wave feminism '"drag" [is] a *productive* obstacle to progress, a usefully distorting pull backward, and a necessary pressure on the present tense' as it rehistoricizes feminist embodiment, both individually and 'in the movement time of collective political fantasy... connecting queer performativity to disavowed political histories'.[27] Akerman's non-linear recounting of the murder and its aftermath, hinged by the funeral and ending with the drag of the motivating incident, has a further temporal drag in its investigation of the past through the accounts of its African American interviewees, who draw contrasts between the era of slavery, of Jim Crow, and the present — contrasts based on the historicization of racial violence, presented as a narrative of progress toward inclusion that is disoriented by the murder of Byrd, Jr.

As Freeman elucidates through her reading of Elisabeth Subrin's experimental video *Shulie* (1997), roughly co-eval with *Sud*, this pull backward may be productively gendered, but it is reductively, even pejoratively, racialized. Reading a scene in which the actor (reperforming Shulamith Firestone's performance from a 1967 documentary about her) delivers Shulie's monologue about 'Negroes' working at the post office, Freeman comments that 'Shulie denies to African American activism and history the disjunctive mode of historicizing that Firestone advocated for feminism. Both the filmic character and the historical author confine African Americans to the waiting room, or perhaps locked post office box, of history', without fully exploring or critiquing Subrin's use of the decontextualized and un[interrupted/interrogated] re-performance in the film, which creates a similar 'drag'.[28] While lesbian feminists may experience a 'usefully distorting pull backward', that 'temporal drag' meets an obstacle to the regressive in American racial politics. Akerman's 'drag', her signature auteurial concern with memory and history, risks denying the intricate present of race relations in Texas in the late 1990s (not to mention in New York, the city where she had spent most time in the US, and which was facing its present of racialized violence in the aftermath of the 1991 Crown Heights riots), and the fact that any change or progress was grounded in generations of activist struggle. Akerman's look backwards, both formal and narrative, is productive in asserting (against forgetting) the long and violent history out of which Byrd, Jr.'s murder emerged, but it also misses the queer proximity, the risky friction of the meeting in the present, that Ahmed identifies.

Byrd, Jr.'s murder was not a re-enactment of something past, but was — and remains — part of a continuum of white supremacist genocidal violence on which America is founded. There is no drag; this is not baggage or belatedness. Rather than being 'confined to the waiting room... of history', racial violence is constitutive of American history, and the experience of African Americans is a signal, if not paradigmatic, continuum of such violence. This is apparent in the account of the murder given by African-American Texan filmmaker Carroll Parrott Blue. In her memoir, she tells the story of James Byrd, Jr.'s murder within her biography of her mother, Mollie Carroll Parrott, a 'race woman', or civil rights activist, in Houston in the 1950s. She offers Byrd, Jr.'s story as evidence that the 'tragedy in [her] mother's struggle is that, in the end, she could not triumph. Instead, she left the battle for equality to us, the living.'[29] Blue closes Byrd Jr.'s story with its continuing consequences, a proximity absent from both of the documentaries:

> in 1999, the headstone on Byrd's grave was defaced and the nameplate was removed. In March 2000, a Ku Klux Klan Imperial Wizard was photographed next to Byrd's headstone with a sticker that he'd placed on the headstone. It read: 'A Ku Klux Klansman was here.' The photograph was published in the April 2000 issue of *Details*, a now defunct Condé Nast magazine once described as a lifestyle magazine for Generation X readers.[30]

On the following double-page spread, Blue reproduces two historical images of a sheriff leading an African American man in chains, and of a charred and flayed body hanging from a tree, observed by white onlookers, listed in the endnotes as 'Lynching, Before and After',[31] opposite a photograph of Byrd, Jr. that was widely reproduced by the Associated Press, and a photograph by Ted Parks of the bloodstains on the road, circled by aerosol paint, a visual motif repeated in both films.[32] The mirroring but non-reflective images require us to ask how racist hate crimes should be documented and memorialized, before Blue continues narrating her childhood in the Third Ward, a Black community in Houston, in the context of her mother's community activism. It is the remediation of James Byrd, Jr. that Blue produces as a queer object, one that brings together stories transgenerationally while not performing temporal drag.

Blue does not reproduce the photograph published in *Details*, but her account makes evident that which is repeatedly effaced in accounts of the Byrd, Jr. case, even though it is in plain view in both films: white supremacy. Unlike the black bodies that are reproduced as 'racial images' in Raengo's term, intended to be 'intelligibly visible objects' with no interiority, complexity or depth, white bodies-as-bodies mainly evade documentation in the mediatisation of the Byrd, Jr. case, and thus also the political and theoretical frameworks of visibility that would produce both whiteness and white supremacy as 'intelligibly visible'. Instead, they are presented as individuals rather than tropes of whiteness. Dow and Williams come closest, including a scene shot by Johnson in the same courtroom where Gray unpacks the chains; he displays another crucial piece of evidence that he compiled, a chart depicting and explaining the symbolism of the white supremacist tattoos worn by the three murderers, including Jasper hometown boy Shawn Berry. It was this diagram that connected and convicted the three murderers, through their shared ideology of white supremacy that was proven as a motivation for their murder of Byrd, Jr.

Akerman's penultimate interview is with John Craig, an FBI expert, on the rise of white supremacy in the South. He describes their ideology as motivated by the idea 'that the white man is the heir to all the promises in the Old Testament; that they are white Israel, in reality'. Parallel to the flash of queerness in the interview with Mohammed, there is a flash of connection here for Akerman as a Jew. Craig goes on to describe how the Aryan imaginary positions itself as true inheritor of the Bible, and thus views the Jews as Satanic impostors to be displaced. White, dressed in beige and seated in a beige armchair framed by beige walls, Craig presents a striking contrast to Akerman's other interviewees; both of the other white male interviewees (the journalist and the sheriff) are interviewed in their place of work, and have their names on signs on or close to their desks. Akerman implicates Craig in the ideology he describes (from a position of expertise) through the distinctive and extreme coloration of the mise-en-scène, and yet she herself remains absent. This interview — which comes very late in the film — is followed by another embodied account of the dragging; white supremacy now frames the crime, like the aerosol spraypaint circles that mark out on the road where parts of Byrd, Jr.'s body were found.

Writing from the perspective of 2017, it is hard not to feel that both films missed the real story in Jasper, which was the clear emergence of white supremacy as a terrorist threat. While one of Dow and Williams' main subjects is a male white supremacist who reconsiders his views after watching the Byrd, Jr. trial, neither film confronts the underlying and foundational presence of this ideology head-on. Yet white historian Alwyn Barr notes that:

> small Klan marches occurred... in Houston and Austin in the early 1990's. Neo-Nazi and skinhead groups appeared in the 1980's, especially in Houston and Dallas. Members burned an African-American church in Ellis County in 1989 and killed African Americans in Fort Worth and Lubbock in the 1990s. The same period witnessed the rise of private militia groups with Klan connections. In 1993, responding to the actions of these groups, the legislature adopted an anti-hate crime law that led to convictions, and the Texas Commission on Human Rights brought suit against Klan groups in 1994, seeking compensation for persons they had harassed.[33]

According to Barr, there was a hate crime law, therefore, under which Berry, Brewer and King could have been prosecuted, had their actions been recognized as those of a white supremacist group from the start (as Berry described in his affidavit, according to Journee in *Sud*). While both law enforcement agents and the prosecution in the case drew attention to the murderers' enrolment in white supremacist groups and successfully argued that their uniting ideology was the motivation for the crime, like them, the films do not quite engage with the bigger picture, the 'racial image' — as opposed to 'image of race' — that would by necessity include and interrogate whiteness.

In being disoriented by the drag of James Byrd, Jr.'s body, which seemed to relate to a past history rather than a present and future continuum of supremacist ideology, both films were thus symptomatic of dominant U.S. media and culture. Yet, as African-American poet June Jordan wrote in 1998:

> White. White. American white supremacist white. The monster is an 'American-looking' white man. This violent, paramilitary hatred is absolutely homegrown and growing...
> The Oklahoma City bombing has lifted the curtain.
> If we do not see ourselves, at last, stripped of all excuse and scapegoat, if we do not recognize the weakness of our connections to other [sic] — all of us different, and different-looking Americans — as the wellspring for white supremacy, then we may as well admit that we are ready to submit to Timothy McVeigh's final agenda for our country: to achieve an Aryan Nation by any means necessary.[34]

Or: 'I don't think history is the past... History is the present', as James Baldwin told Margaret Mead during a 1971 conversation at the American Museum of Natural History.[35]

Concluding *The Third* Eye, her brilliant study of cinema as a persistently ethnographic spectacle, Fatima Tobing Rony uses this conversation between the African American essayist and the white American anthropologist to elucidate the vexed connection between the Eurowestern liberal narrative of progress and the persistence of what she terms 'fascinating cannibalism' in Eurowestern filmmaking, rooted in the anthropological origins of cinema. She describes a visual work by Pat Ward Williams entitled *Accused/Blowtorch/Padlock* (1986) that resonates with Blue's framing and juxtaposition of the textual and visual narration of the murder of James Byrd, Jr.. 'Williams accompanies framed photographs of a lynched African American man taken from the book *The Best of 'Life' Magazine* with text, asking the question, "WHO took this picture? Oh, God, Life answers — page 141 — no credit."... the Observer/Observed dichotomy implodes when the Observer realizes that he or she is the Observed'.[36] Williams' question echoes Blue's use of familial narratives to frame her account of Byrd, Jr., and vice versa (as well as using the image of Byrd, Jr. to give the possibility of a name back to the man in the lynching images opposite it), so that a 'racial image' rather than an image of race appears. By placing herself and her disorientation somewhere within the frame, or around it on the soundtrack, following the possibility of the 'lesbian impression' and the interrogation of American fascism (including its simultaneously anti-Semitic and

Christian-Zionist intents), Akerman could have reoriented *herself* south, showing WHO made this picture by showing more clearly the marks where racism physically presses into the skin of her film.[37]

Notes to Chapter 8

1. Sara Ahmed, *Queer Phenomenology* (Durham, NC: Duke University Press, 2006), p. 160.
2. Marion Schmid, *Chantal Akerman* (Manchester: Manchester University Press, 2010), p. 108.
3. Ahmed, *Queer Phenomenology*, p. 160.
4. See Ricardo C. Ainslie and Kalina Brabeck, 'Race Murder and Community Trauma: Psychoanalysis and Ethnography in Exploring the Impact of the Killing of James Byrd in Jasper, Texas', *Journal for the Psychoanalysis of Culture and Society*, 8.1 (Spring 2003), 42–50; Thomas Wicke and Roxane Cohen Silver, 'A Community Responds to Collective Trauma: An Ecological Analysis of the James Byrd Murder in Jasper, Texas', *American Journal of Community Psychology*, 44 (2009), 233–48.
5. Schmid, *Chantal Akerman*, p. 112.
6. Wicke and Cohen Silver, 'A Community Responds to Collective Trauma', p. 245.
7. Jennifer Petersen, *Murder, The Media, and the Politics of Public Feelings: Remembering Matthew Shepard and James Byrd Jr* (Bloomington, IN: Indiana University Press, 2011), p. 203.
8. Rose Capp, 'Akerman Resists Southern Comfort', *Senses of Cinema* (May 2000). Online: http://sensesofcinema.com/2000/feature-articles/south/.
9. Kay Armatage, 'Material Effects: Fashions in Feminist Programming', in *There She Goes: Feminist Filmmaking and Beyond*, edited by Corinn Columpar and Sophie Mayer (Detroit: Wayne State University Press, 2010), pp. 92–104, pp. 98–99.
10. Capp, 'Akerman Resists Southern Comfort'.
11. Schmid, *Chantal Akerman*, p. 109.
12. Capp, 'Akerman Resists Southern Comfort'.
13. Ahmed, *Queer Phenomenology*, p. 160.
14. Capp, 'Akerman Resists Southern Comfort'.
15. Schmid, *Chantal Akerman*, p. 112.
16. Ahmed, *Queer Phenomenology*, p. 169.
17. Ainslie and Brabeck, 'Race Murder and Community Trauma', p. 49.
18. Schmid, *Chantal Akerman*, p. 111.
19. Capp, 'Akerman Resists Southern Comfort'.
20. Alessandra Raengo, *On the Sleeve of the Visual: Race as Face Value* (Hanover, NH: Dartmouth College Press, 2013), p. 3.
21. Amy Villarejo, *Lesbian Rule: Cultural Criticism and the Value of Desire* (Durham, NC: Duke University Press, 2003), p. 86.
22. Ibid., p. 86.
23. Schmid, *Chantal Akerman*, pp. 108–09.
24. bell hooks, 'Is Paris Burning?', *Reel to Real: Race, Sex and Class at the Movies* (London: Routledge, 1996), pp. 214–26, p. 220.
25. Ibid..
26. Elizabeth Freeman, *Time Binds: Queer Temporalities, Queer Histories* (Durham, NC: Duke University Press, 2010), p. 62.
27. Ibid., p. 64; p. 65.
28. Ibid., p. 80.
29. Carroll Parrott Blue Blue, *The Dawn at My Back: Memoir of a Black Texas Upbringing* (Austin: University of Texas Press, 2003), p. 52.
30. Ibid., p. 53.
31. Ibid., p. 54.
32. Ibid., p. 55.
33. Alwyn Barr, *Black Texans: A History of African Americans in Texas, 1528–1995*. 2nd ed. (Norman: University of Oklahoma Press, 1996), pp. 233–34.

34. June Jordan, 'In the Land of White Supremacy', in *Affirmative Acts: Political Essays* (New York: Doubleday, 1998), pp. 113–16, pp. 115–16.
35. James Baldwin in James Baldwin and Margaret Mead, *A Rap on Race* (New York: Dell, 1971), p. 174, quoted in Fatima Tobing Rony, *The Third Eye: Race, Cinema, and Ethnographic Spectacle* (Durham, NC: Duke University Press, 1996), p. 193.
36. Ibid., p. 216.
37. I would like to thank Alexandra Hidalgo for enabling me to see *The Two Towns of Jasper*, and Katharina Lindner for a productive discussion of Elizabeth Freeman's work on drag.

CHAPTER 9

Vocal Landscapes: Framing Mutable Stories in *De l'autre côté* (2002) and *Une voix dans le désert* (2002)

Albertine Fox

The long, static shots of landscape in *De l'autre côté* (2002) give one the feeling of having been there. Each has its own tone, rhythm and colouring. Akerman's camera puts the spectator into the landscape and although one is brought so close to the experiences of those whose stories are heard, the spectator is never told what to think. The landscape comes to resemble a recording surface marked by an accretion of memories, which bind as they drift with the tracking shots, each story offering recognition and solidarity to another. *De l'autre côté* is interspersed with interviews that Akerman and her cinematographer Robert Fenz conducted with local people living and working in the locations they visit on either side of the US-Mexico border. Fenz has revealed that due to the absence of interviews in *D'Est* (1993), Akerman was urged by her producer Thierry Garrel to include the device in *De l'autre côté*, much to her dismay. However, as Fenz points out, the interviews work beautifully, melding with Akerman's improvisational approach and her welcoming of uncertainty and ambivalence. If the people they met were doing something interesting, he explains, they would 'enter into the story, or the feel of the film'.[1] Fenz's reference to the film's 'story' and 'feel' is suggestive not only of the work's rhythmic quality and intrinsic porosity of boundaries but also of Akerman's fidelity to the creative power of storytelling.

I would like to suggest ways in which *De l'autre côté* and Akerman's 2002 installation *Une voix dans le désert* foster an attitude of deep receptivity, placing the spectator/visitor in an encounter with a compassionate mode of filmmaking that arises from an aural-ethical approach. *De l'autre côté* is forever drawing the spectator into spaces of affective contact, which at their most explicit consist of vignettes of local people who express their hopes, fears, emotional pain, and prejudicial views to Akerman and Fenz, whose strong listening presence is made manifest by the sight of their shadow or the sound of their voices. Both Akerman and Fenz can be heard off-frame conversing with the interviewees. Their slow, intuitive interactions combined with distinctive framing techniques give rise to the kind of 'mutual curiosity' that Ivone Marguiles identifies in *D'Est*, when the camera's inquisitive gaze is returned by the women being filmed.[2] In *De l'autre côté*, the words and feelings of the interviewees extend towards the spectator who is invited into 'the privileged intimacy of the listening situation', thus described by Marion Schmid in her analysis of the film.[3] The persistent gestures of listening that pervade the filmic landscape will be the focal point of this chapter. I conceive of these gestures as part of an interlinked process of 'feeling with', 'speaking with or nearby', and 'listening beside'.

The first part of the film takes place in Mexico, encompassing salient shots of the border wall, the mountainous city of Tecate, and interviews with residents from the city of Agua Prieta in the Mexican state of Sonora, while the second part takes place in the Arizona border city of Douglas. The final few minutes of the film form a coda, as Akerman tells a fictional story about a woman from Mexico who crossed the border to find work but has disappeared. The camera is situated at the front of a moving vehicle as Akerman tells her story, accompanied by Claudio Monteverdi's 'Duo Seraphim' from his 1610 *Vespers of the Blessed Virgin* (transcribed for two cellos and bass by Sonia Wieder-Atherton and Natalia Shakhovskaya), taking the spectator on a night-time musical journey along the well-travelled and heavily patrolled Interstate 5 corridor to Los Angeles.[4] This coda provides some of the material for *Une voix dans le désert* that initially formed part of a 3-part video installation composed of footage from *De l'autre côté*.

Feeling With, Speaking Nearby, Listening Beside

I take my lead from Lisbeth Lipari's concept of 'listening otherwise', a process she situates at the heart of the ethical response. Listening otherwise is committed to receiving otherness, engaging with the unfamiliar and with what is not already understood. For Lipari, listening precedes speaking and it is only *out of* this process of listening that dialogic ethics can arise. When one responds to another one does so through one's capacity to listen — 'a voice that speaks through listening' — as much as through the spoken word.[5] Lipari's study is channelled through the subject of suffering and the associated relational processes of empathy, compassion and understanding. Crucially, she counters the view that rational understanding is a prerequisite to compassion: I can only have compassion for someone if their experience resonates with my own knowledge and understanding. She is also careful to dissociate compassion as an attitude of openness and concern for the other, from ego-centred feelings of guilt, pity and paternalism. Even though one may not identify with or ever comprehend another's suffering, this does not prevent one from being able to 'listen to suffering' and feel compassion.[6]

Lipari's turn to feminist care ethics, namely to Nel Noddings's rendering of empathy as a kind of 'engrossment', and as a process attuned to a state of *feeling with*, offers a fruitful point of comparison with Akerman's method of filming interviews in *De l'autre côté*. Rather than putting oneself in the shoes of the other, taking an objective and projective problem-solving approach to her/his reality, Noddings's ethics of care is attentive to the process of receiving 'the other into myself' and seeing and feeling with them.[7] Listening otherwise as a kind of 'feeling with' can be paired with the act of 'speaking with or nearby', proposed by feminist filmmaker and cultural theorist Trinh T. Minh-ha who discusses the notion of speaking with (not 'about') in her theorising of the interview. Trinh concentrates on the relational space opened up during interviews when standard strategies commonly adopted in broadcast journalism and conventional documentaries are rejected. These include an insistence on authenticity and a reliance on pre-set questions that urge interviewees to comply with 'a preconceived role and a forced itinerary'.[8] Trinh, like Akerman, is sensitive to the creative possibilities and ethical significance of the 'interval' between interviewer and interviewed subject, and of 'the movement between listening and speaking'.[9] The power of the interview is rooted for Trinh in its functioning as a site of multiplicity and its ability to disrupt the dominant act of speaking, disturbing the idea of a unitary self and challenging the norms that govern how we appear to others. She does so by privileging detours, decentred framing, the sounding of multiple voices, and by generating a sense of fluidity and multi-directionality.

This brings me to the final gesture of 'listening beside', inspired by Eve Kosofsky Sedgwick's interest in this preposition in her essays on emotion, affect and performativity. Influenced by Deleuze's theorising of planar relations, her attraction to *beside* as opposed to 'beneath', 'beyond' and 'behind' is due to its spatial resonance that resists narratives of origin and telos and rigid models of cause-effect relations. *Beside* forms a key part of Sedgwick's exploration of nondualistic thought, allowing for 'a spacious agnosticism' about linear causality and offering a means of sidestepping the 'topos of depth or hiddenness, typically followed by a drama of exposure' that she identifies as a staple of critical practices.[10] This narrow and pressured transition from 'hiddenness' to 'exposure' is also a seductive, if aggressive, and highly marketable feature of film and television interviews today, functioning as a popular sensationalist strategy in much journalistic broadcasting. Akerman's films evade this process by concentrating on the meanings that arise through deviation and reverberation, and by prioritising the multiplicity of human experience, demonstrated through her ceaseless probing of the intersecting connections between historical catastrophe, personal tragedy and passages of artistic creation.

Digressions, Distractions and Peripheral Occurrences

The fourth shot in *De l'autre côté* shows the border wall at sunset, bathed in a glistening severity. Vehicle sounds fade and the dust settles to leave a haze of bluish grey, before the camera cuts to the second interview, conducted by Akerman in Spanish with Delfina Maruri Miranda, a 78-year old woman whose son and grandson died while attempting to cross the border at Sonoyta. Delfina's untiring, self-directed style of storytelling parallels the resistant curves of the mountains and rooftops and the criss-crossing marks on the ground, so visible in the previous shot where they were offset against the immutable straight lines of the corrugated steel fence, a wall of violence and pain. The sight of the striated metal wall is reduced in significance and replaced by the shiny, light-green crinkled table covering, on which the television, DVD player and hi-fi system sit in Delfina's house. The scene of storytelling that ensues contests the oppressive system of surveillance outside by shifting the focus to the intimate voicing of personal histories that cannot be tracked or contained.

Akerman asks Delfina about her family history, and then about her son Reymundo and her grandson, progressing in a methodical fashion. We learn of the Spanish origin of her name, and that her great grandfather was among the first Spanish people to arrive in Las Minas with a group of engineers who were sent to the mines of Zomelahuacán in Veracruz. She tells us she worked as a teacher in Barrancones, Progreso, Tepeicán, El Olvido, Zapotitlán and Zomelahuacán, and she talks of the poverty in these regions. When she mentions her son, she focuses on his entrepreneurial spirit and his passion for renovating the school and houses in his local area. When Akerman enquires: 'He wanted to go North?', Delfina continues to refer to her son's ambitious outlook, refusing to talk over the silent trauma of his death. In this way, she speaks with and nearby her subject, inviting spectators to *feel* the tentative process of communication, an experience that prises open a space to imagine and reflect on the identity and existence of her deceased family members.

Delfina's own suffering shows itself quietly when she wipes away tears or sweat from her eyes with her handkerchief, after disentangling it from the microphone in her pocket, a gesture symbolic of her gentle attempts to separate herself from any form of constraint imposed on her from the outside. Akerman is keenly aware of the woman's distress and fragile condition, and in her role as interviewer she keeps a minimal presence and refuses to steer the course of the narrative, never pressing her interviewee for more than she provides. Rather than disavowing Delfina's independence and optimistic outlook, Akerman allows the spectator enough time to appreciate her personal qualities, while receiving and validating the feelings of vulnerability that arise. Moreover, the content of Delfina's story never comes to dominate. Other vital nuances catch our attention and underpin the necessary digressive nature of her speech. These comprise the blank television screen positioned behind her in which members of the crew can be glimpsed, reminding us of the two-way, intersubjective process of this interview exchange. The white plaster on Delfina's arm makes us aware of her worsening ill-health, and her poignant handkerchief, and the sight of her granddaughter Ana who appears in the doorway, create minute breaks in the flow of her story, emphasizing its refusal to adhere to preconceived expectations. In one instance, a single fade to black punctuates the end of her sentence, and then a small bird flutters in front of the camera. These minor disturbances form a cluster of peripheral occurrences that reinforce the woman's long and uneven wandering narrative, to which Akerman and the spectator must listen without turning away.

On a larger scale, the exterior soundscape is presented as a space of sonic excess that continually diverts the spectator's attention from the interviews themselves. A sort of carrying over takes place that sees remnants of the stories recounted reverberate through other images. During a later interview at a barber shop, one of the clients (a 21-year old man from Oaxaca) describes his failed attempts to cross the border. As he speaks, a silhouette appears on the wall beside him, conjuring the idea of an anonymous presence of someone who has disappeared, producing a concrete rendering of what the queer Chicana writer and feminist Gloria Anzaldúa describes as 'life on the borders, life in the shadows'.[11] The unabating reality of the disappearance of undocumented migrants, whose bodies remain undiscovered, is one to which Akerman was highly sensitive as she made *De l'autre côté*. She writes of her wish to find out the names, journeys, and places of death of those without graves who had perished in the desert. For those whose bodies had not yet been found, simply questioning their whereabouts makes them exist already. She affirms: 'Pour le reste, rien que poser la question fait déjà exister le reste, et dit qu'il y a un reste.'[12] Each interviewee's recitation of their name and age at the start of a scene reflects Akerman's concern to restore a measure of dignity to those whose bodies have never been found.

The ethereal presence of the silhouette on the wall is echoed a little later by two associated rustling sounds. The first is produced by the folding of paper and the second by stirring tree branches. A group of Mexican men and women are filmed in a restaurant in Naco. One of the men, José Sánchez, has written a speech on behalf of the group, declaring their status as 'illegal migrants' and explaining their reasons for attempting the treacherous crossing. Once the speech is over, José folds up the paper and the rustling sound passes into the following shot, blending horizontally with the muffled sound of tree branches blowing in the wind, alongside the white fence of the border wall at dawn. The sound lingers on, forging an intimate sonic bond between the voicing of collective experience and the dispassionate landscape outside. The sound infuses the exterior environment with a surplus of heavy sorrow, causing the spectator to recall the resilience conveyed by the man's candid words. Indeed, the slow tracking shot requires the spectator to stay present and bear witness to the suffering of the people whose story was recounted moments earlier. As we listen, it becomes impossible to ignore the pinkish glow cast over the fence which starts to resemble blood.

Free-Floating Listening, Border Music and Hybridity

For Trinh, the prospect of hearing beyond the 'all-too-visible' depends on one's ability to receive 'with more than one's eyes or ears' and hear the reverberations of words and ideas 'on many planes at once'.[13] Her theorizing of music and receptivity entails a 'perpetual inter-tuning', a process whereby 'the rhythm of another person is constantly adopted and transformed while the person untunes him/herself to vibrate *into* the music that is being performed'.[14] This relational understanding of musical experience engenders Lipari's rendering of 'feeling with', in the sense of Noddings's notion of empathetic engrossment, whereby the other's feeling (or rhythm) becomes our own. Inter-tuning prevents us from living 'only in a world external to ourselves, so that when we speak, we only speak *out*; when we point, we point to the world out there from a largely unquestioned subjectivity'.[15] It encourages an openness to difference and a willingness to transform ourselves in response to the other's experience.

This musical process of inter-tuning speaks to Akerman's cinematic methods of reconfiguring binary ways of thinking in *De l'autre côté*. She wanted to capture the complexity of the situation of the people she encountered in a non-judgmental manner, by remaining aware of how the socio-political and economic environment influences their perception of themselves and of others. Transcending the simplistic logic of 'taking sides', what attracts Akerman to documentary is the way in which a composite reality can be represented in a manner that resonates with an aspect of the spectator's personal experience.[16] In a revealing text written by Akerman to convince her producer of the film's legitimacy, she mounts a lengthy defence of *De l'autre côté*, while concurrently elucidating her singular conception of documentary form. The material cannot be pre-planned, she insists, but it should float to the surface during the making of the film. The filmmaker must become a sort of sensitive sponge, receptive to the socio-political tensions and the fragility of social relations within the geographical areas and communities she visits. Akerman relates how during the making of the film she developed a method of impartial, free-floating listening, which she terms 'une écoute flottante', in order to avoid the representational biases intrinsic to portrayals of a certain North-American world and a certain Mexican world.[17]

Let us now consider a short musical excerpt that accompanies one of the film's early tracking shots. This shot interrupts the fourth interview of the film that Akerman conducts with a teenager from Mexico who is residing in a detention centre close to the border. In her study of Akerman's sound strategies, Babette Mangolte singles out this intermediary sequence, referring to the shifting audio dynamics that deflect the spectator's attention from the boy's words.[18] Mangolte describes the gradual decrease in sound level as the camera performs a protracted 360-degree turn that starts and finishes close to the metal fence, before cutting back to the interview. Strangely though, 'No se nos ve', the corrido (a Mexican folk ballad) that quietly accompanies this lengthy digression, written and performed by the popular *norteño* band Los Tigres del Norte, is left unmentioned. And yet it produces one of the most telling scenes of storytelling in *De l'autre côté*, acting as the hidden counterpart to the later speech in the restaurant, presciently corroborating José Sánchez's measured statement: 'there are some who have everything and others nothing'. As Anzaldúa notes in *Borderlands/La Frontera: The New Mestiza*, corridos typically feature 'Mexican heroes who do valiant deeds against Anglo oppressors', serving as 'chief cultural mythmakers', entertaining while also chronicling significant current events.[19]

It is pertinent that lyrics from another corrido by Los Tigres del Norte entitled 'El otro México' launch the opening chapter of *Borderlands*, Anzaldúa's hybrid, multilingual text composed in English, Castilian Spanish, the North Mexican

Fig. 9.1. Tracking shot accompanied by 'No Se nos ve', birdsong and ambient sound in *De l'autre côté* (Chantal Akerman, 2002); © Roches Noires Productions

dialect, Tex-Mex and Nahuatl, and that together in their intertwining fashion a new feminist and political language that she names 'the new *mestiza* consciousness'. Inspired by Mexican philosopher José Vasconcelos's theory of a 'cosmic race' that counteracts the concept of racial purity with one of inclusivity, Anzaldúa proposes that from this 'racial, ideological, cultural and biological cross-pollinization', a new *mestiza* 'consciousness of the Borderlands' is produced.[20] The *mestiza* consciousness demonstrates a 'tolerance for contradictions, a tolerance for ambiguity', owing to the Chicana/*mestiza*'s liminal position straddling two social systems on either side of the border, but never feeling fully accepted by either.[21] The *mestiza* consciousness is committed to a plural, relational and holistic cultural perspective, and to the dismantling of subject-object dualisms that imprison those who live 'torn between ways', between countries, languages, cultures and identities.[22]

Los Tigres del Norte have been labelled 'the leading voice of the immigrant community', often assuming the collective voice of Mexican migrants whose struggles and suffering are reflected in the lyrics of their songs.[23] Released on the band's 1983 album *Internacionalmente Norteños!*, 'No se nos ve' translates into English as 'What we don't show (to others)', an awkward rendering due to the non-standard use of grammar in the original that reflects the colloquial speech of the popular classes.[24] Prior to the song's entrance, which seems to emanate from the tracking vehicle's sound system, the camera swerves unsteadily to the left, moving away from the border wall (on the Mexican side), and as it does so we hear a flourish of sonic activity, including crunching gravel, guitar strumming and people talking and laughing, all of which serves to guide our attention to the soundtrack. The camera then settles into a long tracking shot, passing houses, empty buildings, people's backyards and piles of rubble, as if the landscape is haunted by Delfina's account of her son's building projects.

The lyrics comprise a series of repeated statements: 'Not all of us have two eyes / [...] Not all of us have two arms [...]', before the chorus reveals 'What I do think all of us have / It's what we don't show (to others)'. As the song develops, we discover that this hidden facet comprises a basic human need: 'We're thirsty and we want to drink / [...] We're hungry and we want to eat'. Whilst the song expresses feelings of poverty and inequality, highlighting the disparity between 'us' and 'others', it also evokes a shared aspect of human experience to which each of us can relate, tapping into the Chicana/*mestiza*'s ability to empathize with a panoply of perspectives and sidestep the hollow 'duel of oppressor and oppressed',[25] as Anzaldúa explains.

The essential hybridity of *Borderlands* is also evident in its mixing of essays with poetry. On a par with Akerman's constitutive mingling of documentary and fictional audio-visual forms, Anzaldúa's text comprises essays inflected with a poetic aspect, and poetry inflected with a documentary aspect via the poems' recording of factual detail. If we hear *De l'autre côté* through the prism of *Borderlands*, we come to recognise how its unique aural-ethical poetics embodies a powerful means of challenging oppressive discourses and reworking fixed notions of identity through a commitment to multiplicity. Schmid points out that the mixing of different musical genres in the film, and the three different formats in which it was shot, in addition to its incorporation of archival footage, is reflective of the film's 'deliberate hybridism' that contributes to the 'aesthetic of impurity' that is developed and that gives voice to the work's principal themes of exclusion and alterity.[26] Extending this idea, I believe that *De l'autre côté*'s hybrid montage is directly related to the intertextual relationship that Akerman forges between the political aesthetic of her documentary and the dynamic, multi-layered textual form of Anzaldúa's prose.

She is a Storyteller: *Une voix dans le désert*

An important gender shift takes place at the end of the opening chapter of *Borderlands* that is echoed in the final minutes of *De l'autre côté*, a shift that spotlights the figure of the Mexican woman. One of the stanzas in Anzaldúa's opening poem reads: 'This is my home / this thin edge of / barbwire'. This stanza returns to conclude the chapter in a modified form: 'This is *her* home / this thin edge of / barbwire', with the altered layout of words on the page highlighting the pronominal change from 'my' to 'her'.[27] This is matched by Anzaldúa's concluding focus on the potential dangers encountered by the female Mexican migrant (sexual violence, physical and psychological isolation, and economic exploitation). In Akerman's film, the female figure at the centre of the director's own moving storytelling scene is a woman from Mexico who left behind her family and her son, David, to find work in Los Angeles. As she travels she undertakes a series of low-paid jobs, often working as a cleaner and a waitress. At a certain point, the woman stopped sending letters and money home and one day she disappeared, leaving only her coat and rent money behind.

Fig. 9.2. A night-time musical journey to Los Angeles in
De l'autre côté (Chantal Akerman, 2002); © Roches Noires Productions

Akerman's story stands out as the only migration narrative recounted in the film that features a female subject, whose illusive, anonymous and solitary presence alerts the spectator to a female genealogy specific to Akerman's cinema. We recall the travelling filmmaker Anna in *Les Rendez-vous d'Anna* (1978) and the bourgeois housewife Jeanne Dielman in *Jeanne Dielman, 23 Quai du Commerce, 1080 Bruxelles* (1975), whose tidy appearance and well-ironed clothes chime with those of the woman from Mexico. We recall Akerman's reading of her mother's letters in *News from Home* (1976) and the scene in *Toute une nuit* (1982) when Akerman's mother, Natalia, who makes a fleeting appearance, steps outside to smoke, just as the Mexican woman does in Akerman's story. We also think of *No Home Movie* (2015) when the fuses blow in Natalia's apartment, echoing the moment when the fuses blow as the Mexican woman irons while listening to the radio. We are also always thinking of the Belgian-born artist and of her family's particular history of forced Jewish migration.

At the end of *De l'autre côté*, the non-integrated sound of Monteverdi's 'Duo Seraphim' returns. The music was originally scored for three tenors whose voices represent angels (it begins: 'Two seraphim cried out, the one calling to the other'). The rich instrumental voices of Wieder-Atherton and Shakhovskaya join forces with Akerman's gravelly storytelling voice, producing a spiritual and musical burgeoning that marks the film's culminating act of storytelling that spills over into another art work altogether.

The ending of the documentary forms an osmotic, intermedial interface with the contemporary installation *Une voix dans le désert*, which originally comprised a digital video of a 10-metre wide screen positioned on the US-Mexico border in the Sonoran Desert. Onto this screen, the final six minutes of *De l'autre côté* are projected, including infrared surveillance footage of migrants making their crossing and the concluding Interstate 5 highway sequence, accompanied by Akerman's story, which she now reads in English and Spanish as a sort of homage to Anzaldúa's autobiographical, historico-poetic text. As Akerman explains, the idea at the heart of the installation was that from each side of the border one could *hear* the story of David and his mother, with the embedded segment from the documentary looped to play continuously, accentuating the cyclic temporality of the storytelling act.

Une voix dans le désert shares its title with a composition by Edward Elgar, scored for reciter, soprano and orchestra, that premiered in 1916. The piece constitutes Elgar's response to the war-time suffering of the Belgian people and the lyrics derive from a poem of the same name by the exiled Belgian poet Émile Cammaerts. Cammaerts's *Une voix dans le désert* is set close to the trenches along the River Yser and takes as its subject the devastated landscape and bleak consequences of war. The 'voice in the desert' belongs to a Belgian peasant girl who stands in a cottage damaged by shrapnel. She sings a song of hope for a brighter future when bells will ring, flowers will bloom, and normal life will return. Cammaerts's poem also inspired a 1916 war painting called *The Red Cross*, by the Victorian woman artist Evelyn De Morgan, whose symbolic paintings give expression to her spiritualist, feminist and anti-war beliefs.[28] *The Red Cross* is dominated by the figure of Christ who is dressed in red, a symbol of martyrdom and a reminder of the bloodshed caused by war, and he is surrounded by 'a choir of angels' with bright red wings.[29] Behind this vision, the bland memorial crosses of the graves of dead soldiers appear, tinged with red, foreseeing the pinkish glow that appears on the border wall in *De l'autre côté*.

Themes of martyrdom, suffering, redemption and peace, as evoked by De Morgan's painting, and combined with the faint spirit of hope in Cammaerts's poem, are magnificently recreated in the most minimalist of ways by three female artists, Akerman, Wieder-Atherton and Shakhovskaya, whose voices finally collide during this endless dreamlike journey, surrounded by the fiery red glow of car lights. Their voices are doubled by the imagined song of the Belgian peasant girl and Monteverdi's reciprocal calling of angels, producing a polyvocal new beginning in the feminine. This spiritual opening emerges at the intersection of different art forms and responds to the free-floating ear of the wandering spectator. Akerman's act of storytelling serves as a supreme gesture of solidarity with the interviewees in her film. By openly participating in the creative process of telling stories, she ensures that the freedom to imagine and invent dispels of the necessity to tell a story whose purpose is merely to satisfy the other's desire to know.

Paradoxically, the polite but sombre Mexican woman, who 'said little' and 'never stole', at the centre of Akerman's story, is without a story ('There's really nothing to say about her', the director utters). The woman is disconnected, indifferent to her surroundings and difficult to get close to. Nevertheless, Akerman finds more and more to say *with or nearby* her subject, taking the only route that the woman's life permits her to take. Akerman gathers up the banal traces of a life whose political-poetical force exists through its absolute inconsequence. And yet it fashions a unique pattern that curtails and transforms the stultifying logic of the drama of exposure, whose only concern is the confessional content of the speaker's story. This female figure comes to exist cinematically through the director's telling of her story, which puts her into relation with other traces and trajectories of other female figures. The woman's ex-landlady who thought she glimpsed her one day, but who, as she got closer, saw that no-one was there, confirms to us that the female subject of Akerman's story has passed into cinema. She becomes an indistinct but enduring image whose relational existence depends on the spectator's receptive ability to fall into the rhythm of her story, which in turn depends on the expansive gesture of listening.

Notes to Chapter 9

1. Robert Fenz made these comments during a panel discussion held on 14 April 2016 that formed part of the *Chantal Akerman: Contre l'Oubli / Against Oblivion* retrospective in Los Angeles, curated by Bérénice Reynaud. A video of the discussion is available at <https://vimeo.com/164216133> © Déborah Farnault.
2. Ivone Marguiles, *Nothing Happens: Chantal Akerman's Hyperrealist Everyday* (Durham, NC: Duke University Press, 1996), pp. 201–02.
3. Marion Schmid, *Chantal Akerman* (Manchester: Manchester University Press, 2010), p. 115.
4. Research conducted by The Centre for Immigration Research (University of Houston) reveals that during the 1990s, measures were taken to make migration from Mexico to the United States more costly (financially, physically and psychologically) by increasing enforcement on well-travelled routes such as the Interstate 5 corridor that features in *De l'autre côté*, and by forcing migrants to travel through smaller cities, open countryside and desert areas (for example, the Sonoran deserts of Arizona). See Karl Eschbach, Jacqueline Hagan, and Nestor Rodríguez, 'Deaths During Undocumented Migration: Trends and Policy Implications in the New Era of Homeland Security', *In Defence of the Alien*, 26 (2003), 37–52 (pp. 39–40).
5. Lisbeth Lipari, 'Listening Otherwise: The Voice of Ethics', *The International Journal of Listening*, 23 (2009), 44–59 (p. 45).
6. Ibid., p. 52.
7. Ibid., p. 51.
8. Trinh T. Minh-ha, *Cinema Interval* (London: Routledge, 1999), p. 248.
9. Ibid., p. 4.
10. Eve Kosofsky Sedgwick, *Touching Feeling: Affect, Pedagogy, Performativity* (Durham, NC: Duke University Press, 2003), p. 8.
11. Gloria Anzaldúa, *Borderlands/La Frontera: The New Mestiza*, 4th edn (San Francisco, CA: Aunt Lute Books, 2012), p. 19.
12. 'For the rest of them, just asking the question makes them exist already, and acknowledges that there are indeed others who remain unaccounted for.' See Chantal Akerman, *Chantal Akerman: Autoportrait en cinéaste* (Paris: Éditions du Centre Pompidou/Editions Cahiers du cinéma, 2004), p. 94. All translations are my own, unless otherwise noted.
13. Trinh T. Minh-ha, *Elsewhere, Within Here: Immigration, Refugeeism and the Boundary Event* (New York: Routledge, 2011), p. 56.
14. Ibid., p. 57.
15. Ibid., pp. 55–56 (original emphasis).
16. Akerman, *Autoportrait en cinéaste*, p. 93.
17. Ibid., p. 90.
18. Babette Mangolte, 'The Loudness of the World: Listening to What is Out There: Sound Strategies in Akerman's Fiction and Documentary Films', *Senses of Cinema*, 77 (2015) <http://sensesofcinema.com/2015/chantal-akerman/sound-strategies/> [accessed 15 March 2017] (para. 11 of 16).

19. Anzaldúa, *Borderlands/La Frontera*, p. 83.
20. Ibid., p. 99.
21. Norma Élia Cantú and Aída Hurtado, 'Breaking Borders/Constructing Bridges: Twenty-Five Years of *Borderlands/La Frontera*', in Anzaldúa, *Borderlands/La Frontera*, pp. 3–13 (p. 7).
22. Anzaldúa, *Borderlands/La Frontera*, p. 100.
23. Elena Dell'Agnese, '"Welcome to Tijuana": Popular Music on the US-Mexico Border', *Geopolitics*, 20 (2015), 171–92 (p. 178).
24. I am indebted to Liliana Chávez-Díaz for providing a translation of the song title and for her generous correspondence and conversation on the subject. I am also grateful to Natasha Malherbe for her translation of the lyrics and Alex Raynbird for kindly helping me to identify the song.
25. Anzaldúa, *Borderlands/La Frontera*, p. 100.
26. Schmid, *Chantal Akerman*, p. 118.
27. Anzaldúa, *Borderlands/La Frontera*, pp. 25 and 35 (my emphasis).
28. The De Morgan Foundation, 'Evelyn De Morgan' <http://www.demorgan.org.uk/de-morgans/evelyn-de-morgan> [accessed 15 March 2017] (para. 7 of 7).
29. Ibid., 'The Red Cross'. Online at: <http://www.demorgan.org.uk/The%20Red%20Cross> [accessed 15 March 2017]

CHAPTER 10

❖

'Like a Musical Piece':
Akerman and Musicality

Adam Roberts

Chantal Akerman loved music. At times, she would burst into spontaneous song. She wrote the lyrics for the songs in her musical *Golden Eighties*; who can forget her vigorous conducting of the recording of one these songs in *Les années 80*?

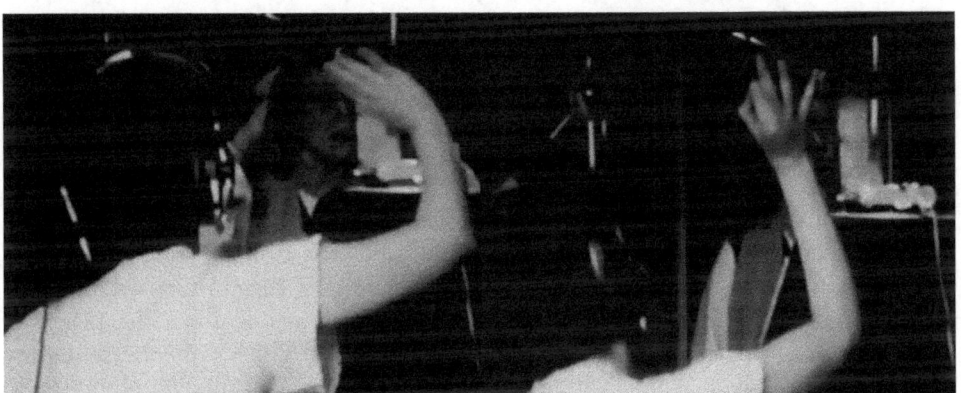

FIG. 10.1. Chantal Akerman conducting Magali Noël in *Les années 80* (1983), Courtesy of Fondation Chantal Akerman © Fondation Chantal Akerman

Akerman's taste in music was eclectic, as evidenced by her use in her films of the classical and romantic repertory (Mozart, Brahms, Beethoven, Schubert or Rachmaninov), twentieth-century composers (Dutilleux), popular songs (touchingly in *Portrait d'une jeune fille de la fin des années 60 à Bruxelles* (1993), *Toute une nuit* (1982), and *Les Rendez-vous d'Anna* (1978)), and the Yiddish songs and tunes in *Dis-moi* (1980) and *Histoires d'Amérique* (1988). Use of music can be regarded as a matter of expression, of a film-maker seeking to qualify rather than structure the experience of a narrative. It is not unusual for film-makers to add music only after the edit is finalised, as enhancement of drama or for the manipulation of emotion.

Akerman was in London during 2015 for preparatory work towards an exhibition of her installation works.[1] I had several conversations with her about music, though sadly did not record them. We touched on Kurtág, Scelsi, Monteverdi, Stockhausen, Morton Feldman, John Cage, Steve Reich and Piaf. Akerman told me that music provided touchstones and points of reference for experience and life. Indeed, Akerman has often made a point by alluding to music, as for instance in a reference to Beethoven's Cello Sonata No. 5 when talking about musical rests: 'You just have to feel [the rest]... it has to go through your own body, then it's your own music.'[2]

Akerman arrived in New York at the start of the 1970s, a young film-maker seeking and finding experimental film on show at Anthology Film Archives. Her encounters with the work of Michael Snow, Andy Warhol and Jonas Mekas were significant. But in New York Akerman also heard music by Philip Glass at an Elizabeth Street loft, as confirmed for me by Babette Mangolte.[3] Akerman's encounter with downtown musical life went deeper, to include Charlemagne Palestine for example, hardly a well-known name.

The questions this chapter will attempt to address include whether music can be said to have had an influence on Akerman's films — that is, on their design, conception and form — and what a musically inflected approach might mean in terms of watching the films, the experience of the films. These are not the same questions, and so the chapter falls roughly into two parts. They are both questions at heart about how the films might be experienced, and about the specific pleasure that makes the works, long and short, such an enduring and relevant body of work.

Structure

Akerman often talked of her work in terms of refusals: the refusal of the reverse angle, the refusal of idolatry, of narrative and characterisation. Beyond this there is her commitment to the quotidian, her commitment to a certain focused attention to such material. If a woman peels a potato, then the act is given the fullest of attention, the peeling of the potato placed centrally for the camera. An empty corridor will be given as much time and emphasis as a human subject. Nondescript letters full of the looping anxieties of a worried mother will be given a commanding place in a sound track.

To give such attention is, I suggest, linked to receptivity: a term embraced by the composer John Cage and others to describe their musical projects. This term marked a revolution in the conceptualisation of what music was. This revolution unfolded principally in New York, informed by encounters with Zen Buddhism, with classical Indian and Indonesian gamelan music, and by developments in fine art. About his seminal work *4'33"* Cage wrote:

> The piece is not actually silent... it is full of sound, but sounds which I did not think of beforehand, which I hear for the first time the same time others hear. What we hear is determined by our own emptiness, our own receptivity; we receive to the extent we are empty to do so.[4]

As early as 1937, Cage had stated:

> Wherever we are, what we hear is mostly noise. When we ignore it, it disturbs us. When we listen to it, we find it fascinating. The sound of a truck at 50mph.

> Static between stations. Rain. We want to capture and control these sounds, to use them, not as sound effects, but as musical instruments.[5]

And, in another text: 'Noises are as useful to new music as so-called musical tones, for the simple reason that they are sounds.'[6]

Cage cited several sources for this thinking, including Zen Buddhism and Robert Rauschenberg's blank white canvases.[7] What they share is that they emphasise music as a phenomenon experienced in the moment, and that there is no sound unworthy of the attention of composer and audience, no hierarchy setting one kind of material above another. Cage made works that employed the sounds of water poured from one vessel to another, or the sounds of radios randomly tuned and switched on and off, or the sounds of a piano which had been 'prepared' so that its familiar classical sonority was sabotaged and made fresh to our ears. And of course, in 1952, he made a break-through work that proposed silence as material.

Cage's *4'33"* structures a set of three silences. One version of the score employs the musical term *tacet*, a term conventionally used to mark a passage where a voice or instrument is silent. There are three *tacets*, of 30", 2'23", and 1'40".[8] These silences are structured by performative gestures; when first performed by a pianist, the keyboard cover was opened and closed. In this way, the audience knew when a 'movement' started and when it stopped. What is the effect? The first 30" silence is tolerable, and novel, even for the most anxious listener. The second silence is an expanse in which thoughts have space and time to erupt, then perhaps subside. A growing and attentive listening to the (never-silent) specific occasion of any performance is what Cage asks of the listener. The third silence is just short of half the duration of the second part, but without a time-piece the experience of time is subjective, defined by (if by anything at all) one's own breath, one's own body and its rhythms. Sounds in the auditorium, or even the weather outside become part of the work.

In this light, it is impossible not to think of the durations and deliberate ratios of Akerman's film-making: for example, that the last shot of *News From Home* (1976), the view from the ferry as it departs from Manhattan, is one ninth of the film. There is no specific reason for this, other than the feeling that it is right given what has come before, which is to say shots whose durations and edit points are not determined by the needs of continuity editing, creating a set of proportions, out of which expectations are established. Everything is arrived at, as Akerman has insisted, by a procedure in which she watches and waits for a feeling within herself that it is time to cut.

A sense of the work as being 'structured', as an object with design, is emphasized by subtle strategies, ranging from the use of formal framings, of non-synch sound, and a sound mix that sometimes omits sound that one might expect (I return to this below).

Cage had relinquished much: 'No harmony. No melody. No counterpoint. No rhythm.'[9] This conception stands in stark contrast to another view of music, what might be termed a romantic ideal, as exemplified by E.T.A. Hoffman:

> Music discloses to man an unknown kingdom, a world having nothing in

common with the external sensual world which surrounds him and in which he leaves behind him all definite feelings in order to abandon himself to an inexpressible longing.[10]

Akerman harboured no such romantic ideals:

> Tu as envie de suivre une fiction parce que tu as été formée comme ça. Tout ce qui fait habituellement fonctionner le spectateur, c'est l'identification au personage. Or, dans mon film, il n'y a pas de héros et pas de narration classique. Ça fonctionne ailleurs, sur des rhythmes, des pulsations, sur le regard, une image en amène une autre, c'est comme dans la musique, tu sais des notes, là tu suis des images, tu ne peux faire qu'une chose, regarder, écouter, et cela te met en question comme spectateur.[11]

Akerman often spoke of 'holes' and 'silences', alluding on the one hand to the gaps in her mother's narrative of her life in the Nazi death camps, but by extension also to her foregrounding of marginalized and silenced voices, and the invisible labours and performances of women and the overlooked inhabiting unremarkable lives (a Brussels housewife, a Mexican factory worker, a community silenced by fear of lynching). Akerman actively sought out and attended to silenced subjects, then devised structures around and depending on silences: silence and absence as materials to work with, the *tacets* of her work invoking the *tacets* of Cages' *4'33"*. Silence is never about the absence of sound, but only ever about that which is unsaid, because something unsaid becomes audible, or visible, in the space made by time.

Form

This moment of experimentation in music was also a moment of experimentation for film-makers in New York, as Akerman witnessed at Anthology Film Archives. Her practice (if the two short films made before travelling to New York in 1972 may be called that) was transformed — *News From Home* and *Hotel Monterey* (1972) reveal her encounter with Snow and Warhol. But, of course, Akerman could be no mere formalist; as a European Jew she was committed to the value of story-telling (*Dis-moi* for example — the clue is in the title).

Since *4'33"* definitions of music have emphasized bodily experience: 'music is the actualization of the possibility of any sound whatever to present to some human being a meaning which he experiences with his body — that is to say, with his mind, his feelings, his senses, his will, and his metabolism.'[12] Akerman, who talked of time experienced in her body as filmmaker, and then in the body of the audience, might well agree. But this definition of music offers no account of form, which Percy Scholes formulated in the *Oxford Companion to Music* as strategies designed to find a successful mean between the opposite extremes of perpetual change and perpetual repetition.[13] That is to say, repetition is a key structural component, with change or difference its counterpart. Cinema had rarely presented such an overtly repetitive structure as Akerman presented in *Jeanne Dielman, 23 quai du Commerce, 1080 Bruxelles* (1975), even if repetition is set up only then to be disrupted. What emerges from such a large scale, and from such carefully foregrounded repetition, is a sense of structure — and I would say musical structure in particular. This matters because it may explain why the experience of *Jeanne Dielman*, and Akerman's films in general, feel so light — the expanse of time, the denial of conventional film narrative, characterization and character interaction simply do not weigh heavily.

More Musically than Realistically

To reiterate, music is a term that proposes difference working against repetition, composition as the placing of musical components so that repetition is relieved. This conception applied to Akerman's practice provides a key to the specific and remarkable pleasure offered by her filmmaking.

Traditionally, and unrelievedly so, cinema chases the story, chases the white rabbit of action. To frame is to frame an action; to cut is to pursue a change; to move from wide shot to close up is to close in on what is of interest. Akerman is not like that. Akerman, to make use of Tarkovsky's useful notion, 'sculpts time'.[14] She is working with rhythm, pulse and timing. She choreographs bodily movement as if working with dancers, creating patterns that have more to do with timing than narrative. Her accounts of directing Delphine Seyrig in *Jeanne Dielman* spring to mind:

> [Delphine Seyrig and I] rehearsed everything in the morning with video. It was very precise: how much time it takes to do this or that... we would look at the tape together, and I would say, "Don't come so close, do that faster, get closer when you do that, do this more smoothly, do that more forcefully". Then it was ready.[15]

This assembling and placing of material is akin to composition, the laying out of activity (or the lack of it) in time. The description above is like the preparation of a score with markings; it is far removed from the conventional film script, which gives dialogue and action only. Perhaps for this reason Akerman often began with a prose text or novel before she devised a shooting script — not because she was working with narrative per se but because a film script was arguably irrelevant to her practice.

Music figures directly in many of Akerman's films. In *Les années 80* (1983) she enters the frame to conduct her singer. She even sings a song herself. From her first film, Akerman demonstrated an acute awareness of sound. Sound became an arresting characteristic of her entire body of work. First we heard her whistling and noted the otherworldly sound mix of *Saute ma ville*, then the percussive foley sounds and footsteps of *Jeanne Dielman* that engrave themselves inescapably into memory of the film, and finally the tormented tree of the opening shot of *No Home Movie* (2015) that has survived harsh desert wind, and is embodied not so much as a visible presence but by the audible roar that buffets the microphone of Akerman's Blackberry, and deafens us in the auditorium. In so many ways sound defines these films. And if sound has value, so does silence: if Akerman decides to play a film or passage mute, it is for a good reason. Both *Hotel Monterey* (1972) and *La Chambre* (1972) play 'silent',[16] although the lesson of 4'33" is that there is no such thing as silence; the audience inevitably brings its own sound track by virtue of being alive — we breathe, we fidget, we cough...

Watching Akerman's films, questions invariably spring to mind: how did she know how long to hold that shot, or why wait so long, but then when change comes, why does that feel so right?

Are these questions about editing, that is, about the joining together of parts of actions to create flow and continuity? I suggest not. These are instead questions about abstract concerns — about proportion, change, rate of change, pulse, time and duration — what can be called musical concerns. Thinking musically (not as an editor creating a sequence) is embodied, for example, in advice from a composer: 'not only must there be rate of change, but the rate of change must change'[17] — a kind of thinking that seems to point best to an answer to the question about shot duration.

Akerman, talking about the soundtrack for her *News From Home*, once pointed out that: 'It was like a musical piece. We see one car — but the sound is not totally [in] synch... I put the sound more musically than realistically.'[18]

Indeed, looking closely at the film — for which the sound was recorded 'wild' (that is, recorded separately from the shooting of the pictures and only later fitted to the edited sequences) — we can see that sound may well look like it is in sync, as we might expect if picture and sound were recorded at the same time. But then we see that it is not, and that the fact is not hidden. In fact, even within a single shot, the expected sound may at times be present and correct for one pass of a car, but then be missing in the next. Moreover, sound comes and goes, not always on the cut, as Akerman was carefully pointing out.

Turning now to the sound mix in *News From Home*: the voice — Akerman's own voicing of her mother's words — drifts in and out of audibility, drowned out at times by rising city sounds, but revealed again as the city sounds fade. It is as if the murmured maternal *obbligato* is a constant. It is the city sounds — the sounds of the observable world — that rise and fall; it is the city's sounds that are provisional. They are — to use a musical term — *ad libitum*. This is the reverse of usual editing practice in film making, where the picture is conventionally cut along with the dialogue track. Only later are *ambient sounds* and the *spot sound effects* added — these are sounds that we take for granted, not intended to be noticeable but giving the illusion of reality. Indeed, they are often added by an assistant, someone other than the picture editor. In *News From Home* by contrast, it is Akerman's voice that is laid in throughout, like a drone track, sound that can be taken for granted.

The soundtrack level changes, the coming and going of the various sounds, discernibly so, produce for me a picture of Akerman in the sound studio moving faders up and down as if playing a piano. The effect is of sound patterns woven, worked with like warp and weft, as if making a rug whose pattern becomes visible only with a step back. The phase of the patterns and the play of the patterns are a design that we apprehend, that I feel to be as important as the choreographic coming and going of the cars, or the opening and closing of automatic doors, or the to and fro of passengers idling on a platform.

I believe it is the missing aural elements that give the clue to this act of weaving. Without the absent synch, I suspect, the film's procedures, its structure, would not register in the same way. These observations have a bearing on all of Akerman's work. The pleasures of the work derive in great part from the sense of design, and purposeful design at that, the sense of time lending value to the moments, and the rhythms of the structure overall lending vitality to the parts.

Patterns

So much for the sense in which the warp and weft of Akerman's work can be said to be musical. What of the audible presence of the musical in her work?

Sonia Wieder-Atherton is a cellist of the top rank. Since the early 80s she was also Akerman's companion and collaborator. Wieder-Atherton appears first in the enigmatic short *Rue Mallet-Stevens* (1986), where she is both protagonist and performer. Music, as embodied by Wieder-Atherton, is presented as a matter of hard work, of technique, as a striving for mastery. We know that because she must practice, or at least repeat. Music, as a practice and a discipline, is part of what bodies can do, demonstrating a mysterious inner potential. But music can be beguiling and expressive.

In another short film, *Trois strophes sur le nom de Sacher* (1989), Wieder-Atherton enters, cello in hand, to perform the music by Henri Dutilleux. The music is extraordinarily beautiful, beguiling, sinuous and utterly disarming in its apparent simplicity. Wieder-Atherton, wonderfully, performs this with complete focus and poise, her cello tuned to other-worldly scales. Akerman places Wieder-Atherton in a room, with drapes, evoking a proscenium arch. In the background are windows, looking across to the wall and windows of another building. The windows reveal other rooms, interiors, with inhabitants. These characters appear and disappear, coming and going. They interact, in a play of minimalist gestures and meticulous choreographies. The music, the performance, the actions are carefully organized in counterpoint (counterpoint is usually defined as the relationship between parts or voices that are interdependent harmonically yet independent in rhythm and contour). Those are the heterogeneous materials that Akerman is working with. No narrative intent, though narrative may be guessed at: no chasing of actions and incident, no hierarchy of interest. It is a film built around a structure, surely a totally musical structure.

Another little screened yet marvellous film is a performance/lecture — *Les Trois dernières sonates de Franz Schubert* of 1989 — by one of the greatest pianists of any age, Alfred Brendel. Brendel talks about the musical features of the three piano sonatas by Schubert. He talks of the music's melodic charms and relationship with the work of other masters. He touches on the fact that these are Schubert's three last works for piano, but points out that Schubert could not have known when he wrote them that they would be his last works. He also relates how these works were not performed in Schubert's day, how they were then lost, only later to be recovered, and, how in modern times, their nature and importance as compositions were grasped and now are taken for granted.

Brendel's manner throughout is calm, striking in its simplicity and directness; his composure the fruit of life-long absorption in his subject. Akerman's filmmaking is in a similar vein — simple, direct, nuanced, and rhythmical without excessive force or emphasis. Every edit is perfectly judged, the ebb and flow of attention perfectly supportive. This is a film in tune. It is a musically felicitous construction — a counterpoint of attention, polite distance and receptive interest — that allows the insights of Brendel's talk to shine. Akerman's restraint is that of an accompanist who knows she must support the soloist, and yet success always depends on balance. Brendel says that he finds in the sonatas, 'a combination of the formal and psychological as there should be in all great music', a striking generalisation that might seem to capture something of Akerman's art.

Le Déménagement (1992) was shot for ARTE, the European TV station, one of a series of monologues commissioned from various filmmakers. Akerman directed and wrote the script for her film. She makes use of a restrained number of shots and angles on a man who has just moved into a new apartment, but who has yet to unpack because he is afflicted by uncertainty and doubt: 'Je n'aurais jamais dû, jamais dû déménager. Qu'est-ce qui m'a pris? J'étais bien dans l'autre. Presque. Non, la plupart du temps, j'étais mal, pas là. Fallait déménager.'[19]

Le Déménagement is a densely woven soliloquy of indecision and regret, of a dread sense of predicament that is inescapable. Through this protagonist, Akerman reflects on the impossibility of making decisions, on the forlorn hope of certainty. It is a project that seems to owe much to Samuel Beckett, that great dramatist of indecision and the inescapable. But what strikes the viewer is the patterning of the shots, the frequent cuts to black, the rhythm and pacing of the text. Sami Frey's performance as a man imprisoned by existential despair is remarkable, a bravura performance depending on subtle and nuanced use of voice and timbre. His control is absolute as he works within Akerman's structure. He provides the audible pulse, while Akerman works with image and timing. The past is a prison that must be remembered and raked over forever, for there is nothing else. This is to say that the music Akerman conjures up is an inescapable melody, composed with such precision, that to start is to be held (surely?) in its grip until the close.

La Captive is a late feature film by Akerman, released in 2000, a reworking of the fifth volume of Proust's *À la recherche du temps perdu* (*In Search of Lost Time*), called *La Prisonnière* (*The Prisoner* or *The Captive*). Put simply, the film tells the story of a wealthy dilettante named Simon, living in a fine apartment with his elderly grandmother and housekeeper. A group of workmen are noisy, moving ladders and tools around for reasons that are never clear. Living here too, on a not so comfortable looking divan, is Simon's lover Ariane, called at night to Simon's bed by means of an intercom, where she invariably falls asleep (or seems to) while Simon indulges in stolen kisses and frottage, lying astride her like some nightmare vampire. Having exhausted himself, Simon wakes Ariane to send her back to her cramped divan.

But Simon's mastery is an illusion. Simon is driven to distraction by jealousy and curiosity. He is not above stalking Ariane if she leaves the apartment, or sending friends to escort Ariane, and then to quiz them as to every detail of Ariane's movements. If Ariane takes a singing lesson, Simon wants to know who else attended and exactly what was sung. He is convinced above all that Ariane is a lesbian and that she is in love with another woman, in particular with an actress of fame (played by Akerman's regular collaborator Aurore Clément). Crisis comes when Simon listens on the radio to a live transmission from the theatre where he knows Ariane is watching the actress take the lead in a play. Rapturous applause is intolerably loud in Simon's ears, and in a torment of jealousy he rushes to the theatre to pull Ariane away and beleaguer her with questions. The situation cannot continue and he ruthlessly despatches her from the apartment. Or rather he does so only then to change his mind, and whisk her off to a hotel in Biarritz, offering her the promise of travel to exotic places. Ariane agrees to his every suggestion, before going for a swim. She never returns. Simon believes her drowned. His desire and jealousy have come to nothing.

The film is remarkable for many reasons, but best seen in an auditorium where the Dolby optical sound track can be heard as intended: uncompressed and played back at a high level without distortion, as it was mixed and intended to be heard. Loud soundtracks with great dynamic range (that is the interval between loud and quiet), are now the norm in mainstream commercial cinema, yet in the classic era of cinema sound tracks could not reproduce greatly varied volume levels, and cinema until the advent of Dolby was a cinema of compressed sound. A crash was not much louder than a whisper. When digital technology arrived, a huge expansion of dynamic range became possible. Explosions can now be felt, let alone heard.

Arthouse cinema has not much worked with sound outside of the demands of the naturalistic sound track. That is to say, soundtracks are made to provide a pleasing sense of 'being invisibly present', of sitting in the best seat in the house, able to hear what is important, without disruption of the illusion. Every sound is explicable, and adds to the carefully contrived suspension of disbelief. Even the birdsong heard in the distance will be season and location appropriate. At times, music may displace other sounds, but the mix is always genteel. Sounds made by the rub of fabric or the fall of footsteps are placed discreetly amid atmospheric background noises. Distant waterfalls are heard in the distance. A close-up of fingers tapping are heard as if from inches away. Voices are always heard front and centre. The perceived geography is rarely confounded by the sound world.

Akerman's *La Captive* is strikingly different, perhaps without peer, resulting in an experience that is overwhelming. The stifling claustrophobic apartment with its creaking eighteenth-century floorboards, with its many doors noisily opening and closing, with its parade of bothersome workmen coming and going, with its impossible to chart geography in an airless, confined labyrinth — this is a luxuriantly furnished prison. The viewer simply cannot find the exit. No one can move unheard; voices from other rooms can be heard from everywhere. From his bed Simon several times talks with his grandmother even though she is elsewhere in her own bedroom. The laws of nature do not apply here — this is a non-Euclidian space, revealed by aural means only. The shortest trajectory may not be a straight line.

Protagonists come and go, though if they do, they walk briskly. Especially out of doors. Paris by night is a terrain of shadows, blind alleys, inexplicable connections and intersections. To try and recreate the nocturnal stalking, the route taken, would be folly. The Paris of this film is a nightmare imagined by De Chirico. The sounds tell us that progress is made, but the visible world does not confirm that. In one brilliantly memorable shot, the shadow of Ariane moves one way across a wall, yet is seen moving in the other direction at the same time. The sound meanwhile does not recede. Seeing and hearing this, Simon is dumbstruck. What exotic metaphysics is this?

The thing that sets this film ablaze however is the sound world. To note:

- Foreground and background sound mixed equally loudly.
- All sounds democratically organised — nothing dramatic displaces anything less so.
- Sounds are not shaped within scenes — if present they stay evenly until the scene ends.
- If one sound predominates it is played full volume.
- Quiet passages are very quiet.
- Rustles and footsteps are loud, in the foreground.
- Sound is not much panned to follow action, as is the norm for naturalistic soundtracks.
- Loud and quiet are set in stark contrast.

The soundtrack builds to climaxes in volume and density of sound, which then ebb away. If one charts sound levels against time, a three-part structure is revealed: thirds separated by two quiet passages. The last third is busy with wild extremes in sound level, and marked by two discernible, measurable crises. This much is visible in the graph, and reflects subjective experience of the film: emotion and intensity a matter as it were of measurable phenomena. The sound crew should be applauded,[20] although very sadly the names of the studio foley artists (those who make the rustles and footsteps for the sound track) are not listed in the credits, though their performances define the film.

This sound track is self-conscious. It does not strive for the invisibility of a naturalistic sound track. It presses itself upon the film spectator, startling in its strange and painfully acute registration of every nuance. It is brash. It is about underlying structural features — we are supposed to notice everything, we have no choice. It is like the painfully detailed and sharp experience of the clinically depressed, where the sound of a sweet paper screwed up at the other end of a bus can be unbearable. The sound world relentlessly highlights the noises that are made, that tap out rhythmically, that impose themselves. The sound world shapes all, conducts experiments and enquires, imposes its technological mastery to separate and create order. Sound enfolds all and creates unity. The option to separate and disappear into silence, to remove ourselves without audible clue is absent. Above all, the questioning will never cease. The film portrays perfectly a very male mode of enquiry — brash and inescapable.

La Captive also includes music. Rachmaninov's great romantic symphonic poem *The Isle of the Dead* is much used, part of it repeated over and over again (as well it should in a modernist project that wishes us to register the presence of design). The music never blends in: it blares, with the full weight of the dynamic range of the soundtrack technology and of the orchestra. Schubert's *Arpeggione Sonata* is played too, turned on and off, on screen, by Simon using a remote control. The volume level is set always high. Simon and Ariane listen: so must we.

And Mozart's opera *Così fan tutte* supplies an aria, sung by the (caged bird) Ariane from her open window in duet with an unseen neighbour, much to the irritation of Simon who catches it on his way out. In the opera, Dorabella and Fiordiligi sing about playing games with their lovers (*Prenderò quel brunettino*), taking more pleasure in their conspiracy than in the men's affections they so casually sport with. For the film, the singing is without accompaniment, sung into the night, from separate spaces, the sound reverberating from walls. It is without direction, and inexplicably placed. The singing is untutored, in Italian — and unsubtitled (at it least not so for the French release). We are supposed to hear, not listen — the plot of the opera is irrelevant, unless we know it as the duet about how women conspire and enjoy each other — but then Simon's reaction gives us all that.

The word 'disquiet' is about a feeling of worry or unease. It suggests as much by invoking the idea of sound — to dis-quiet is to mar silence. The silence that Ariane might presumably long for is marred by the tyranny of sound. *La Captive* is a film above all about anxiety, about the predicament of a woman caught and forced to respond to questions, given no space to answer, no time to answer — and about a man who cannot stop speaking or asking, who gives no time, and demands control of time. His sound is endless, her silence denied. The dis-quiet we experience becomes the embodiment of the situation. The dyad is insufferable. We hear, and feel, as much — in our bones.

Coda

To conclude, sound in Akerman's films is a material to work with. It is stuff just as much as angle and point of view. But the structures which Akerman weaves are made in ways that invoke a sense of the musical, a sense of having been composed. Rhythm, for example, is a matter of proportion, not of accent, as the pianist Artur Schnabel said.[21] And in Akerman's films, rhythm is just like that.

Akerman, like Cage, did not repudiate the body — not her own, nor that of her subjects, nor that of the audience. Time, Akerman said often, was to be felt in every body, in the bones. Akerman raises all gestures to an equal standing, and organises her material musically in order to maintain her grip and command that we might see every gesture as it is for what it is. Without such compositional methods to peel a potato might then be simply to peel a potato.

Notes to Chapter 10

1. *Chantal Akerman: NOW*, curated by Adam Roberts & Joanna Hogg (A Nos Amours), Michael Mazière (Ambika P3), 30 October–6 December 2015 at Ambika P3.
2. <https://mubi.com/notebook/posts/interview-with-chantal-akerman>, interview by Ricky D'Ambrose.
3. Mangolte, a noted photographer, was the first person Akerman met in New York. Mangolte introduced Akerman to the downtown scene, and became Akerman's cinematographer, shooting, among others, *Jeanne Dielman*.
4. John Cage letter to Helen Wolff, April 1954. (c) 2013 John Cage Trust.
5. 'The Future of Music: Credo' (1937), in John Cage, *Silence: Lectures and Writings by John Cage* (Middleton, CT: Wesleyan University Press, 1961), p. 3.
6. John Cage, 'History of Experimental Music in the United States', in *Silence*, p. 68.
7. Rauschenberg's *White Paintings* (1951), whose emptiness Cage noted (in *Silence*, p. 98), made them a means to register nuanced and subtle circumstances of light, dust in the air and so on.
8. Woodstock score (1952), Source Edition (1967), Kremen MS (1953) & Peters edition 6777a, 1993. The Tacet Editions (1960, 1986) give 33", 2'40", 1'20". For an assessment of the various scores see <http://solomonsmusic.net/4min33se.htm>.
9. John Cage, 'Lecture of Something', in *Silence*, p. 132.
10. 'Beethoven's Instrumental-Musik', in E.T.A. Hoffmann, *Sämtliche Werke*, ed. by C. G. von Maassen, transl. by Bryan R. Simms, 9 vols (Munich: G. Müller, 1908), I, p. 127.
11. 'We follow stories because this is what we are trained to do; as spectators we habitually identify with characters. With my films, on the other hand, there are no protagonists and no familiar stories. What is happening lies elsewhere: in the rhythm, in the pulse, in the point of view. One image precedes another, like notes in music. Images are notes. You have only to look and listen — and that calls into question your role as spectator' (Martine Storti, 'Un entretien avec Chantal Akerman', *Libération*, 20 June 1977).
12. Thomas Clifton, *Music as Heard: A Study in Applied Phenomenology* (New Haven: Yale University Press, 1983), p. 1.
13. Percy Scholes, *Oxford Companion to Music*, ed. by John Owen Ward, 10th edn (Oxford: Oxford University Press, 1970), p. 370.
14. Andrey Tarkovsky, *Sculpting in Time: Reflections on the Cinema*, trans. by Kitty Hunter-Blair (London: Bodley Head, 1986).
15. Unpublished interview with Janet Bergstrom, 27 June 1989, quoted in Gwendolyn Audrey Foster, ed., *Identity and Memory: the Films of Chantal Akerman* (Carbondale: Southern Illinois University Press, 2003), p. 108.
16. Akerman had no clear memory or interest in an alternative sound track version of *La Chambre*, though the text of it survives.
17. Kevin Volans, unrecorded conversation in London, 2000.
18. Interview with Akerman by Ricky d'Ambrose, November 2013: <https://vimeo.com/78547046> [accessed 26 March 2018].
19. 'I should never, never have moved. What got into me? I was happy before. Well, almost. No, mostly I was not. Not good at all. I had to move.'
20. Nicolas Becker (sound effects editor), Thierry de Halleux (location sound), Jean-François Schenegg (location sound assistant), Valérie Deloof (supervising sound editor — as Catherine de Loof), Assia Dnednia (assistant sound editor), Agnes Rave (assistant sound editor — as Agnès Raves), Nicholas Becker (sound engineer), Eric Ferret (post synch sound recording engineer), Martin Boissau (post synch sound assistant), Stéphane Thiébaut (sound mixer). The sound mixing facility was *Les Audis de Joinville*, built by Paramount Studios in the 1930s, in the suburbs to the east of Paris. It played a key part in the making of so many French films; its logo was all but ubiquitous in the end credits. It was closed in 2010, the work rolled up into the *Studios de Boulogne*, near the Pont de Saint-Cloud on the other side of the city. The team that made this sound track were old hands, whose credits are countless.
21. Clifford Curzon, who had been a pupil of Schnabel's, quoting his master in John Gillespie and Anna Gillespie, *Notable Twentieth-Century Pianists: A Bio-Critical Sourcebook*, 2 vols (Westport, Conn: Greenwood Press, 1995), II, p. 793.

CHAPTER 11

Light out of Joint

Cyril Béghin

In 2009, in a poetical director's statement for her video installation *Maniac Summer*, Chantal Akerman describes a sort of burst of images prior to their extinction, like an ultimate remanence before darkness. *Maniac Summer* is the mysterious vision of a ruin of light. It is, she writes, 'un film qui se multiplie au moins quatre fois, parfois cinq quand il est pris dans la catastrophe, quand la vitesse de la lumière semble être dépassée. Comme à Hiroshima. Et comme à Hiroshima, il laisse des traces, mais en devenir. Un film qui explose et glisse avant de mourir.'[1]

The mention of Hiroshima is surprising on several levels. First, there is, with reference to another disaster, the use of disproportionate analogies, metaphors and allusions that make the spectre of the Nazi death camps and the tragedies of Jewish history a key reference point in many of Akerman's films, under often terrible (*D'Est*) and sometimes displaced or grotesque traits — even the everyday smoke from chicken roasting in a kitchen unleashes tragic associations, in *Demain on déménage*. The other surprise is that the catastrophe summoned up in the exaggerated confines of the small installation isn't the genocide of Europe's Jews. This is a trend of the last years of Akerman's work, which opens itself up to different historical memories, including racism in the United States (*Sud*), illicit Mexican migration (*De l'autre côté*) and colonialism in Asia (*La Folie Almayer*).

Still, whichever way you look at it, *Maniac Summer* doesn't portray the actual impact of an atomic bomb. What follows, starting from and in juxtaposition with everyday views of Paris or the interior of the director's apartment, in summer, is a series of visual events: blow-ups, negatives and high-contrast monochromes by which we eventually see, in the distorted images projected onto the walls, a defamiliarized resemblance to the shadows that explosion's flash burned on the ground and walls, replacing the vaporized bodies and objects with a final trace. Sometimes these images fall or slide along the walls, disappearing towards the ground like something being shed. Without the note from the director, however, it would have been difficult to make the metaphorical leap between installation and bomb. Akerman's pointer is deliberately over the top. In setting out a link between elements that are factually and morally incommensurate, she attempts to harness the power of their smallest similarity: the uncontrollable overflowing of light and the threat of distortion. Rather than the analogy with photographic print that is generally evoked with regard to Hiroshima's shadows, the installation favours this deadly 'becoming'. Trivial views of a Parisian summer join Hiroshima's tragic summer in a visual burning.

The Jewish tradition of forbidding representation — often cited, including by the director herself, to account for her minimalism, her productions of absence and her taste for oral evocation — doesn't result in total prohibition or iconophobia. Light, in particular, is an intermediary fact, between representation and abstraction, liable to open up aesthetic feeling to an apprehension of the invisible.[2]

In cinema, and in the arts of projection in general, dazzlement is an aesthetic apogee, in which the excess of the image's presence, in the sense of its 'praesens' as defined by George Didi-Huberman, merges with its destruction.[3] In the nuclear metaphor outlined in the director's statement for *Maniac Summer*, the mysteriously 'overwhelmed' speed of light accomplishes, in a certain sense, what is forbidden immediately after having produced the traces. Does this notion of a smashed light speed, taken 'off its hinges', or, to use the Shakespearean phrase, '*out of joint*', eventually testify to, and amplify, an aspect of Akerman's work that is rarely commented upon — the work of light in its various relationships to the possibility of representation? Akerman perhaps has a secret relationship with the Mosaic precept, which manifests itself in her use of light as a tool with which to put into question the production of images, at once a motif of contemplation and a motif of dazzlement or fascination that prevents seeing — light, before illuminating forms, can seize the gaze and block it, 'making a screen'.[4] Light has always been discreetly unbalanced in Akerman's films, but *Maniac Summer* inscribes it furiously on the gallery walls, like long-emitted radiation suddenly accelerated.

What Real Time?

Why say that light has always been subtly broken down, in the work of a director known above all for her scrupulous realism, to say nothing of 'hyperrealism', of documentary truth and real time? Even before considering this apparent paradox, we encounter two obstacles. For one, there's the rarity of aesthetic studies that are wholly consecrated to light in a director's work, outside the more historical application of broader characteristics associated with movements or techniques. The field is fallow and leaves little to work with. For another — and the two are linked — there's a reticence in the face of a body of work that, considered from the point of view of light, seems radically uneven, constantly switching between natural light and the artifice of studio filming, varying directors of photography, and devising installations as a further way to organize light in space and time. Given this disunity, we will take a transverse view of Akerman's oeuvre, not splitting it up, and we will take it as read that her films and installations explore the same aesthetic problems. In the absence of a conceptual framework, we must fall back on describing the films and installations with light in mind, such that this chapter will often resemble a series of case studies more than an argument.

We could start our journey very early, right from the overly vivid white kitchen of *Saute ma ville*, but it's from the 1990s above all that Akerman's light-craft becomes

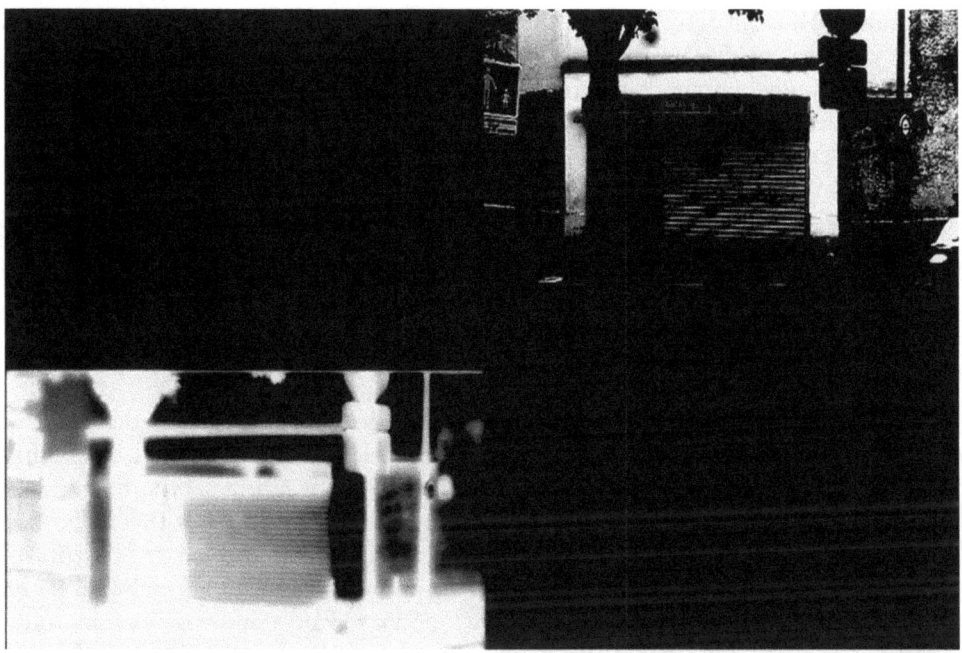

Fig. 11.1. Chantal Akerman, *Maniac Summer* (2009), Courtesy Marian Goodman Gallery, Paris/ New York/ London © Fondation Chantal Akerman

more explicit, growing ceaselessly more complex right up to recent years, in *La Folie Almayer* (2011), *No Home Movie* (2015) and the installation *Now* (2015). Akerman's first video installation, *D'Est. Au bord de la fiction* (1995) is often designated as a pivot point, leading to a resurgence of experimentation twenty years after the American ventures of *Hotel Monterey* (1972), *La Chambre* (1972) and *News From Home* (1976). But with light in mind, one ought instead to consider the installation *D'Est* as a part of a series that began with *Nuit et jour* (1991), of which the script (a young woman sustaining two lovers, one by day, the other by night) is the pretext for tight cutting between natural and artificial lighting, the night-time scenes often filmed outdoors in Paris, the daytime scenes indoors and in the studio, with a clear taste for artifice and the proliferation of different ambiences. In *Je tu il elle* (1975), *Jeanne Dielman* (1975) and *Les Rendez-vous d'Anna* (1978), Akerman smooths the joins between natural and artificial, corresponding more or less with the shifts between outdoor and indoor shots — the films weren't primarily concerned with their alternation. And in *Toute une nuit* (1982), *Golden Eighties* (1986) and *Histoires d'Amérique* (1988), artificial lighting served a unity of time (night) or place (the shopping mall). *Nuit et jour*, by contrast, and often playfully, messing around with the resources of the studio and paying homage to the theatrical tricks of painted backdrops and atmospheric reenactments, transforms the natural cycle of light into a collage of small sensations, depicted mainly as unique moments, in the hinge between stylization and illusionism. Here, the feeling of presence that some shots produce has nothing to do with 'praesens' but with 'reality effects' that strangely combine with reality itself. We see in it the overly gilded, overly static brightness of an evening 'mock sun' bathing someone's face, or the touched-up blue dawn passing through openwork shutters over the bodies of lovers in a studio, while the night-time strolls of the characters are dominated by the various flutterings and multi-coloured reflections of car headlights and Paris streetlights. These rapid switches between night and day supply no solution to the love triangle, the usual metaphors being out of order: the seductions of the night aren't diluted by the clarity of the day, no more than the cruelty of daylight is softened by nocturnal comfort. The outcome is that, on 'another day', under a real early morning sun, the female character exits alone, in a long closing tracking shot, just as *Golden Eighties* concludes with a step into natural light after having wallowed entirely in the electric light of the shopping mall.

In this way *Nuit et jour* makes a strange proposition: what is presented as the real time of light — that, for example, of its earth cycle — is fundamental, inscribing itself in the title, but also misleading, necessitating a way out in the form of an escape. Light's foundational temporality becomes a stifling fiction. Even the fact of nature requires renewal, in an aesthetic sensibility controlled by repetition, obsession and haunting.[5] Opposed to the composite cycle of nights and days is the duration of the final shot, which allows the woman to find a sense of freedom under another light, enjoying her walk alone as much as the serene insistence of a sun that seems more real. The light, not yet quite 'off its hinges', is therefore doubled, and this duplicity isn't reducible to a straight contrast between natural and artificial or significance and insignificance, such binaries being complicated by the play of cycles, durations and speeds.

When it comes to light, Akerman isn't a purist in the manner of Straub and Huillet, in whose work practices mix only very seldom, even in a hybrid film like *Amerika*. In Akerman's films, what is natural or artificial degrades gently and awaits sudden bursts. We see it shortly after *Nuit et jour* in *D'Est* (1993), in which the geographical journey toward Russia is figured as a plunging into night and electric lighting. The first shot, after the credits, shows a roadside and a tree through an open window somewhere in a generic countryside. It's in broad daylight, and the prolonged duration of the fixed shot allows a gradual shift in the quality of the sunlight, a 'false tint' that in cinema is one of the most powerful ways to capture real light in its duration, a sort of ontological hallmark. This, however, proves to be the only one in the film, establishing a limit beyond which the invariability of pale skies and urban lighting prevails. Over the course of its silent tracking shots, *D'Est* captures the waiting and despondency of the innumerable bodies that loiter, as much as the chill of the lights under which they stand: it is a 'journey to the end of the night' after the fall of the Wall, but a night of street lights and greenish neons, of wan lighting in vast train stations, and wide muddy streets punctuated by dirty glimmers. We expect a switch to daytime that seems as if it will never return, or the emergence of a sign among the repetitive sequence of lights, but in the duration of the shots a few pale mornings and infinite variations of street lighting have replaced the event of a solar flush and a false tint. Light's temporality has turned into a slow hypnotic blinking organized by the movements of the camera and the editing.[6]

Fig. 11.2. Chantal Akerman, *D'Est* (1993)

Nuit et jour and *D'Est* thus established, at the start of the 1990s, a vague but suggestive principle of Akerman's cinema, already present in some earlier films but never with such simplicity. In these films light becomes a dramaturgical element purely by the effect of its difference, or relationship, to itself, and rarely by its straightforward symbolic link to the thing it illuminates or obscures. This is what we earlier called its 'duplicity'. The daytime lover could be the night-time lover and it would change nothing; and throughout the pale nights of *D'Est* all types of postures and situations are captured. There are, of course, fundamental metaphors: going out in broad daylight or sinking into the night. But without duplicity they will stay flat or short of effect. Light, in its apparent indifference, more or less polished and sublime, comes to produce significations and emotions it initially lacks, by dint of its insistence, its rhythms and its metamorphoses, variously developed in the duration of the shots and in the duration of the films and the spaces that host these shots. This principle was carried to the full in the 2000s, in the installation *Une voix dans le désert* (2002) and the film *Là-bas* (2006). In the first, the nocturnal finale of the documentary *De l'autre côté* (a long tracking shot on an American highway, accompanied by the voice of Akerman recounting the story of a Mexican migrant) is projected onto a screen raised at the border between the United States and Mexico at sunrise: the film's night gradually disappears in the growing light, while the shot's uncut duration melts in the real-time dawn. In diluting the film that is being projected onto the screen, the light seems to vaporize its story in space, as the sound reverberates around the installation, joining the memory of those who have died in the desert as victims of smugglers and the politics of immigration. The film becomes a monument to the moment of its luminous death, pursuing a calm dazzlement.

In *Là-bas*, the relationship is that between the shadow inside an apartment in Tel-Aviv in which the director is holed up alone, and the violent sun outside, modulated by the Venetian blinds through which Akerman films almost exclusively the buildings opposite, the street, a few distant silhouettes that become the basis of an autobiographical *dérive* in voiceover, and an evocation, at bottom, of the neuroses of Israeli society. The apartment is transformed into a 'camera obscura' in which the shutter serves as a filter or interface, blurring the burning of daylight and imprinting it with different rhythms, by the graphical play of the horizontals between which the gaze circulates, or by its movements, when a breeze disturbs it. The prolonged duration of the shots is that of a stubborn fascination, at once childlike and depressive, with the micro-variations of the light and the surface of the image, that threaten to drown the viewer's attention in a myopic and hypnotic torpor even more brutal than that of *D'Est*. Without the shutter, the imperturbable fragment of sunshine would be dazzling, it would prevent sight; but with the shutter, the temporality of the light perverts itself, boggling perception, diverting from what it illuminates while enabling meditation from every detail, every anonymous silhouette on what the director is talking about, the history of Israel. The contrast has never been greater, between grand history and minuscule play of light, between the sun reigning everywhere and the device that allows one to filter it for oneself.

We must go back. Because the destiny of dazzlement and the intellectual plunge of light is already fully formulated in the last key work of the 1990s, the installation *D'Est, au bord de la fiction*. A first room shows the film *D'Est* in its entirety, the second disperses it over twenty-four different video monitors, and the final room adds to it a long shot ('the 25th image') accompanied by Akerman's voiceover, the image passing slowly from the view of a street at night, under the light of a street lamp, to a sort of luminous abstraction 'quand cette lueur arrivée en très gros plan est comme à son tour irradiée par la neige de l'image vidéo'.[7] The confrontation with the screens in the second room, arranged in a triangle pointing towards the background, keeps the singularity of each shot out of sight and ushers us into a chaos of movement and brightness. The views of night and day, of street illumination and domestic lighting rub shoulders without apparent logic, forcing connections, demolishing the sense of slow progression through the darkness produced by the film. Above all the installation imposes on the film a *permanent explosion of light*. This dislocation prepares us for the final room, where there remains, at the end, nothing but the faint light of the video and the voice intoning, among other things, the Mosaic precept 'Tu ne feras pas d'idole...' (You shall not make for yourself an idol...), confirming the strange duplicity established between the phantasmal return, over the different shots, of the *'primal scene'* of exoduses and evacuations in the Second World War, and its recovery by something akin to an abstract version of that which Akerman calls 'des images plus lumineuses, et mêmes radieuses' (brighter, even radiant images).[8] The time that the visitor has taken to move from room to room becomes that of a sinuous rise of light until the first shot, in which the only illumination comes from the video itself. In this way the installation sets up, like a slow process, an affinity between dazzlement and the prohibition of the image.

Forms of Light

It would, however, be too easy to link, in the entire oeuvre, the fate of light to the accomplishment of the unrepresentable. Duplicity never resolves itself in ethical terms, just as hypnotic fascination doesn't systematically end with an elevation of its subject, far from it. Simon, at the start of *La Captive*, plays and replays a few silent shots from a holiday film, home alone in the dark, with a projector that he manipulates to rerun the 'bright images' of the woman he loves, Ariane, and to make her say a 'je vous aime bien' that she perhaps hasn't said. He sets up a flickering that shatters the duration of the shots to give them another rhythm before taking place in front of the projected image appearing to us in black silhouette, under the effect of the backlight. Simon's obsession could thus come down in abstract fashion to a desire to imprint a shape in the light — a vain, excessive desire that comes to pass in the film's closing shot of a bleak dawn in which he has lost Ariane.

Before introducing the spectator to the smallest visual sensations; before enabling reverie and thoughts and perhaps even associative visions following procedures close to hypnosis; before leading to an eventual dazzlement that is redemptive or catastrophic; before all that, the rhythms of the light can, more trivially, numb and stupefy, absorb and flatten perception. *Nuit et jour* already recounted the fear of endless repetition. In the first room of *Maniac Summer* and in *Now*, Akerman arranges at the bottom of the screens, as if a peripheral detail, coloured neon lights next to two fake, brightly lit fish tanks, in which plastic fish bob ceaselessly against a photographic backdrop of rainbow-coloured corals. These tanks are light's equivalent of 'muzak', the repetitive background music that supermarkets use to comfort and stupefy customers, which we also hear in the first room of *Maniac Summer*, where the short film *Tombée de nuit sur Shanghai* (first made for the collective film *L'État du monde*) is screened. 'Muzak-light' is a constant of Akerman's work, much in evidence in the parades of traffic lights and car headlights, from the strange reflection blinking calmly across the sitting room windows in *Jeanne Dielman*, to the neon lights of the bar at the start of *La Folie Almayer*. Even so, *Tombée de nuit sur Shanghai* marks an added step, devoting to it an entire film in which several forms of light confront each other. Akerman, placing the camera on the edge of the bay of Shanghai, takes long static shots of boats coming and going in the hazy, greying dusk, before filming two buildings daubed in vast illuminated advertising hoardings at night. Between these shots she interjects rapid cuts, from inside and outside a bar, showing silhouettes caught against other electric backdrops. In the bay, a boat points its orange headlights towards the camera, while another carries a gigantic advertising board that the camera's sensitivity can grasp only as an overexposed rectangle passing slowly from one side of the frame to the other: in this aquarium world, the dazzlement is reduced to a floating detail. Over the buildings — transformed into screens — passes an absurd succession of 'stock images', of birds, fish, flowers, some adverts and even reproductions of Picassos, Manets and Van Goghs that have become giant, bright surfaces. The mind can't grasp this flux that has replaced the real time of nightfall, in the duration of the shots, following the aforementioned logic of 'duplicity'.

Still, although it looks like a catastrophe, in its suspension of meaning and deadening of perception, muzak-light exhibits a form of a kind. Simon's quest, at the start of *La Captive*, can't succeed because he doesn't understand muzak-light's impersonal character, seeking to create it as an act of will. Muzak-light, as harnessed and constructed by Akerman's films, is autonomous, automated, uncontrollable. The flickering, moving light, crystallizing into motifs and even faces, dances to its own tune. In the closing shot of *La Folie Almayer*, the title character is devastated by the departure of his daughter, an event that signals all at once his solitude, his ageing and the failure of his life. On screen, he is streaked by light, because a strange movement of the chair he sits on makes him move from shadow to sunshine, his devastating pain sculpting itself in accordance with the shadows which, cast by the leaves, caress his face and overlay it with a kind of chaotic weft, which the actor warps with a few movements of his head. He discreetly alternates his suffering grimace with the simple pleasure of soothing warmth, the brief glare that stuns him and the return of his inner pain. The chance play of light gives a rhythm to Almayer's emotions, despite himself.

The character's face bears 'depressive shadows', or 'maniac shadows', to use the title of one of Akerman's last installations. Shadows, as Akerman understands them, aren't only a dark counter form. We already saw from *Maniac Summer*, and its reference to Hiroshima, that an entire image could produce a kind of trace. The installation *Maniac Shadows* continues this work across a system of five projections: a central triptych, laying out mundane images of interiors and daily life filmed in New York, Tel Aviv and Brussels, often with Akerman and her mother; and an irregular projection on either side, each doubling up a different shot from the triptych, but on dark grey walls that do much to erase the vividness of the images, sometimes putting them at the limit of visibility. A neighbouring space shows a video of Akerman reading her book *Ma mère rit*, in a static shot against a dark background; and a third space hosts, fixed on a wall, a montage of 96 small photos that look like screengrabs from the videos, quickly taken, composing a litany of the everyday light that accompanies our existence, between muzak-light and minor aesthetic miracles of daily life: the blurred aura created by steam on a windowpane, the glimmer of a white curtain, the burst of sunlight across a grill of a mosquito net or reflected by the wooden walls of a house, some street lights at night, a shapeless grey stain in an anonymous darkness — or rather her own shadow, that's to say Akerman's, filmed moving in the water, at the seaside. On one side, therefore, with the first room, it is a destiny of bright blurring of images that occurs: the doubling on the grey walls makes of 'duplicity' an uncertain reflection, whose apparitions intervene without

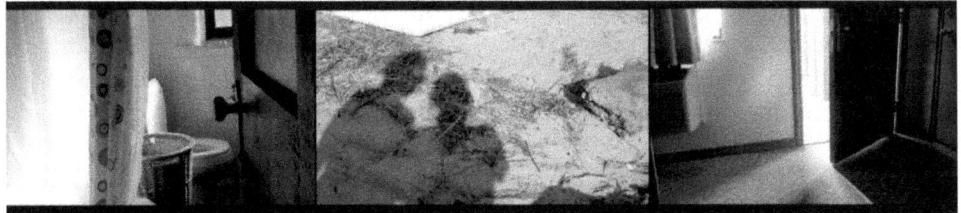

Fig. 11.3. Chantal Akerman, *Maniac Shadows* (2013), Courtesy Marian Goodman Gallery, Paris/ New York/ London © Fondation Chantal Akerman

logic, as if in a mirror very far away. On the other side, the bright snapshots stuck to the wall rather evoke a gathering of familiar figures, an inventory of friends.

In a way, *Maniac Shadows* manifests a tension found throughout Akerman's oeuvre: what is the difference between 'forms of light' and 'luminous forms'? Blurring, flickering, nightfall, sunrise, and sunrises, variation and flash are forms of light, that affect the integrity of shots in their frame and in their duration, while the drawing of shadows, the filigree of flashes or the flattening of reflections are luminous forms that possess a shape. The two forms are, however, interdependent. Witness, for example, how in *No Home Movie* over-exposure and under-exposure disturb the account of relations between Akerman and her elderly mother, filmed with a small video camera that amplifies certain contrasts, drowning the details in zones wholly white or black. The Brussels apartment of Natalia Akerman is hollowed by faults and deadly abysses, as shown by a shot cut perfectly in two, in which one sees the mother reading in an armchair, on the right, against a background of a bright curtain, while the left half of the frame is plunged into the thick darkness of a hallway. The tracking shots of the desert that punctuate *No Home Movie* metaphorize this radicality of eroded lights that, terribly, 'create voids'; but at the same time these desert views oppose to the graphic forms taken by the shadows and flashes in the apartment a calmer, more nuanced light, subjected to the shifting blur of clouds and dusty winds. One finds similar tracking shots in the five screens arranged in a V in the installation *Now*, their brightness heightened to produce the 'permanent bright explosion' mentioned earlier regarding the installation *D'Est*. There once more, duplicity consists of a relation between the forms of light displayed by the shots, and two abstract luminous forms, the whitish flashes and lightly vibrating projections on the ground between the screens. These, literally, are 'white shadows', which one can construe as the reflection of the living lights of the desert on the ground, but which assert their own development, independently and automatically — a sort of shutter coming at regular intervals to slowly cut the halos. Light manifests itself, in this autonomous mystery of a white shadow, as disarticulated and 'out of joint'.

Here, at the end of this journey, we see the dialectic we have attempted to sketch: on one side a dazzlement that performs a prohibition of the image, or which responds to the ethical demands of the unrepresentable; on the other, the silent rising of 'luminous shapes', like a return or an uncontrollable insistence of figuration, however minimal, created by light. The waves filmed in the night, at the very beginning of *La Captive*, before even the aforementioned scene with Simon and his projector, sweep the screen with pale foaming stripes that will be radicalized at the night-time start of *La Folie Almayer*, where the black swirls produced by a river's current draw incessant white calligraphies on the black background. Nearly forty years earlier, in *Hotel Monterey*, a slow back-and-forth tracking shot, in a corridor lit at one end by a window, conjures a reflection on a wall that seems to lift from the wall and transform into a floating halo. Of course, the obsession with luminous shapes can tend towards hypnotic devices, it fully commands the perceptive engagement of the spectator within the duration of the shots; one could also rightly say, in Lacanian fashion, that with Akerman the luminous form is the projection into the shot of the spectator's gaze or body.[9] To end there, however, would be to miss the autonomy, the terrible 'out of joint' that arrives at the moment in which the light escapes even the director and takes shapes that exceed her, like the 'exceeded speed' of the light at Hiroshima.

It is why, for example, the long sequence of *De l'autre côté* portraying the lines of Mexican migrants passing the American border, at night, taken by a helicopter with a thermal camera, is so strong: the shots haven't been filmed by Akerman's crew but their luminous logic incorporates itself into the work like an aesthetico-political ready-made. The bodies are reduced to white shadows on the dark background, inside the camera lens of the border guards, and the sinuous trace of the lines seems to prefigure the white inscriptions at the start of *La Folie Almayer*. The sequence has been preceded by other night-time moments in which reign a few halos and distant flashes of torches, operating a discreet dislocation of space under the points of light. These sparse glimmers crystallize in the pale silhouettes of the migrants, which seem born of the night, at once brutally real, as the archival record of images attests, and phantasmal, if one follows the aesthetic process of their apparition. The shadows of Hiroshima could thus also serve as metaphors, the thermal camera substituting for the nuclear light in the negation of lives and the creation of traces. And it is later in the installation *Une voix dans le désert* that the film 'slips before dying', under the effect of the day fading the projection, bathing the screen, and in which we once more encounter the confrontation between forms of light and luminous forms. Despite everything, Akerman might have thus reformulated Godard's famous dictum: il y aura toujours un éblouissement pour sauver l'honneur de tout le réel.[10]

Notes to Chapter 11

1. 'A film that multiplies itself at least four times over, sometimes five when it is gripped by disaster, when it seems that the speed of light is exceeded. As at Hiroshima. And as at Hiroshima, it leaves traces, but traces that are emerging. A film that explodes and slips before dying'. Chantal Akerman, press release for *Maniac Summer*, Marian Goodman Gallery, 2009.
2. Cf. for example Catherine Chalier, 'L'image dans le judaïsme. L'invisible en proximité', *Nouvelle revue théologique*, 120.4 (1998), 590–604. Charlier borrows eloquent examples from Freema Gottlieb, *The Lamp of God. A Jewish Book of Light* (Lanham, MD: Jason Aronson Inc., 1996).
3. On 'praesens' as a visual event, raised to the front rank of the image's 'opposite', cf. George Didi-Huberman, *La peinture incarnée* (Paris: Minuit, 1985), p. 12. On the double valence of the flash, see Régis Durand and Dominique Baqué, eds., *Éblouissement* (Paris: Editions du Jeu de Paume, 2004).

4. It's the jouissance of the 'scopic field' defined by Jacques Lacan in his chapter on 'the split between the eye and the gaze' in *Les quatre concepts fondamentaux de la psychanalyse* (Paris: Seuil, 1973). We come back to it briefly at the end of this chapter.
5. For ease, we grouped these three traits under the word 'mastery' [*emprise*] in an earlier text on Chantal Akerman. Cf. Cyril Béghin, 'The Long Take, Mastery', *Film Quarterly*, 70.1 (2016), 48–53.
6. On the hypnotic character of Akerman's long shots and repetitions, see Raymond Bellour, *Le Corps du cinéma. Hypnoses, émotions, animalités* (Paris: P.O.L, 2009).
7. 'When this light arrived in extreme close-up as if irradiated in its turn by the snow of the video image.' Raymond Bellour, 'Sauver l'image', in *L'Entre-images 2* (Paris: P.O.L, 1999), p. 72.
8. 'Et c'est petit à petit que l'on se rend compte que c'est toujours la même chose qui se révèle, un peu comme la scène primitive. Et la scène primitive pour moi — bien que je m'en défende et que j'enrage à la fin — , je dois me rendre à l'évidence, c'est loin derrière ou toujours devant, de vieilles images à peine recouvertes par d'autres plus lumineuses et même radieuses. De vieilles images d'évacuation, de marches dans la neige avec des paquets vers un lieu inconnu, de visages et de corps placés l'un à coté de l'autre, de visages qui vacillent entre la vie forte et la possibilité d'une mort qui viendrait les frapper sans qu'ils aient rien demandé. Et c'est toujours comme ça.' (And bit by bit, we come to see that it's always the same thing that is revealed, a little like a primal scene. And the primal scene for me — although I deny it and get angry by the end — I have to face facts, it's far behind or always ahead, old images barely covered by others that are brighter and even radiant. Old images of evacuations, of walking in the snow with packages to an unknown place, of faces and bodies placed one beside another, of expressions that waver between a strong life and the possibility of a death that would come to strike them without their having asked for anything. And it's always like that). Chantal Akerman, 'La vingt-cinquième image', *Trafic* 17 (1996).
9. 'In what is presented to me as space of light, what is gaze is always some play of light and opacity'. Cf. Lacan, 'La ligne et la lumière', in *Les quatre concepts fondamentaux de la psychanalyse*, pp. 109–11.
10. 'There will always be a flash to save the honour of all reality'. Cf. Godard 'Même rayé à mort, un simple rectangle de 35mm sauve l'honneur de tout le réel' (Even scratched to death, a simple rectangle of 35mm saves the honour of all reality); Jean-Luc Godard, *Histoire(s) du cinéma, 1A: Toutes les histoires*, 1998.

CHAPTER 12

Chantal Akerman: Filmmaker, Video Artist, Writer

Marion Schmid

Known above all as one of cinema's boldest visionaries and a pioneering video artist, Chantal Akerman was also a highly original writer. The author of several books — including her acclaimed autoportrait *Ma mère rit*, shortlisted for the 2013 Prix Médicis — she is part of a distinguished lineage of Francophone *écrivains-cinéastes* that stretches from André Malraux, Jean Cocteau and Sacha Guitry in the first half of the twentieth century, via Marguerite Duras, Alain Robbe-Grillet and Georges Perec in the 1960s and 70s, to contemporary artists such as Catherine Breillat, Jean-Philippe Toussaint and Virginie Despentes. Artists for whom writing and making films are not only complementary, but intertwined practices. For almost half a century, Akerman seamlessly criss-crossed between media, extending her experiments from film to literature and, since the mid-1990s, to video installations. Forging new pathways between the arts, she was engaged in an experimental project 'in progress' where traditional media boundaries are undone and new forms of (self-)representation are being invented. Akerman's creative practice was resolutely in-between media, yet the disciplinary habit of separating the arts tends to make us consider her moving-image work as if it existed in isolation from her writing. If it is time to discover Chantal Akerman the writer, we must also pay tribute to a great intermedial artist, who proposed new forms of narrating, seeing and experiencing at the intersection between writing and the moving image.

The Written and the Cinematic

Paradoxically perhaps for a celebrated moving image artist, Akerman never made a secret of her predilection for literature over film. 'The book was doubtless always more important for me than the cinema. The cinema always remains somehow "impure". [...]. You shall not make for yourself a carved image', she states in a text accompanying her installation *Marcher à côté de ses lacets dans un frigidaire vide*.[1] Similarly, in an interview with Alain Veinstein about her book *Ma mère rit*, she remarks, 'C'est moins indécent l'écriture que le film'.[2] And, commenting on the solitary gesture of writing versus the collective nature of filmmaking, she adds:

Quand tu écris, tu apprends à comprendre ce que tu as vu, ce que tu es, ce que tu as vécu et pourquoi tu l'as vécu et comment tu l'as vécu. [...] Et c'est quand même plus fort que quand tu fais un film, pour moi.³

As she explains in a 1979 interview with Jean-Luc Godard, as a Jewish director with a religious upbringing, her cinematic practice was profoundly shaped by the prohibition against visual representation from the book of *Exodus*. Even if she readily transgressed this injunction in her artistic work, her visual aesthetic is inflected by a deep distrust of the spectacular or the sensational, making her privilege what she calls 'distilled' images over more direct representational strategies.⁴ Tellingly, this oblique representational ethics that characterizes her work is aligned with written forms of expression. Thus, when the cinephile Godard teases her for drawing on metaphors like 'inscription' or 'writing' to speak about her films, Akerman persists in using a graphological trope: 'I say that, yes, there are images already inscribed, and it is exactly *under* those that I work: over the inscribed image and the one I would love to inscribe.'⁵ Writing here, unlike in the *auteurist* discourses of the New Wave, is not merely used to valorise the cinematic; it is invoked as a purer form of representation that can to a certain extent counterbalance the idolatrous, 'impure' nature of the cinema.

Akerman initially wanted to become a writer until, aged fifteen, she discovered Godard's *Pierrot le fou* (1965), and, with it, the expressive possibilities of a 'total cinema' no longer in the shadows of its literary ancestor: 'ça touchait à la poésie, ça touchait à la peinture, ça touchait à tout'.⁶ Literature and philosophy played an important part in the construction of her imaginary as well as in her creative practice. In interviews and her self-portrait *Autoportrait en cinéaste*, she mentions Proust, Kafka, Faulkner, Isaac Bashevis Singer, James Baldwin, Vasily Grossman and Varlam Shalamov as authors that had an influence on her work, alongside thinkers such as Walter Benjamin, Lacan, Deleuze, Guattari and Levinas. An *auteur* in the tradition of the *Nouvelle Vague* — even though her own trajectory was shaped by the New York avant-gardes of the 1970s — , Akerman authored most of the scripts for her films herself. Some, including her free adaptation of Proust, *La Captive*, and *Un divan à New York*, are co-written. The boundary between script, personal writing and film is an altogether fluid one in her work: her first feature *Je tu il elle* originates in a novella; the documentary *D'Est* began as travel notes. 'Il faut toujours écrire quand on veut faire un film', she insists, even in the context of her documentary work.⁷ By publishing the scripts for *Les Rendez-vous d'Anna* (Albatros, 1978) and *Un divan à New York* (L'Arche, 1996), in the footsteps of artists like Marguerite Duras and Alain Robbe-Grillet, Akerman bestows a literary status on texts which, traditionally in film production, occupy a purely utilitarian function.

The written, especially in the form of letters, is omnipresent in her films, be it as a feature of the filmic diegesis (in for instance *Saute ma ville, Je tu il elle, Jeanne Dielman, Un divan à New York, Demain on déménage* and *De l'autre côté*), or, more radically, as the main narrative device. Both *News from Home* (based on Natalia Akerman's letters to her daughter) and *Letters Home* (a recording of a play centred around Sylvia Plath's letters to her mother) are epistolary films. Though, unlike

Fig. 12.1. Chantal Akerman, *Un divan à New York* (1996)

Godard, Akerman never had a mania for citation, literature is evoked repeatedly in her works as an artistic form with which her characters grapple. In *Jeanne Dielman*, Sylvain's (Jan Decorte) hackneyed rehearsal of a Baudelaire poem with his mother (Delphine Seyrig) drains the writing of its rhythm and beauty, reducing it to mere words to be parroted. In *Un divan à New York*, the uptight New York psychoanalyst Henry (William Hurt) struggles to make sense of Rimbaud's 'Roman' (*Romance*), a poem about the elation of youthful love. All three characters appear singularly insensitive to literary writing, a condition shared to comic effect by Charlotte (Sylvie Testud) from *Demain on déménage*, who tries to make a living from composing pornographic novels.

Akerman made creative forays into the hybrid zone between writing and film in the short *Contre l'oubli: Pour Febe Elisabeth Velasquez (El Salvador)*, in which Catherine Deneuve speaks a prose poem in memory of the Salvadorian trade unionist written by Akerman, and in the documentary *De l'autre côté*, which ends on the story of David who has lost trace of his migrant mother written and spoken by Akerman.[8] If her plans to adapt Isaac Bashevis Singer's epic tales *The Manor* and *The Estate* unfortunately never came to fruition, she revitalized the interstitial genre of adaptation with her acclaimed reworkings of Proust and Conrad, *La Captive* and *La Folie Almayer*. Far from stifled by the literary prestige of these texts, Akerman creatively revisits them, 'creolising' them with other, non literary sources: in the former, Proust's meditation on an obsessive jealousy is conjugated with Hitchcock's *Vertigo* (1958); the latter reimagines Conrad's debut novel from a feminine perspective, crossing it with F.W. Murnau's *Tabu* (1931) as well as aspects of Akerman's biography.[9] We can only regret that she wasn't given the time to adapt Dostoevsky's *The Idiot* — a project which, according to Claire Atherton, she contemplated after the death of her mother.[10]

Yet Akerman was not merely a filmmaker who engages literature and the written in her cinematic oeuvre. In tandem with her moving image work, she veered into experimental forms of writing, first in the play *Hall de nuit* (1992), followed by the autofictional 'récit' *Une famille à Bruxelles* (1998) and the already mentioned autoportrait *Ma mère rit* (2013). Together with *Autoportrait en cinéaste*, these latter two texts pursue in a different medium her triptych of cinematic autoportraits from the 1980s and 90s (*Lettre d'une cinéaste, Portrait d'une paresseuse, Chantal Akerman par Chantal Akerman*). In *Lettre d'une cinéaste*, Akerman describes her written and her audio-visual offerings as complementary activities which allowed her to surmount the inhibitions she had in one medium: 'Si je fais du cinéma, c'est à cause de ce que je n'ose pas accomplir dans l'écriture.'[11] This desire to explore medial boundaries with a view to overcoming the limitations of a single medium eventually led her to installation art, where writing and film are allowed to intermingle more freely in a heterogeneous, 'impure' multi-media space.

While her cinematic self-representations have generated considerable interest,[12] her verbal self-portraits have hardly had any critical response to date. In what follows, I will read *Une famille à Bruxelles* and *Ma mère rit* in tandem with her moving-image work to draw attention to the manifold circulations, displacements and cross-fertilisations in her oeuvre across media. I also want to highlight the unbroken creativity and appetite for experimentation that characterize Akerman's work in the last two decades of her life, a period in which she gave a new impetus to the genre of self-writing and renewed self-portraiture in both film and installation art.

Expanding Self-Portraiture

Written some one and a half years after the death of Akerman's father, *Une famille à Bruxelles* centres on a Jewish family's coming to terms with the illness and death of the husband and father, the only character to be named in the narrative. Firmly anchored in the everyday, the text gives voice to the solitude of the mother, a Holocaust survivor whose family members are dispersed all over the globe. Though parallels to Akerman's own family abound (the father is called Jacques, the older daughter lives in Ménilmontant, the younger daughter has settled in Latin America), the text evades any clear-cut autobiographical assignation.[13] Like in her filmic work (notably *Les Rendez-vous d'Anna* and *Portrait d'une jeune fille de la fin des années 60 à Bruxelles*), Akerman blurs the boundaries between autobiography and fiction; as suggested by the deindividuated title, personal experience is distanced in favour of a wider engagement with questions of loss, mourning and family relations.

Une famille à Bruxelles absorbs readers into what Serge Doubrovsky — the writer and theorist who coined the term 'autofiction' — calls 'l'aventure du langage, hors sagesse et hors syntaxe du roman, traditionnel ou nouveau'.[14] Reminiscent of Beckett, Duras and Thomas Bernhard in its brooding style, the text espouses the mother's ruminating thought without fear of platitude or sentimentality. The stream-of-consciousness-type narrative moulds itself to the maternal speech pattern in its embracing of idiosyncratic locutions ('ça faisait du bien aux os'), oral-type expression and de-structured, often labyrinthine syntax. As Akerman explains in conversation with Alain Veinstein, her writing emulates the particular ways of speaking, but also the silences of the 'first generation', that is, the generation that directly experienced the Holocaust: 'c'est comme on se parle, et c'est aussi ce qu'on se cache. C'est comment parlaient ceux de la première génération'.[15]

The book opens on a markedly visual scene:

> Et puis je *vois* encore un grand appartement presque vide à Bruxelles. Avec juste une femme souvent en peignoir. Une femme qui vient de perdre son mari. C'est drôle je ne *vois* pas cette femme dehors pourtant elle sort parfois, elle marche dans la rue, elle attend le tram. Je la *vois* surtout au téléphone et devant sa télévision couchée dans un divan avec parfois un journal devant elle.[16]

Given the identity of the author, it is difficult not to visualize this incipit as the first establishing shots of a film — an uncanny variation on *Jeanne Dielman*, which similarly staged the lonely existence of a widow in her Brussels flat. The strangely placed 'encore' in the opening sentence reinforces the sense of 'déjà-vu', corroborated some ten pages later by a passage about the autonomy women can gain from driving a car, which resonates with one of the letters from *Jeanne Dielman*. Like in her play *Hall de nuit*, which echoes scenes from *Hotel Monterey* and *Nuit et jour*, personal, literary and filmic narratives enter into implicit dialogue.

Initially, the story seems to be told from the perspective of the older daughter, whom we identify as the 'je' of the opening paragraph, yet, rapidly the point of view shifts to an omniscient perspective before embracing that of the mother figure. Throughout the text, 'je' is occupied alternately by mother and daughter in a criss-crossing of voices and perspectives which undoes any stable notion of identity. Sudden changes in possessive determiners ('ma fille' / 'sa fille') further destabilize the narrative point of view in a vertiginous toing and froing between internal and external focalisation, 'moi', 'toi' and 'elle', closeness and distance. The double occupancy of the 'je' by both mother and daughter hints at a crisis of emancipation with regard to the mother, which already informed the earlier *News from Home*. Akerman comments, 'I haven't managed the transition to adulthood, as one says. It seems that this is strongly visible in *Une famille à Bruxelles* where one doesn't know whether it is the mother or the daughter who speaks. So it seems that the separation has not been successful.'[17]

Une famille à Bruxelles exists in triple medial form as a book, a play (performed by Akerman herself in theatres in Paris, Brussels and New York) and a CD. It was also incorporated into the video installation *Selfportrait/ Autobiography: A Work in Progress,* one of the artist's first video works exhibited at the Frith Street Gallery, London, in 1998. Consisting of edited scenes from four iconic Akerman films (*Hotel Monterey, Jeanne Dielman, Toute une nuit* and *D'Est*), the installation is distributed over six monitors, organized in the form of a triangle. Each extract is accompanied by its own soundtrack, overlaid by the voice of the artist who reads *Une famille à Bruxelles*. The reading time corresponds to a complete cycle of the installation. Delivered orally, the family story sutures and puts in relation the disparate moving images — people queuing in the snow from *D'Est*, Jeanne Dielman attending to her domestic tasks, guests emerging out of a hotel lift in *Hotel Monterey* and so forth — pointing to their interconnectedness as traces of our diverse human existence. The biographical, the fictional and the documentary are welded together in a displacement between 'I' and 'they', opening up new connections between sound and image, between the self and the Other. This *Selfportrait/ Autobiography* is 'in progress' in the sense that it is constantly evolving, never closing in on any fixed meaning.[18] Cyril Béghin observes:

> Le père, on le cherche partout dans les images; la mère, elle occupe les écrans de *Jeanne Dielman* mais aussi chaque apparition de femme sur les lignes de fuite de l'installation. Le sens est en constante expansion: les textures très riches de ce qui est dit comme de ce qui est vu s'entrecroisent non pour se serrer et trouver des nœuds de montage, mais au contraire s'espacer, relâcher dans leurs tensions respectives la maille des attributions de corps, d'actions et d'histoires.[19]

In its multi-media format, the installation allows Akerman to put in conversation the heterogeneous materials of her creation — documentary 'bordering on fiction', feature, experimental writing — and, through this (self-)relational process, to broaden them out to new significations. By recomposing texts and images in space, the installation creates a new context for the reception of already existing works, revisiting and expanding them outside the confines of the cinema or the theatre. As Vivian Sky Rehberg explains, visitors to the museum or the gallery space no longer apprehend the work through the collective, frontal viewing experience that is afforded in the cinema projection room; rather, they explore it as passers-by, thus entering into a different temporal and spatial register.[20] This new context of the installation space encourages spectators to reimagine existing works within a wider historical and art-historical frame:

> When Akerman reworks a film for an installation, she invites the spectator to participate in a collective act of historical and autobiographical re-reading and re-interpretation of her own production. Displaced from imposed chronologies, and released from the linear temporal progression of 24 frames per second, as well as from the conventions of storytelling in narrative and documentary cinema, Akerman's installations appear as fragments in a constantly moving history in the making, one that engages the history of art and the history of cinema, as well as her own life story.[21]

Distanced but nonetheless intimate, shifting its point of view and opening itself up to new configurations, the moving image installation affords an openness to which all of Akerman's work ultimately seems to aspire: no story is ever closed; no meaning arrested. Past and present, personal and collective histories, the written and the cinematic are allowed to interpenetrate in what with Jean-Luc Nancy one could call an 'être singulier pluriel' [being singular plural].[22]

Writing and Filming Truthfully

Akerman's 2004 video installation *Marcher à côté de ses lacets dans un frigidaire vide*, created for the Marian Goodman Gallery, Paris, and subsequently shown in the Jewish Museum, Berlin, and the Camden Arts Centre, London, tends to be considered as a changing point in her project of self-portraiture. If, in works like *Histoires d'Amerique* and *D'Est*, the artist grappled with her traumatic family history indirectly — Alisa Lebow calls them 'transitive autobiographies'[23] — here she for the first time moves to a more overtly autobiographical stance. The installation revolves around the diary of Akerman's maternal grandmother who was murdered in Auschwitz. In the first room, reflections about the cinema written by Akerman as well as selected passages from the diary are projected onto a diaphanous tulle spiral. The semi-obscurity and the shadows spectators' bodies throw on the walls and spiral suffuse the space with a spectral, mournful atmosphere. As Edna Moshenson explains, this part of the installation is

> a cinematic autobiography of sorts, which contains her [Akerman's] thoughts about the cinema and the power of the cinematic image; about the Second Commandment that forbids the making of graven images; about her work and about what has nourished and motivated her.[24]

At the centre of the second room is a projection of the diary on the same diaphanous material. Behind this screen, audiences access another projection: a split-image documentary of the director and her mother, Natalia Akerman, who translates her mother's diary from Polish and, for the first time, shares her experience in Auschwitz with her daughter. 'Taken together', Moshenson observes, 'the two parts of the installation [...] summarize years of creative work in which Akerman searched for a way to replace an invented memory and autobiography with a reconstruction of her family biography through a process of opening up and talking, acceptance and reconciliation with the past.'[25]

Some ten years later, Akerman pursued this autobiographical project with two works that, though not initially intended as such, retrospectively form a diptych: her confessional autoportrait *Ma mère rit* and the video essay *No Home Movie*.[26] According to Akerman's own testimony, *Ma mère rit* was written over the course of several years, virtually without corrections.[27] The artist read from the book at the Théâtre du Châtelet, Paris, and at The Kitchen, New York, in 2013 and it has since been the subject of performative readings by professional actors (notably Natacha Régnier, who played the pregnant woman in *Demain on déménage*). *No Home Movie* originates in recordings of Natalia Akerman in her Brussels home taken during the final two years of her life. After her mother's death in 2014, Akerman contacted her long-time editor and collaborator Claire Atherton to see whether 'quelque chose est possible'.[28] Based on some 20 hours of footage, first shaped into 8, then 6 and eventually just under 2 hours, the film, in Atherton's words, was an attempt to 'retenir la mère de Chantal avec nous'. 'Le film s'est imposé à nous comme un cri', she movingly notes in an interview with Albane Penaranda.[29] In their stark honesty and uncompromising style, the two portraits constitute some kind of *summa* of Akerman's work, returning to some of the central preoccupations of her oeuvre:

Fig. 12.2. Chantal Akerman, *Marcher à côté de ses lacets dans un frigidaire vide* (2004), Courtesy Fondation Chantal Akerman & Marian Goodman Gallery, Paris/ New York/ London © Fondation Chantal Akerman

the relations between mother and daughter; the female domestic space; the shadow of the Holocaust; exile, nomadism and family life. Pursuing her experimentation in both written and cinematic forms, they have become the testament of an artist whose whole oeuvre was fuelled by the mother figure.

In *Ma mère rit*, Akerman asserts, she wanted to 'écrire vrai, chercher au plus loin'.[30] Interweaving the artist's grappling with the illness and near-death of her mother with the breakdown of a love relationship, the text plunges us, in the words of one commentator, 'into the confrontation with oneself and the other, that is, with that other that is inside us.'[31] The candour with which Akerman shares deeply intimate aspects of her life is singularly courageous, even in a culture where the exposure of painful filial or love relationships and the experience of personal illness or loss have become an integral part of women's self-representation.[32] Yet for this artist for whom vision and style are inseparable interwined, 'écrire vrai' is more than just a matter of personal frankness. Just like her moving image art challenges the cinematic language of the mainstream, so her writing undocs standard rules of French syntax, vocabulary and grammar. In the tradition of 'minor writing' analysed by Deleuze and Guattari,[33] Akerman coins an idiom that evades the dominant linguistic practice — a raw, living language unburdened by the stifling norms of 'literary style'. Readily dispensing with standard punctuation alongside other linguistic markers of literariness, her prose captures the ruminations of the mind.

Repetition, a preference for noun phrases, incomplete sentences, predominantly familiar register, spoken rhythms and interjections designate the style as oral. As in *Une famille à Bruxelles*, beneath the French language we hear the echoes of other tongues: rhythms and constructions from Polish, Hebrew or Yiddish; the melody of prayers Akerman heard at the synagogue when she was a child; the distinct music of Natalia Akerman's voice inflected by her Jewish-Polish origins.[34]

If in the earlier book the point of view alternated between mother and daughter, here other voices — notably that of the sister and the lover, but also many others — join in a truly polyphonic chant. Their voices erupt amidst the first person in a strange conflation between direct and indirect modes, that, at times, can make it difficult to identify who speaks. Thus, for instance, in a passage on the mother's impending operation:

> Plus que quatre semaines maintenant avant l'opération.
> C'est ce qu'elle a dit hier.
> Mais ce matin après le petit déjeuner elle était déjà fatiguée.
> Elle s'est couchée sur le divan.
> Quand je suis allée voir, c'est ce qu'elle m'a dit, manger m'a fatiguée.
> Mais est-ce que j'ai le droit de me reposer ? J'ai lui ai dit c'est pas un droit c'est un devoir.
> Et moi est-ce que je vais tenir ici quatre semaines.[35]

Or, later, on the mother's habit of phoning her daughters regardless of their day-time occupations :

> Ma sœur me dit ne fais pas attention, il ne faut pas faire attention, moi je ne fais pas attention. Je vais je viens, je ne lui dis pas où et je ne lui donne pas le numéro de mon portable.
> Ma mère veut absolument téléphoner à ma sœur. Pourquoi tu veux lui téléphoner, elle travaille. Laisse-la. J'ai quand même envie de l'appeler pour savoir quand elle rentre.[36]

Ubiquitous in the narrative, this collision between narrative voices hints at a deeper concern over proximity and distance in interpersonal relationships. Like the neurotic filmmaker in the autofictional *L'Homme à la valise* (played by Akerman herself), who barricades herself in her room to escape the presence of a male friend, or the aseptically distanced Jeanne Dielman, who unsuccessfully tries to keep the outside world at bay, the artist speaking in the first person seems permanently engulfed by those around her. Unable to delineate clearly its boundaries as a subject, the 'je' is at risk of melting into the other.

While *Ma mère rit* is framed by Natalia's quasi miraculous recovery, *No Home Movie* is a loving portrait of the mother's final years. As intimated in the title, this is not a 'home movie' in the proper sense of the word — that is, a family portrait made by an amateur filmmaker — although the texture of the digital video gives it a deceptively amateur feel. It is the work of an artist sadly bereft of the home and person that afforded her anchorage, even if so much of her oeuvre is marked by a strong ambivalence towards the home. In an interview two months before her own death, Akerman confides:

> Even if I have a home in Paris and sometimes in New York, whenever I was saying I have to go home, it was going to my mother. And there is 'no home' anymore, because she isn't there. When I came last time, the home was empty.[37]

With its overtly autobiographical focus, *No Home Movie* at first seems closer to the artist's written and installation work, yet in its preoccupation with domestic spaces, daily rituals and the female body it seamlessly inserts itself into her filmography. In formal terms also this is signature-style Akerman in its privileging of long takes, preference for symmetrical framing, and combination of fixed-angle and tracking shots (punctuated by several hand-held camera sequences as well as extreme close-up shots of Natalia's face on Skype).

Given that *Jeanne Dielman* was inspired by Natalia Akerman, it is perhaps not surprising that parts of *No Home Movie* resemble a documentary remake — some forty years on — of what remains Akerman's most famous film. Not only is the kitchen where mother and daughter are often filmed eating and chatting almost identical to that of Dielman and do the glass-walled display cabinets with their knick-knacks in the sitting-room remind us of her collection of bibelots. Beyond such similarities of decor, snippets of conversation (Natalia and Chantal talking about potatoes at the beginning of the film) and rituals (the mother's evening walk) allude to the life of the fictional protagonist. What is more, the use of amplified sound (passing traffic, Natalia's footsteps or humming, the white noise of the radio), repeated shot compositions through door frames, and the opening or closing of shots on parts of the interior not yet or no longer inhabited by a human presence convey a similar sense of osmosis between the domestic space and its female inhabitant. Bearing the imprint of Natalia's body (evoked by the unmade bed or a casually abandoned spread on the armchair), the domestic space absorbs, and to a certain extent defines the mother.

For readers of *Ma mère rit* many a scene from *No Home Movie* will seem strikingly familiar. At times, it feels as if the film afforded visuality to the book or, inversely, as if the book put into words what is only intimated in the film, in particular Akerman's anguish about her mother's passing voiced so poignantly in the autoportrait: 'Le vieil enfant se disait que si sa mère disparaissait, il n'aurait plus nulle part où revenir. [...] Qu'est-ce qui va me retenir à la vie après'.[38] Yet, if the film is in many ways a mirror of the book, its focus is firmly on the mother. For most of its 118 minutes, Chantal Akerman remains hidden from view, only furtively to be glanced in the dialogue window of Skype or as she walks in and out of frame; when mother and daughter sit at the kitchen table, Chantal's body is half-covered by Natalia or filmed from behind. Akerman alludes to subterranean links between the two works in an insert shot of her shadow reflected in water, derived from the installation *Maniac Shadows*, which figures as a photogram in *Ma mère rit* (p. 115).

Assembled from footage which initially didn't have a precise destination, *No Home Movie* was sculpted into a dramatic structure which, once more, recalls *Jeanne Dielman* in its upending of the regime of habit shown in the first half of the film, followed by an inexorable move towards catastrophe in the second. Exactly half-way through the film, the first of a series of tracking shots across a desert region in Israel

Fig. 12.3. Chantal Akerman, *No Home Movie* (2015)

marks a caesura in the narrative.[39] The intercut sequences originate in an installation entitled *De la mèr(e) au désert* Akerman was preparing for an exhibition in Jerusalem (a smaller version of what would become her last installation, *NOW*).[40] Devoid of human presence and battered by wind, the barren landscapes metonymically speak of exile and displacement. They remind us of the Arizona desert in *De l'autre côté*, Akerman's documentary about Mexican migrants trying to cross over into the US, but also of Natalia's recollection earlier in the film of how members of her husband's family fled Nazi Germany in 1939. Intercut between the documentary footage, the shots from the installation with their threatening sound environment collide with the images of Natalia in her Brussels flat. Conversely, sound from *No Home Movie* was reused in *NOW*, though it is almost imperceptible in the installation piece.[41] The installation and the film, then, are constructed of the same materials, speaking of continued persecutions, across time and space. As in the documentary trilogy *D'Est*, *Sud* and *De l'autre côté*, landscape and soundscape become a privileged vehicle for conjuring up memory traces beneath the images of our present.[42] For Akerman, as for Walter Benjamin who was a life-long inspiration, the truth of an image lies above all in this capacity to make visible, in a dialectical process, the connection between past and present. She cites Benjamin in *Autoportrait en cinéaste*: 'La manière dont le passé reçoit l'empreinte d'une actualité plus haute est donnée par *l'image* en laquelle il est compris. Et cette pénétration dialectique, cette capacité à rendre présentes les corrélations passées, est l'épreuve de vérité de l'action présente'.[43]

Desert images punctuate the second half of the film, as we witness Natalia's steady decline. If, in the first part, the interiors were bathed in warm summer light, now darkness invades the image in repeated shots of the flat and its inhabitants at nightfall. Two haunting sequences in which Chantal immerses herself into the inner recesses of the apartment mark the shift from a realistic-documentary to an oneiricsymbolic mode. We hear her heavy breathing and occasionally see her shadow reflected on a piece of furniture; we note the clicking sounds of a door, footsteps on a stair, but struggle to make out her spatial surroundings, eerily dissolved by the rapid movements of the hand-held camera. Accompanied by the painful sound of Natalia's coughs, this is an immersion into a twilight-zone, between light and darkness, the living and the dead. We are metaphorically transported into the *sheol* of the Old Testament, that subterranean underworld inhabited by the shadows of the departed — a land guarded by gates and divided into compartments, one beneath the other. In both the inserts from the installation and the documentary footage, the appearance of entirely black or white screens pushes the cinematic image towards abstraction. At one point, the hand-held camera ventures outside, onto the balcony and from there towards the street, but the over-exposed, shaky image hardly affords any visibility any more. In staging a crisis of vision, the film marks a limit point.

Inside, Natalia has slowly slipped away. Her daughters try to keep her awake, yet we sense that she is no longer anchored in the world of the living. If the opening shots of a windblown old tree that bends, but does not break had celebrated resilience, two almost motion-less fixed-angle shots of the desert some eight minutes before the end convey a sense of stillness. Something has happened between these shots and the subsequent one of Akerman getting ready to leave; faithful to the oblique ethics of her work, it remains unspoken. The scene where she closes the curtain of her room, walking out of the frame while the camera remains fixed on the semi-obscure space, is heart-wrenching. In the last symmetrical shot of Natalia's sitting room, the mother's absence is palpable. Chantal's footsteps echo in a space of emptiness. *No Home Movie* is a film of silent exits, a sober and deeply moving mise-en-scène of disappearances.

In light of the artist's own death shortly after the release of the film, it is difficult not to read this ending as a double parting, yet we may find comfort in the last shot of nature, intercut just before she draws the curtain. In stark contrast to the desolate landscapes shown earlier, it affords the tranquil image of a corn field gently swaying in the breeze. In the backdrop nestles the modern skyline of a city, somewhere in Israel. We are reminded of the mother's joy about her first visit to Israel from *Une famille à Bruxelles*: 'Je me suis sentie si bien là-bas quand on y a été la première fois, c'est vrai que je me suis sentie là-bas comme nulle part au monde'.[44] There is solace here, a sense of homecoming.

Notes to Chapter 12

1. Chantal Akerman, 'Neben seinen Schnürsenkeln in einem leeren Kühlschrank laufen', in Astrid Ofner, Claudia Siefen and Stefan Flach, eds., *Retrospektive Chantal Akerman* (Vienna: Schüren, 2011), p. 73.
2. 'Writing is less indecent than film' (all translations unless otherwise stated are mine). 'Chantal Akerman pour son livre *Ma mère rit*', *Du jour au lendemain*, France Culture, 7 November 2013.
3. 'When you write, you learn to understand what you have seen, what you are, what you have experienced and why you have experienced it and how you have experienced it. [...] And, for me, that's certainly stronger than when you make a movie.'

4. See Janet Bergstrom, 'Invented Memories', in Gwendolyn Audrey Foster, ed., *Identity and Memory: The Films of Chantal Akerman* (Carbondale: Southern Illinois University Press, 2003), pp. 94–116 (p. 94).
5. Akerman and Jean-Luc Godard, 'Entretien avec Jean-Luc Godard', *Ça Cinéma*, 19 (1980), p. 11.
6. 'It touched on poetry, it touched on painting, it touched on everything.'
7. 'You always need to write when you want to make a film.' Akerman cited in Jacqueline Aubenas, 'Des mots pour une cinéaste', in Jacqueline Aubenas, *Hommage à Chantal Akerman* (Brussels: Commissariat général aux Relations internationales de la Communauté française de Belgique, 1995), p. 7.
8. The poem is reproduced in Chantal Akerman, *Autoportrait en cinéaste* (Paris: Editions du Centre Georges Pompidou/ Editions Cahiers du cinéma, 2004), pp. 65–66.
9. For detailed readings of these adaptations see Martine Beugnet and Marion Schmid, *Proust at the Movies* (London: Ashgate, 2004), chapter 5, and Marion Schmid, 'The Cinema Films Back: Colonialism, Alterity and Resistance in Chantal Akerman's *La Folie Almayer*, *Australian Journal of French Studies*, 51 (2014), 22–34.
10. 'Nuit Chantal Akerman — 2ème partie de l'entretien avec Claire Atherton et Vincent Dieutre', *Les Nuits de France Culture*, France Culture, 11 February 2018.
11. 'If I make movies it's because of what I dare not accomplish in writing.'
12. See for instance Alisa Lebow, 'Memory Once Removed: Indirect Memory and Transitive Autobiography in Chantal Akerman's *D'Est*', *Camera Obscura*, 18 (2003), 34–83 and Maureen Turim, 'Personal Pronouncements in *I...You...He...She* and *Portrait of a Young Girl at the End of the 1960s in Brussels*', in Foster, ed., *Identity and Memory*, pp. 9–26.
13. Philippe Lejeune postulates that, for an autobiographical pact to be sealed, the author, narrator and principal protagonist must be identical (Lejeune, *Le Pacte autobiographique* (Paris: Seuil, 1975), p. 14).
14. 'The adventure of language, outside wisdom and outside the syntax of the novel, be it traditional or new.' Serge Doubrovsky, *Fils* (Paris: Galilée, 1977), back cover.
15. 'it's how we speak to each other and also what we hide. It's how those of the first generation spoke'. 'Entretien sur *Une famille à Bruxelles*', *Du jour au lendemain*, France Culture, 19 March 1999.
16. 'And then I still *see* a big, almost empty flat in Brussels. With just a woman, often in a bathrobe. A woman who just lost her husband. It's strange I don't *see* this woman outside yet she sometimes goes out, she walks in the street, she waits for the tram. I *see* her mostly on the phone and in front of her television lying on a couch with sometimes a newspaper in front of her.' Chantal Akerman, *Une famille à Bruxelles* (Paris: L'Arche, 1998), p. 7 (my emphasis).
17. Akerman, 'Neben seinen Schnürsenkeln', p. 75.
18. On the installation see Cyril Béghin's excellent 'Selfportrait — Autobiography in Progress', in Akerman, *Autoportrait en cinéaste*, p. 218.
19. 'We look for the father everywhere in the images; the mother occupies the screens of *Jeanne Dielman*, but also every female appearance on the vanishing lines of the installation. The meaning constantly expands: the very rich textures of what is said and what is seen are intertwined, not to tighten and find knots of montage, but on the contrary to space out, to release in their respective tensions the mesh of the attribution of bodies, actions and stories' (ibid.).
20. 'Tant qu'il est encore temps/ While There Is Still Time', in Dieter Roelstraete and Anders Kreuger, eds., *Chantal Akerman. Too Far, Too Close* (Antwerp: Ludion, M HKA, 2012), p. 56.
21. Ibid., p. 52.
22. Jean-Luc Nancy, *Être singulier pluriel* (Paris: Galilée, 1996).
23. For an excellent discussion of oblique strategies of (self-)representation in Akerman's *D'Est*, see Lebow, 'Memory Once Removed'.
24. Edna Moshenson,'Chantal Akerman: A Spiral Autobiography', in Edna Moshenson, ed., *Chantal Akerman: A Spiral Autobiography* (Tel Aviv: Tel Aviv Museum of Art, 2006), p. 16.
25. Ibid., p. 19.
26. Autobiography also strongly informs the video installations *Maniac Summer* (2009) and *Maniac*

Shadows (2013). *Maniac Summer* is composed of footage shot in and from Akerman's Paris flat. While the central panel is largely documentary, the surrounding ones enter a more allegorical realm with their manipulated, at times almost abstract images. In the press release for the piece, the artist relates this work on traces to the after-images left by the radiation of the Hiroshima bombing. *Maniac Shadows* shows Akerman in various living spaces where she has temporarily or more permanently taken residence, alongside shots of her mother in her Brussels home, projections of Akerman's shadow, New York street scenes and images from Obama's 2008 election. The sound of the three video projections mingles with that of the artist reading from *Ma mère rit*. A work on presence and absence, *Maniac Shadows* is mournful in its evocation of death and disappearance.

27. 'Chantal Akerman pour son livre *Ma mère rit*'.
28. 'something is possible'.
29. 'to keep Chantal's mother with us'; 'The film imposed itself on us like a cry'. 'Nuit Chantal Akerman — 2ème partie de l'entretien'.
30. 'To write truthfully, to search as far as you can'. 'Chantal Akerman pour son livre *Ma mère rit*'.
31. Jean-Michel Vlaeminckx, '*Ma mère rit* de Chantal Akerman', *Cinergie.be*. For a detailed discussion of *Ma mère rit* as an experiment in self-writing see my 'Self-portrait as Visual Artist: Chantal Akerman's *Ma mère rit*', *MLN*, 131.4 (2016), 1130–47.
32. See for instance works such as Annie Ernaux's '*Je ne suis pas sortie de ma nuit*' and *Se perdre* which, respectively, chronicle her mother's death from Alzheimer and her obsessive relationship with a Russian man; or Sophie Calle's installation 'Rachel, Monique', inspired by the loss of her mother.
33. Gilles Deleuze and Félix Guattari, *Kafka, pour une littérature mineure* (Paris: Minuit, 1975).
34. See Akerman's comments on the layering of languages in the two works in the interviews 'Chantal Akerman pour son livre *Ma mère rit*' and 'Entretien sur *Une famille à Bruxelles*'.
35. 'Only four weeks left before surgery. That's what she said yesterday. But this morning after breakfast she was already tired. She lay down on the couch. When I went to see, that's what she told me, eating made me tired. But am I allowed to rest? I told her it's not a right it's a duty. And I, will I last here four weeks.' Chantal Akerman, *Ma mère rit* (Paris: Mercure de France, 2013), p. 26.
36. 'My sister says don't pay attention, you mustn't pay attention, I don't pay attention. I go I come, I don't tell her where and I don't give her my mobile number. My mother absolutely wants to call my sister. Why do you want to call her, she's working. Leave her alone. I still want to call her to find out when she's coming home' (Akerman, *Ma mère rit*, p. 93).
37. Akerman cited in Nicolas Rapold, 'Chantal Akerman Takes Emotional Path in Film about "Maman"', *The New York Times*, 5 August 2015.
38. 'The old child thought if her mother disappeared, she would have nowhere to go back to. [...] What will keep me alive afterwards?' (Akerman, *Ma mère rit*, p. 25).
39. To be precise, the film starts with the image of a tree battered by the wind, which also originates in the installation, but contrary to the later ones, this is a fixed-angle shot reframed several times.
40. The inauguration of the Jerusalem installation in 2014 was accompanied by a reading from *Ma mère rit* and footage from what was to become *No Home Movie*.
41. 'Nuit Chantal Akerman — 2ème partie de l'entretien'.
42. Cf. Claire Atherton's comments on the importance of sound in *NOW*: 'Chantal said that she wanted us to experience fear, war, flight, imminent disaster through the entanglement of the soundtracks in space. She wanted us to experience chaos, to feel the extent to which our world is unhinged by violence.' http://myartguides.com/exhibitions/chantal-ackerman-now/ (last accessed 1 July 2018).
43. 'The way in which the past receives the imprint of a higher present event is determined by the *image* in which it is contained. And this dialectic penetration, this capacity to render present past correlations, is the test of truth of the present action' (Akerman, *Autoportrait*, p. 44).
44. 'I felt so good there when we first went there, it's true that there I felt like nowhere in the world.' Akerman, *Une famille à Bruxelles*, p. 61.

WORKS BY CHANTAL AKERMAN

Films

1968   *Saute ma ville* (Blow up My Town), 13 min., b/w.
1971   *L'Enfant aimé ou je joue à être une femme mariée* (The Beloved Child, or I Play at Being a Married Woman), 35 min., b/w.
1972   *La Chambre 1* (The Room 1), 11 min., col.
       La Chambre 2 (The Room 2), 11 min., col. (silent).
       Hotel Monterey, 63 min., col. (silent).
1973   *Le 15/08*, 42 min., b/w (co-directed with Samy Szlingerbaum).
       Hanging out Yonkers, approx. 40 min., col. (unfinished).
1975   *Je tu il elle* (I... You... He... She...), 90 min., b/w.
       Jeanne Dielman, 23, quai du Commerce, 1080 Bruxelles, 200 min., col.
1976   *News from Home*, 89 min., col.
1978   *Les Rendez-vous d'Anna* (Meetings with Anna), 127 min., col.
1982   *Aujourd'hui, dis-moi/ Dis-moi* (Tell Me), 45 min., col.
       Toute une nuit (All Night Long), 90 min., col.
1983   *Les Années 80* (The Eighties), 79 min., col.
       L'Homme à la valise (The Man with the Suitcase), 60 min., col.
       «*Un Jour Pina a demandé...*» (One Day Pina Asked Me), 57 min., col.
1984   *Family Business*, 18 min., col.
       J'ai faim, j'ai froid (I'm Hungry, I'm Cold), 1984, 12 min., b/w.
       Lettre d'une cinéaste: Chantal Akerman (Letter from a Filmmaker), 8 min., col.
1986   *Golden Eighties* (aka Window Shopping), 96 min., col.
       Letters Home, 104 min., col.
       Le Marteau (The Hammer), 4 min., col.
       Portrait d'une paresseuse/ Le Journal d'une paresseuse/ La Paresse (Sloth), 14 min., col.
       Rue Mallet-Stevens, 7 min., col.
1988   *Histoires d'Amérique: food, family and philosophy* (American Stories/ Food, Family and Philosophy), 92 min., col.
1989   *Les Trois dernières sonates de Franz Schubert* (Franz Schubert's Last Three Sonatas), 49 min., col.
       Trois strophes sur le nom de Sacher ('Three Stanzas on the Name Sacher', by Henri Dutilleux), 12 min., col.
1991   *Pour Febe Elisabeth Velasquez, El Salvador*, 3 min., col.
       Nuit et jour (Night and Day), 90 min., col.

1992 *Le Déménagement* (Moving In), 42 min., col.
1993 *D'Est* (From the East), 110 min., col.
      Portrait d'une jeune fille de la fin des années 60 à Bruxelles (Portrait of a Young Girl from the Late Sixties in Brussels), 60 min., col.
1996 *Chantal Akerman par Chantal Akerman*, 63 min., col.
      Un divan à New York (A Couch in New York), 105 min., col.
1997 *Le Jour où*, 7 min., col.
1999 *La Captive* (The Captive), 107 min., col.
      Sud (South), 70 min., col.
2002 *Avec Sonia Wieder-Atherton*, 52 min., col.
      De l'autre côté (From the Other Side), 102 min., col.
2004 *Demain on déménage* (Tomorrow We Move), 110 min., col.
2006 *Là-bas* (Over There), 78 min., col.
2007 *Tombée de nuit sur Shanghai* (Nightfall over Shanghai), 15 min., col.
2008 *Femmes d'Anvers en novembre* (Women from Antwerp in November), 20 min, col.
2009 *A l'Est avec Sonia Wieder-Atherton*, 43 min., col.
2011 *La Folie Almayer* (Almayer's Folly), 127 min., col.
2015 *No Home Movie*, 118 min, col.

Installations

1995 *D'Est, au bord de la fiction* (From the East, Bordering on Fiction).
      Video installation in two rooms; 24 monitors and one single monitor, colour, sound.
      Composed of footage from the film *D'Est* (1993).
1998 *Selfportrait/ Autobiography: A Work in Progress.*
      6 monitors, colour, sound.
      With images and sounds of: *Hotel Monterey* (1972); *Jeanne Dielman, 23 quai du Commerce, 1080 Bruxelles* (1975); *Toute une nuit* (1982); *D'Est* (1993); and the sound of Chantal Akerman's voice reading *Une famille à Bruxelles*.
2001 *Woman Sitting after Killing.*
      7 monitors, sound.
      Composed of footage from the last sequence of the film *Jeanne Dielman, 23 quai du Commerce, 1080 Bruxelles* (1975).
2002 *De l'autre côté: une voix dans le désert* (From the Other Side: A Voice in the Desert).
      Single-channel video projection, sound.
      Composed of footage from the film *De l'autre côté* (2002).
2004 *Marcher à côté de ses lacets dans un frigidaire vide* (To Walk Next to One's Shoe Laces in an Empty Fridge).
      Part 1: Sculpture of spiral tulle with two video projections and one soundtrack; Part 2: Double-image video projection on a wall and a single-image video projection on a tulle screen.

2007 *Dans le miroir* (In the Mirror).
   One projection, b&w, sound.
   Composed of footage from the film *L'enfant aimé ou je joue à être une femme mariée* (1971).
2007 *Je, tu, il, elle, l'installation*.
   Three projections, b&w, sound.
   Composed of footage from the film *Je tu il elle* (1974).
2008 *Femmes d'Anvers en novembre* (Women from Antwerp in November).
   2 projections, colour and b&w, silent.
2009 *Maniac Summer*.
   3 part video installation, colour and b&w, sound.
2009 *Tombée de nuit sur Shanghai* (Nightfall over Shanghai).
   One projection, colour, sound.
   Composed of footage from the film *Tombée de nuit sur Shanghai* (2007).
2012 *La Chambre*.
   One projection or 5 monitors, silent.
   Composed of footage from the film *La Chambre* (1972).
2013 *Maniac Shadows*.
   3-channel video installation, HD video, colour and b&w, sound.
2014 *De la mère au désert* (From the mother to the desert).
   Three projections, sound.
2015 *Now*.
   Multiple channel, HD video installation, colour, 5 soundtracks, various objects.

Books

CHANTAL AKERMAN, *Les Rendez-vous d'Anna* (Paris: Albatros, 1978).
——*Hall de nuit* (Paris: L'Arche, 1992).
——*Un divan à New York* (Paris: L'Arche, 1996).
——*Une famille à Bruxelles* (Paris: L'Arche, 1998).
——*Chantal Akerman. Autoportrait en cinéaste*, ed. by Claudine Paquot (Paris: Editions du Centre Georges Pompidou/ Editions Cahiers du cinéma, 2004).
——*Ma mère rit* (Paris: Mercure de France, 2013).

SELECT BIBLIOGRAPHY OF WORKS ON CHANTAL AKERMAN

Books

AKERMAN, CHANTAL, CATHERINE DAVID, MICHAEL TARANTINO, *Bordering on Fiction: Chantal Akerman's D'Est* (Minneapolis: Walker Art Centre, 1995).

AUBENAS, JACQUELINE, *Hommage à Chantal Akerman* (Brussels, Commissariat général aux Relations internationales de la Communauté française de Belgique, 1995).

FOSTER, GWENDOLYN AUDREY, ed., *Identity and Memory: The Films of Chantal Akerman* (Carbondale and Edwardsville: Southern Illinois University Press, 2003).

MARGULIES, IVONE, *Nothing Happens: Chantal Akerman's Hyperrealist Everyday* (London: Duke University Press, 1996).

MOMCILOVIC, JÉRÔME, *Chantal Akerman: dieu se reposa, mais pas nous* (Nantes: Capricci, 2018).

MOSHENSON, EDNA, ed., *Chantal Akerman: A Spiral Autobiography* (Tel Aviv Museum of Art, 2006).

PRAVANDELLI, VERONICA, *Performance, Rewriting, Identity: Chantal Akerman's Postmodern Cinema* (Turin: Otto, 2000).

ROELSTRAETE, DIETER and ANDERS KREUGER, eds., *Chantal Akerman: Too Far, Too Close* ([Ghent]: Ludion; [Antwerp]: M HKA, 2012).

RONDEAU, CORINNE, *Chantal Akerman, passer la nuit* (Paris: Editions de l'éclat, 2017).

SCHMID, MARION, *Chantal Akerman* (Manchester: Manchester University Press, 2010).

SULTAN, TERRIE, ed., *Chantal Akerman: Moving Through Time and Space* (Houston: Blaffer Gallery, the Art Museum of the University of Houston, 2008).

Special Journal Issues and Dossiers

Frieze, 176 (2016).

LIPTAY, FABIENNE and MARGRIT TRÖHLER, eds., 'Chantal Akerman', *Film-Konzepte*, 47.7 (2017).

MARTIN, ANGELA, 'Chantal Akerman's Films: A Dossier', *Feminist Review*, 3 (1979), 24–47.

REYNAUD, BÉRÉNICE, ed., 'Chantal Akerman: La passion de l'intime/an intimate passion', *Senses of Cinema*, 77 (2015).

RICH, RUBY B. and IVONE MARGULIES, eds., 'Dossier Chantal Akerman', *Film Quarterly*, 70.1 (2016), 11–84.

INDEX

Agamben, Giorgio 44, 45, 46, 50, 78
ageing 5, 54–64, 146
Akerman, Chantal:
   and abstraction 18, 139–40, 144–48
   adaptations by 58, 90–98, 151–52
   choreography 44, 48
   in Israel 13, 14, 15, 17, 22–23, 63, 144, 160–61
   in Russia 142
   in the United States 2, 11, 21, 110, 130
   influences on 2, 67, 102, 151
   installation works 4, 9, 11, 13–24, 48–50, 60, 77, 84–86, 97, 123–25, 127, 139–48, 150, 154–55, 156–61
   interviews with 19, 21, 29, 41, 43, 48, 92, 150, 151, 156, 158
   Jewishness 4, 11, 14–16, 23–24, 35, 69, 73, 80, 82, 109, 123, 140, 151
   light in films of 139–48
   Mexican border 115–16, 120, 124
   multimedia work 48, 123–24, 155
   music in films of 17, 93–96, 120–22, 127–38
   realism 68, 128, 140
   and self-portraiture 2, 13–24, 151, 153–56, 156–61
   sound in films of 131–32
   and television 69
   unrealized projects 91, 152
   see also specific Akerman works
Akerman, Natalia (Nelly) 15, 20, 22, 43, 44–46, 57, 63, 85, 123, 147, 151, 156–61
Les années 80 (*The Eighties*) 127, 133
Atherton, Claire 3, 18, 22, 152, 156, 164
Aujourd'hui, dis-moi (*Tell Me*) 61–63
autofiction 153
Autoportrait en cinéaste 2, 91, 94, 95, 98, 100, 151, 153, 160

Bachmann, Ingeborg 5, 90, 91–92, 96, 98
Bausch, Pina 1, 7
Beauvoir, Simone de 55–56, 62, 63
Béghin, Cyril 155
Benjamin, Walter 61, 68, 72, 79, 108, 151, 160
Bernhard, Thomas 6, 153
Bourgeois, Louise 34, 55
Brendel, Alfred 1, 133–34
Bruno, Giuliana 50, 60, 84
Butler, Judith 46, 50
Byrd Jr., James 110

Cannes Film Festival 6, 105
Cage, John 127, 128–29, 130, 131, 137
La Captive (*The Captive*) 90–96, 134–37, 146, 148
La Chambre (*The Room*) 11, 67
Chantal Akerman par Chantal Akerman 23, 153
Clément, Aurore 22, 57–58, 59, 60, 66, 77, 95, 135
collaborations 18, 48, 55, 66, 103, 118, 151
Conrad, Joseph 58, 91, 98, 152
Constant, Régine 66

daughters 4, 43, 58–64, 80–88, 154–55, 157, 158–60
death 15, 20, 26, 32, 35, 47, 54, 56, 91, 95–98, 102, 118, 119, 139, 153–55
De l'autre côté: une voix dans le désert (*From the Other Side: A Voice in the Desert*) 119, 123–24
Demain on déménage (*Tomorrow We Move*) 56, 58, 66–76, 77, 80–87, 139, 152, 156
Le Déménagement (*Moving In*) 67, 134–35
diaries 21, 22, 26–39, 83–86, 156
Didi-Huberman, Georges 78, 79, 140
Un Divan à New York (*A Couch in New York*) 67, 70, 79, 80, 151
Doane, Mary Ann 42
documentary 78, 80, 81, 102–12, 120, 122, 123–25, 143–44, 151–55, 156–61
Doillon, Jacques 2
Dostoyevsky, Fyodor 91, 152
Doubrovsky, Serge 153
Duras, Marguerite 30, 37, 99, 150, 151, 153

Ehrenberg, Sidonie 27
Elgar, Edward 124
Elliott, Nicholas 1
D'Est (*From the East*) 3, 9, 15–17, 48–49, 77–78, 80–81, 83, 86, 108, 115–16, 139, 141, 142–43, 144–45, 151, 154–56, 160
D'Est: au bord de la fiction (*From the East: Bordering on Fiction*) 15, 77, 141
Eustache, Jean 2
exile 3, 15, 19, 20, 73, 108, 157, 160

Une famille à Bruxelles (*A Family in Brussels*) 58, 153–58, 161
Fassbinder, Rainer Werner 1, 2
feminism 109–10, 116–17, 121
Femmes d'Anvers en novembre (*Women from Antwerp in November*) 48–50, 60

Index

Ferreira, Leonardo Luiz 2
La Folie Almayer (*Almayer's Folly*) 56, 58, 91, 98, 141, 145, 146–48, 152
Frampton, Hollis 7
Frank, Anne 26–27, 29–30, 32–33
French New Wave 2, 151

Garrel, Philippe 2
gender 24, 42, 57, 64, 79, 105–09, 122–23, 152
Godard, Jean-Luc 1, 2, 151, 152
  interview with Akerman 151
Golden Eighties 127, 141, 142

Hiroshima 37, 97, 139–40, 148
Histoires d'Amérique (*American Stories*) 15, 16, 17, 23, 127, 141, 156
Holocaust 3, 15–24, 27, 30, 31, 36, 43–44, 61–62, 69, 72, 73, 81, 84, 87, 91, 96, 108, 153, 154, 156–67
homosexuality 108–09
Horvilleur, Delphine 4, 24
Hurt, William 152

Jacquot, Benoît 2
Jeanne Dielman, 23, Quai du Commerce, 1080 Bruxelles 7–8, 15, 24, 35, 42, 44–45, 58, 67–69, 71, 123, 130, 131, 141, 145, 151–52, 154, 155, 158, 159
Je tu il elle (*I, You, He, She*) 49, 57, 66, 67, 151
Johnson, Kirsten 105

Kuyper, Eric de 66, 101

Là-bas (*Over There*) 5, 11, 13–15, 17–19, 68, 71, 143, 144
Lambert, Marianne 14, 20, 22
  I Don't Belong Anywhere 14, 20, 22
landscape 9–11, 13–14, 18, 19, 63, 80, 86, 102, 104, 115–25, 160
Lanzmann, Claude 78, 87
  Shoah 78, 87
Letters Home 67, 151
Lipari, Lisbeth 116–17, 119

Ma mère rit (*My Mother Laughs*) 1, 11, 42, 46–47, 48, 97, 146, 156, 159
Maniac Shadows 91, 146–47
Maniac Summer 97, 139–40, 145–46
Marcher à côté de ses lacets dans un frigidaire vide (*To Walk Next to One's Shoe Laces in an Empty Fridge*) 150, 156–67
Marielle, Jean-Pierre 72, 82
Marti, Christian 66
Minh-ha, Trinh T. 117
memory 17–22, 57, 63, 68, 78–79, 110, 160

mothers 4, 11–12, 13–24, 26–39, 42–43, 43–47, 55–57, 58–64, 70, 78–80, 82, 84–86, 87, 95, 123, 132, 154, 156

New York 43, 110, 129, 130, 146, 151, 152
News from Home 129, 130, 132, 141
No Home Movie 4, 12, 13–14, 20–22, 23, 35, 55, 56, 62–63, 67, 79, 103, 123, 141, 147, 156–60
Now 145, 147

Obama, Barack 104
Ottinger, Ulrike 108–09
  Exile Shanghai 108

Plath, Sylvia 152
Portrait d'une paresseuse (*Sloth*) 41–43, 153
post-New Wave 2
Proust, Marcel 151, 152
  La Prisonnière 91–98, 134

racism 102–13
Les Rendez-vous d'Anna (*Meetings with Anna*) 9, 56, 57, 59, 60, 71, 77, 95, 96, 98, 123, 127, 141, 151, 153
Resnais, Alain 2, 37, 78, 88

Saute ma ville (*Blow up My Town*) 1, 2, 54, 57, 68, 69, 74, 131, 140, 151
Sedgwick, Eve Kosofsky 117
sex 49, 57, 60, 73–74, 83, 85, 91–94
Seyrig, Delphine 24, 131, 152
silent film 74–75
Singer, Isaac Bashevis 151, 152
slapstick 74–75
smoking 41–50, 66, 71
Snow, Michael 2, 7, 67
Storck, Henri 71
Sud (*South*) 81, 102–13

Tarkovsky, Andrei 131
Techiné, André 2
Testud, Sylvie 58, 66, 77, 92, 100, 152
Tombée de nuit sur Shanghai (*Nightfall over Shanghai*) 9, 10, 145
Toute une nuit (*All Night Long*) 9, 42, 45–46, 127
trauma 11, 14, 15, 19, 24, 43, 44, 79, 81–82, 87, 104–06
Les Trois dernières sonates de Franz Schubert (*Franz Schubert's Last Three Sonatas*) 133–34

Valla, Marie-Laure 66
Varda, Agnès 55

Wieder-Atherton, Sonia 1, 66, 116, 123–24

www.ingramcontent.com/pod-product-compliance
Lightning Source LLC
LaVergne TN
LVHW061252060426
835507LV00017B/2029